WILLIAM III'S ITALIAN ALLY

Piedmont and the War of the League of Augsburg
1683–1697

Ciro Paoletti

'This is the Century of the Soldier', Fulvio Testi, Poet, 1641

Helion & Company

Helion & Company Limited
Unit 8 Amherst Business Centre
Budbrooke Road
Warwick
CV34 5WE
England
Tel. 01926 499 619
Fax 0121 711 4075
Email: info@helion.co.uk
Website: www.helion.co.uk
Twitter: @helionbooks
Visit our blog at http://blog.helion.co.uk/

Published by Helion & Company 2019
Designed and typeset by Serena Jones
Cover designed by Paul Hewitt, Battlefield Design (www.battlefield-design.co.uk)
Printed by Henry Ling Limited, Dorchester, Dorset

ISBN 978-1-911628-58-3

For details of other military history titles published by Helion & Company
Limited, contact the above address, or visit our website: http://www.helion.co.uk

We always welcome receiving book proposals from prospective authors.

Contents

List of Illustrations & Maps

Illustrations

Maps

Foreword

The War of the League of Augsburg, also known as the Nine Years' War and as King William's War (after William III), is one that has received insufficient attention due to the tendency to focus on the subsequent War of the Spanish Succession. This is unfortunate at a number of levels, although it has created a marvellous opportunity for Ciro Paoletti in his excellent new book. First, the War of the Spanish Succession cannot be understood, militarily or politically, without considering the preceding struggle. Indeed, the diplomacy that gave rise to the War of the Spanish Succession was, as Paoletti shows, set by the Nine Years' War. yet, there is far more to this book. Paoletti's work indicates the significance of Italian factors in the great power diplomacy of the period. Moreover, he shows that Victor Amadeus II was able to use his position in order to advance his interests, in short that the second-rank powers had agency. The continuing importance of Italian issues to Austria and France emerges clearly, but so also do their significance for the rising power, England. As far as the last is concerned, Paoletti offers a careful and interesting account of the importance of the Waldensian issue for relations between the two powers.

The military dimension is to the fore and in a number of respects. Paoletti considers the nature of early modern warfare itself before pressing on to assess the Savoyard army, to devote particular attention to its logistics, and subsequently to consider operational issues. Issues are carefully introduced, for example the frequency and nature of sieges, the accuracy of infantry fire, the role of cavalry, and the impact of disease. This valuable account deserves attention.

Jeremy Black – University of Exeter

Part I: The Peace

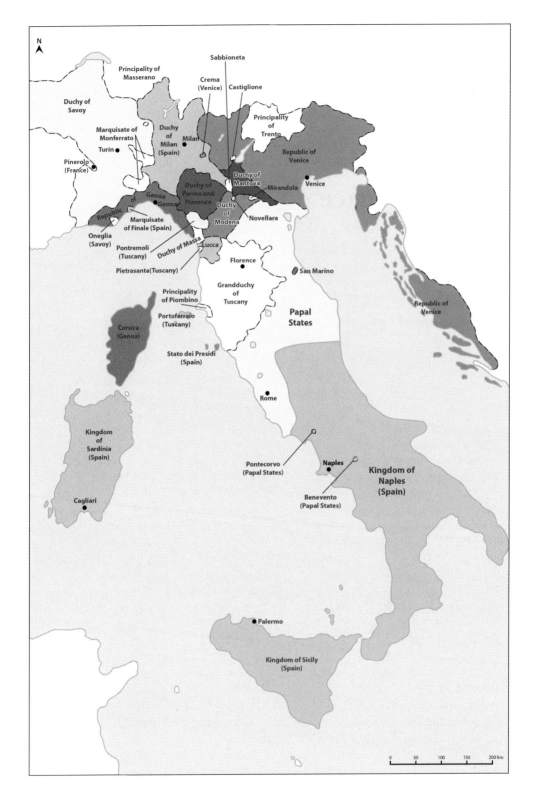

N

Principality of
Masserano

Duchy of
Savoy

Marquisate of
Monferrato

Turin ●

Pinerolo
(France)

Duchy
of
Milan ● Milan
(Spain)

Crema
(Venice)

Sabbioneta

Castiglione

Principality
of
Trento

Republic of
Venice

Duchy of
Mantova

Mirandola

Venice ●

Republic of
Genoa

Genoa ● Genoa

Marquisate
of Finale (Spain)

Oneglia
(Savoy)

Pontremoli
(Tuscany)

Duchy of Massa

Duchy of
Parma and
Piacenza

Duchy
of
Modena

Novellara

Lucca

Pietrasanta(Tuscany)

Florence ●

San Marino

Corsica
(Genoa)

Principality
of Piombino

Portoferraio
(Tuscany)

Grandduchy
of
Tuscany

Papal
States

Republic of
Venice

Stato dei Presidi
(Spain)

Kingdom
of
Sardinia
(Spain)

Rome ●

Cagliari ●

Pontecorvo
(Papal States)

Naples ●

Kingdom of
Naples
(Spain)

Benevento
(Papal States)

● Palermo

Kingdom of Sicily
(Spain)

0   50   100   150   200 km

Map 1. Italy in the 17th century

1

A Satellite of the Sun

I. The Origin of a Modern State

The Duchy of Savoy was a small state on both the sides of the western Alps. Its dukes belonged to the oldest ruling house of Europe, but, being locked between the two most powerful crowns of their time – France and Habsburg – during the 17th century was reduced to mere clients of Louis XIV's France.

This is the story of how the last Duke succeeded in avoiding absorption by France, regaining the independence his ancestors lost, and how he succeeded in completing the first step towards the unification of Italy under his house.

The Duchy of Savoy had been ruled since the eleventh century by the House of Savoy. According to the sources, Humbert 'Whitehand', the first Count of Savoy, was of probable Saxon descent. In 1034 he led an Imperial army from Italy across the Alps, for he had to reconquer Burgundy for Emperor Conrad II.

It is not important to learn how Humbert's descendants increased their possessions, how they became dukes in 1416 and what they did in the following centuries; but it is important to say that their little state occupied in Europe a prominence altogether out of proportion to its small size and its resources. For this, it was chiefly indebted to its geographical position. The Dukes of Savoy were the gatekeepers of the Alps. The eastern part of their states gave access to Italy, the western to France, the northern to Switzerland, thus their alliance was constantly of vital importance to their more powerful neighbours, and the dukes always balanced themselves in between.

At the end of the 15th century, Charles VIII of France went to Italy, starting what was later known as the Italian Wars, a long period of clashes between France and Spain, ending with the victory of the latter. An indirect consequence of that clash was the French occupation of the States of Savoy. In the first half of the 16th century, Emmanuel Philibert of Savoy, who seemed to be the last duke, because his father had been completely deprived of his possession, played his last card in a game of death and life. His mother, a Portuguese princess of the Royal House of Aviz, was the sister of Charles V's wife, thus he went to his uncle's court, and started fighting in the Imperial

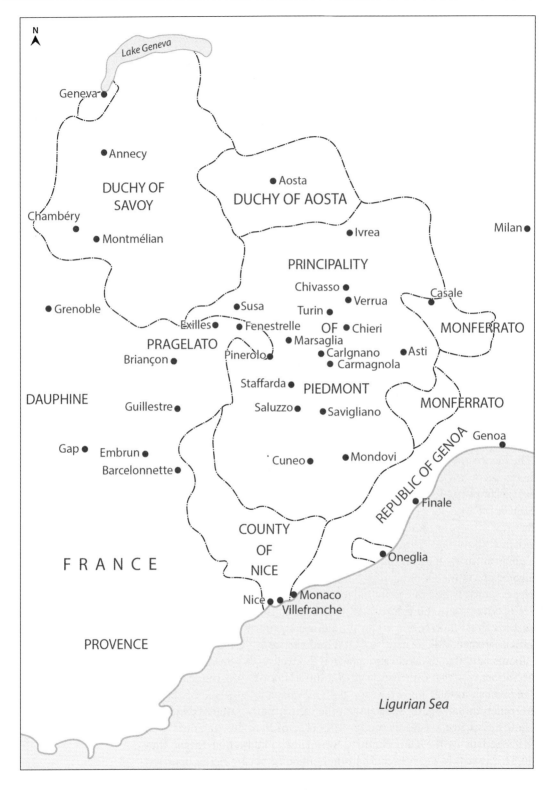

Map 2. The Duchy of Savoy

army. He fought so well, that he soon was appointed a commanding general, and, as the commander of the Spanish army, on the day of Saint Lawrence, 10 August 1557, he definitively and dramatically defeated the French army at Saint Quentin, not far from Paris, and presented his cousin Philip II with an open route to the French capital.

Saint Quentin was probably the worst defeat the French suffered in the whole century, but Phillip II did not exploit it as he was expected to do. He did not march to Paris, nonetheless two years later he signed the Peace of Cateau-Cambrésis. A clause in the treaty gave back Emmanuel Philibert the Duchy his father had been deprived of by the French.

Thus in 1559 a new era started in Piedmont. The Duke decided to strengthen his states. They were, unfortunately, between France and the Habsburg-ruled lands. Hence, whenever a war between the two, their armies had to pass through.

Emmanuel Philibert's Duchy was actually a mosaic of different smaller states on both sides of the Alps. He was the Duke of Savoy, and the Count of Maurienne, and the Count of Nice, on the western side of the Alps, but also the Prince of Piedmont, and the Count of Aosta on the eastern side of the Alps; moreover he was the Prince of Oneglia, a small coastal city not far from Genoa, enclaved in the Republic of Genoa's territory, because he purchased the Principality of Oneglia in 1576, and, according to some well-based dynastical pretensions, he was the King of Cyprus and Jerusalem too. Regardless, he was known as the Duke of Savoy, and the ensemble of his domains was known as the Duchy of Savoy, or as the States of Savoy, and that is why we shall speak of the Duchy of Savoy.

1. Emanuel Philibert. 'Ironhead'. Duke of Savoy in 1560

Cyprus and Jerusalem were too far, but all the other domains were close, and still locked between France and the Habsburgs of Spain, and needed protection. Protection meant an army, and money to feed it. So, Emmanuel Philibert reorganised taxation and created an army. He had served in the Spanish military system and knew it perfectly. The Spanish military organisation was the most effective of that time, hence he organised his army on the Spanish model.

A French threat was more likely than a Spanish one, but nobody knows the future. The French were on the other side of the Alps, the Spaniards were in the Duchy of Milan. The Alps werc hard to cross, nonetheless they could be crossed. Milan was on the other side of a border on an open flat plain, which was very easy to cross. How to hold it? Emmanuel Philibert ordered the building in Piedmont of a ring of fortresses, having that of Turin as its centre. Had the French crossed the Alps in spite of all the opposition

2. (above): The peace of Cateau Cambresis, 1559

3. (right, top): Ferrara in the 17th century; 4. Mirandola

4. (right, below): Mirandola

by Savoy's army, the fortresses would be the next obstacle and they could hold as long as needed to get reinforcements from Milan. Vice versa, had the Spaniards attacked from Milan, the ring could hold as long as needed to allow the French allies to cross the mountains; for Emmanuel Philibert knew that he had not to trust either the enemies nor the friends, and who is a friend today, can easily be an enemy tomorrow.

The army could be used for defence and for attack, supporting foreign policy. And Emmanuel Philibert had a clear political programme. His dynasty had to increase her power. This meant they had to get more territories. Expansion was impossible on the western side of the Alps, because France was too strong, but it was still possible in a politically fragmented Italy, hence, the House of Savoy started looking at Italy as the ground of her next expansion.

On the other hand, there was a risk. The Duchy was locked. Northern borderers were the Swiss, who were officially neutral. The western borderer was France. The Republic of Genoa was in the south, and was a close ally to Spain, because it served as the bank of the Spanish crowns. And Spain herself directly ruled the Duchy of Milan, in the east.

Actually Milan belonged to the *Reichsitalien*, Imperial Italy. Imperial Italy included the whole northern part of the Italian peninsula between the Alps and the Papal States, except for the Republic of Venice. It was a heritage from Charlemagne's Holy Empire. Once shared among his heirs, Germany and Northern Italy composed the Holy German Empire. So, the small duchies of Modena, Parma, Piacenza, Ferrara, Guastalla, Mirandola and Mantua, the Duchy of Milan, that of Tuscany, as well as the Republics of Genoa and Lucca, and the Principality of Piedmont, were officially under the Holy Emperor's rule, and the Holy Emperor was a Habsburg too.

This was enough to render Emmanuel Philibert's domains one of the battlegrounds of the next clash between Spain and France, but unfortunately there was something more. He ruled in Italy the County of Aosta and the Principality of Piedmont, but did not rule some areas within Piedmont, as the marquisates of Saluzzo and of Monferrato. The former was independent and protected by the French, the latter depended on the Duchy of Mantua,

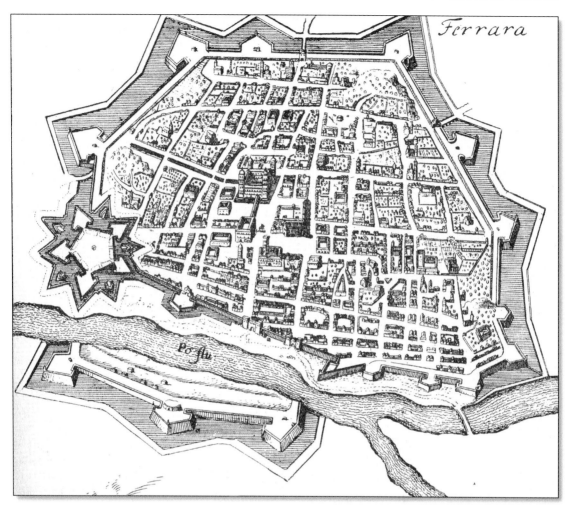

5. Piacenza

whose capital, Mantua, was some 150 miles far from Turin, on the opposite side of Lombardy. Both the two small feuds were important.

Saluzzo was the French strongpoint on the Italian side of the Alps; but in 1601 there was an exchange. Henry IV of France ceded Saluzzo to Savoy, now ruled by Emmanuel Philibert's eldest son and heir, Charles Emmanuel I, and gained Bresse, Bugey, Gex, and Valromey, the future French department of Ain.

France was now cut off from Italy, whilst the House of Savoy still had power on both sides of the mountains, having retained her ancestor's nest, the Duchy of Savoy itself, and the County of Nice. And Monferrato, well, Monferrato and its capital Casale need a long story to be told.

Since very long before, France wanted to break the Habsburg ring. Traditionally Cardinal Richelieu is credited as the original planner of the French grand strategy in the early 17th century; implemented during the Thirty Years' War and successfully pursued by his successor Mazzarino until the Treaty of the Pyrenees in 1659.[1] It is still unclear how much of this strategy was originally developed by Henry IV and what was Richelieu's creation. What is important is the general line stated at that time. France was encircled by the Habsburgs. When not considering the English Channel and the Mediterranean, French borders were more or less parallel to the Rhine, the Alps, and the Pyrenees. It was foolish to attack Spain through the Pyrenees, it was not a good idea to try to pass the Rhine under Spanish troops' eyes in Rhineland and Burgundy, and it was not a good idea to do the same across the Alps.

---

1   *Traité de paix dit des Pyrenées entre le Roi de France et le Roi d'Espagne*, signed in the Ile des Faisans on 7 November 1659, in Solaro della Margarita (ed.), *Traités publics de la Royale Maison de Savoie avec les puissances étrangères depuis la paix de Château-Cambresis jusqu'à nos jours*, 6 vols. (Turin, 1836), vol. II.

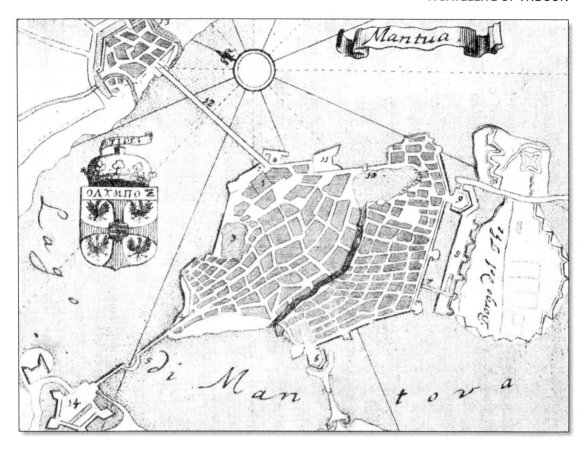

6. Mantua – fortifications

What could France do? The real strategic problem facing it was the extent of the Habsburg domains. Spain ruled Flanders, and Burgundy in Rhineland, that is to say France's back yard. But the Spanish military system had its core far away: in Spain and in Naples. The Spanish navy ruled Mediterranean, and whenever Flanders and the Rhineland needed troops the Spaniards moved by sea from Barcelona and Naples to a small Italian coastal town named Finale, west of Genoa and south of Piedmont. Once landed in Finale, the Spaniards marched along their traditional route, the at that time famous Spanish Road.

Actually, Spanish land military power was based in Italy, and centred on the Kingdom of Naples. Naples consistently provided Spanish Habsburgs with great quantities of money and military manpower. When needed, more troops could be concentrated in Naples from Sicily and occasionally Sardinia. They would march northwards along the Adriatic coast, but normally took ship on the Tyrrhenian Sea. After an intermediate stop in the *Stato dei Presidii* – the 'State of the Garrisons' – on the Tuscan coast, they landed near Genoa and marched north along the River Ticino to the central Alps. Passing through Grisons–Swiss-owned Val Tellina, they reached the Rhine–Danube watershed. If they had to go to the Low Countries, they marched along the Rhine Valley. If they had to reach Austria or central or eastern Germany, they marched along the Danube Valley. Here what was the so-called *Cammino di Fiandra*– literally 'the Path of Flanders' – better known in English as 'The

7. Charles Emanuel II, Duke of Savoy

Spanish Road'. It was the vital strategic artery of the whole Spanish military and political system, and this was the objective that probably Henry IV and surely Richelieu wanted to sever.

And here comes Monferrato and its capital Casale. This small walled town was just on the western flank of the Spanish Road, in the part between its landing point in Finale and the entrance to Switzerland. Whoever had Casale commanded, or at least heavily threatened, the Spanish Road and could cut it, and cut the logistic route feeding the Habsburg forces in northern Europe.

Practically every French campaign in Italy during the Thirty Years' War was tasked to cut the Spanish Road, and failed. No success in Valtellina to close the entrance to Switzerland; no success against Genoa to cut the Spanish landing point in Finale; no success in Piedmont to cut the northbound route along the River Ticino, and, finally, no success in Naples when supporting the failed 10-month insurrection in Southern Italy known as the Masaniello Revolt in 1647.

And, moreover, Saluzzo was no longer in French hands, thus crossing the Alps was harder than before. What to do? But the French at least got a result. In 1627 the main branch of the Gonzaga family ruling Mantua – and Casale – ended. Her possession came to her French branch, the Gonzaga-Nevers. All the Habsburg's horses, and all the Habsburg's men came to Italy to avoid it. Mantua was seized and pillaged in 1629, but what the soldiers did, was changed by diplomats, and the Treaty of Westphalia gave Mantua back to its rulers, along with Casale. This meant that a French prince ruled the main strongpoints – Casale and Mantua – holding a horizontal track from the Alps eastward, which, through Piedmont, reached and ideally cut the Spanish Road.

It was not enough. The French wanted it all, and campaigns went on in a continued conflict with Spain, which lasted 11 years more and concluded with the Treaty of the Pyrenees in 1659. The French gain in Italy was the establishment of the Duchy of Savoy as a client state. French garrisons were placed in Pinerolo – on the Italian side of the western Alps – and in many other strategic towns, in order to keep the horizontal track eastward, which, once crossed the Alps, had a first strongpoint in Pinerolo, then reached Casale and at last Mantua, and ideally cut the Spanish Road.

Charles Emmanuel I died during the Thirty Years' War. and his eldest son, Victor Amadeus I, who had married Christine of France, the sister of Louis XIII, died early in 1637. He had one son, and two daughters. The son, Charles Emmanuel II, found his state more or less preserved by his mother.

In spite of all the strong attempts her brother, Louis XIII, had made to seize it, Christine had succeeded in keeping a formal independence and thus

Right:
8. (top): Victor Amadeus II Duke of Savoy, portrayed in his childhood

9. (below): Jane Baptiste of Savoy-Nemours – Regent of Savoy

a crown for her son, but the Duchy was and remained a client state of France. So, during his reign, Charles Emmanuel did nothing – and by the way he could do nothing – to change it. It was impossible to challenge his cousin Louis, and he enjoyed his life as he could. He married a cousin from a French branch of his family, Mary-Jane Baptiste of Savoy-Nemours, had a son, christened as Victor Amadeus, and died in June 1675.

Mary-Jane became the regent. She was a total disaster. She collected lovers one by one, and, unfortunately, sometimes also two by two; she felt French, depended more and more on France, that is to say on Louis XIV's will, and did whatever Louis liked.

She liked the idea of keeping the power, the sole problem being her son. One day he had to be the ruler. How to avoid it?

II. An 'English' Marriage

The young duke was born on 14 May 1666, and was just a bit more than nine years old when his father died. He was a delicate boy. During his childhood it had been feared that he would never live to grow up, and, according to tradition, he owed his life to a village doctor, whom the Duchess called in, and who, having vetoed various drugs prescribed by the Court physicians, ordered his little ducal patient to be brought up on the very simplest fare, and thus saved his life. He was very precocious, and showed signs of gravity and strength of character really unusual in so young a boy. Samuel Chappuzeau, formerly tutor to William of Orange, visited Turin in 1671, and was greatly impressed by the little prince, who was only five at that time.[2]

---

2   Chappuzeau, Samuel, *Relation de l'estat present de la maison royale et de la cour de Savoye* (Paris, 1673), p. 50.

10. Louis XIV of France

Victor Amadeus soon realised he had to be cautious, very cautious. His mother Mary-Jane cared about power and her lovers. The shadow of his uncle, Louis XIV, was on Turin and on Savoy, ready to seize them as soon as an opportunity came. The French ambassador in Turin was simply a sentry, waiting to warn his master when the prey was ready to be eaten, and thus there were no good prospects left.

When Victor Amadeus was only 13, the Abbot d'Estrades, the French ambassador in Turin, wrote to the minister of foreign affairs, the Marquis de Pomponne:

> This prince is reserved and secretive; it is difficult to divine his real sentiments, in spite of all the troubles that one takes to ascertain them; and I have observed that he admits to his friendship people whom I'm aware he has regarded with aversion.[3]

In other words, Victor Amadeus was already a different character from his pleasure-loving father, and he bitterly resented the subjection in which he perceived his mother intented to keep him. As he grew up he was more and more irritated by her gallantries, as well as by the humiliating position to which his country had been reduced by the French. Actually Louis XIV considered Savoy as a client state – as it was – whose condition of servitude, heavily pushed by French War Minister Louvois, was slowly becoming absorption by France.

In 1681, when Victor Amadeus was 15, an alarming turning point happened: Louis XIV purchased Casale from the Duke of Mantua. The French now had the free passage across the Alps, watched by Pinerolo in their hands, and the direct command of the western flank of the Spanish Road. Moreover, Piedmont was locked in as never before. Victor Amadeus did not like it, but there was not that much he could do. However he had a more urgent and important problem to face: his wedding.

As said, Mary-Jane, the regent, liked very much the idea of keeping the power. In spite of what the usual non-Italian reader may like to think, Italian princes only very rarely used daggers and poisons, or killers, to make an obstacle disappear. This was something used mostly by the Borgia family – which, by the way, was a Spanish one – and by consequence is supposed to have been used by all the Italian princes. Wrong: being Italy, the land of Machiavelli, the Italians were usually trickier, and more clever, and unless it was really necessary they wasted far less blood than was supposed. Thus

---

3   Abbé d'Estrades, reported in de Léris, G., *Etude historique sur la comtesse de Verrue et la cour de Victor Amédée II de Savoie* (Paris, 1881), p. 38.

Mary-Jane never tried to kill her son. She simply thought of a more effective way, also known as *promoveatur ut amoveatur*, 'to be promoted in order to be removed'. A duke of Savoy started ruling as soon as he was 13 years old. That day was still far, but fast approaching when, in 1677, Mary-Jane had a wonderful idea. Her sister, once married to King Alphonse VI, and after his death to his younger brother Pedro II, was Queen of Portugal. They had no male heirs, only a daughter, the Infanta, Princess Doña Isabel Luisa, for whom a husband was needed. The two sisters arranged the engagement. A fundamental Portuguese law prohibited an Infanta who was also heiress to the throne from marrying a foreign prince, but the obstacle was overcome. Victor Amadeus was a direct descendant of Emmanuel Philibert, whose mother had been a princess of the ancient Royal House of Aviz, once kings of Portugal, and, Emmanuel Philibert had also been offered that crown in 1580, hence, Victor Amadeus was not a foreign prince.

Where was the catch? Simply, the Portuguese insisted that both the Infanta and her husband must reside in Portugal at least until the birth of an heir, an event which was unlikely to take place for several years. If Victor Amadeus was born in 1666, Isabel Luisa was three years younger. Had they married as planned in 1682, how long could Victor Amadeus stay in Portugal before the birth of a son? Meanwhile, his mother would continue to exercise her uncontrolled influence, her rule, at Turin, as a regent in her son's name.

One may be surprised that Mary-Jane forbore to tell her son her plans for his future until the affair was so advanced that it would be difficult for him to draw back, but she knew her son much more than one could expect. On the other hand, Victor Amadeus was soon informed by other sources what was in the wind. He was as able as needed to disguise his feelings, and showed nothing which might be interpreted either as approval or the reverse. He knew he had to be trickier than his mother, no matter of how wide the anti-wedding party at his court could be. Mary-Jane was the regent, and it was unclear whether and how her plans were supported or inspired by Louis XIV or not. Thus, Victor Amadeus allowed his mother to rule, with his all consent, also after the day of his majority. Apparently, he simply signed the decrees which she laid before him. In fact he had a large correspondence with his ambassadors abroad, and exploited the time to strengthen the party of his followers.

Originally planned for 1679 – just on time with his majority – the wedding had been postponed on Victor's request to 1682, and, being him so lovely a son, so mild and respectful to his mother's will, no clash occurred and the delay was graciously accorded.

In spring 1682 a Portuguese squadron entered Villafranca – the small galley squadron harbour the House of Savoy had not so far from Nice – and a Portuguese ambassador, the Duke of Cadaval, reached Turin. And, suddenly, the poor Victor Amadeus felt sick, very sick, as the Court physicians said. He was so sick that he could neither afford nor survive a journey, any journey. Cadaval waited from spring to autumn, but on 1 October, having seen instructions from Portugal, very upset he sailed back to Lisbon, and the marriage vanished on the horizon with his ships.

Mary-Jane had seen her plans vanishing with the marriage, so immediately organised a second opportunity: a marriage with Maria Anna

ANNE MARIE D'ORLEANS
Fille de Mons.r Philpe de France Duc
et de Henriette Stuard d'Angleterre
a este epousée Par Mons.r le Duc
de S.A.R le Duc de Savoye le Dix.me
faite par Mons.r le Cardinal de Bouillon
Versailles En presence de sa May.té de Monsieur, de Mad.e la Dauphine, de M.r et de Mad.e
du Duc de Chartres, Et de Mad.elle sa Soeur, des Princes Et princesses du Sang de l'Ambassé
de Savoye, Et des Principaux Seig.rs de la Cour, &c,

DUCHESSE DE SAVOYE
d'Orléans Frere Unique du Roy
Nacquit le 27.e d'Aoust 1669, et
du Maine, au Nom Et Coé Procureur
d'Avril 1684, la Ceremonie En a esté
en la Chapelle du Chasteau Royal de

11. Anne Mary d'Orléans, Charles I Stuart's granddaughter and Duchess of Savoy

Luisa de' Medici, the sole heir of the Grand Duke of Tuscany. But the worst was yet to come. The Portuguese story had been so long, that Louis XIV had been alarmed, and as soon as his spies told him of the Florentine project, his anger exploded. The King did not conceal his high displeasure on learning that the House of Savoy was contemplating an alliance which suggested a desire to weaken – this was the pretext – the authority of the Regent, threatened by the frictions between her and her son, or his supporters. In fact Louis disliked any attempt of Savoy to free itself from his control. No matter the reason, the result was the same: Louvois gave order for 3,000 French troops to enter Piedmont, which, them being in Pinerolo and Casale, was a matter of minutes, just open the gates and go.

Mary-Jane vigorously protested against this action, and thus gave Victor Amadeus an opportunity to annihilate her power. Whilst his mother complained, protested, and objected to the French ambassador intimating to her that it was his master's desire that her son wed a princess of the Royal House of France, Victor Amadeus secretly summoned the same ambassador and informed him that, not only he had abandoned the idea of any Tuscan marriage, but that he was prepared to accept the hand of the whichever princess His Most Christian Majesty might be pleased to give him.

Louis XIV did not know he was going to make one of his biggest mistakes, and Victor Amadeus did not know he was going to have one of his highest pieces of luck. The princess had already been chosen, of course. She was Anne Marie d'Orléans, a niece of Louis XIV, the daughter of his brother Philip Duke of Orléans and of his first wife, the wonderful and charming late Henrietta of England: Henrietta, the daughter of Charles I Stuart, the sister of the King of England, Charles II, and of the next king, James II. This meant to render Victor Amadeus, by his wedding, a first cousin of Mary, the wife of William of Orange, and the next – although not supposed yet – Queen and King of England, and of Anne Stuart, the following but still unpredictable, Queen of England in one of the most important periods of the history of England herself and of the whole world.

Anne was pretty, mild, and clever. Victor Amadeus was handsome, tough, and clever. He was pretty lucky with his wife. She was not that lucky with her husband, he was always respectful, but had so many mistresses that she certainly did not have a really happy life. Nonetheless, it was also, if not mostly, thanks to her, and to her relatives on her mother's side, that he received his royal crown in 1713 and the House of Savoy started a long alliance with England, which lasted with no interruption until World War II.

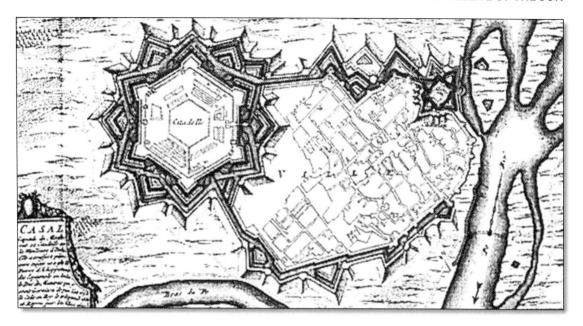

III. Victor Amadeus II's State

12. Casale – map of
fortifications

The state Victor Amadeus ruled was in fact a mosaic, and a weak one. It was a mosaic for it was composed of different peoples speaking different languages. The people on the other side of the Alps, the loyal and faithful Savoyards, spoke French and in fact were French, even if they disliked France and did not feel French at all. France had also heavily influenced the language on the Italian side of the Alps, thus the inhabitants of Piedmont spoke a half-French and half-Italian dialect, but those in the County of Nice, and in the Principality of Oneglia spoke a Ligurian dialect, closer to what was spoken in the Republic of Genoa than to the language commonly used in the other parts of the Duchy.

Not all the inhabitants of Piedmont were subject to the Duke of Savoy: some of them (as in Pinerolo) were ruled by France, whilst others (as in Monferrato), were ruled by the Duke of Mantua, and a portion, living on the western bank of the Ticino river – the future border with Milan – were ruled by Spain, whose king there was simply a feudatory of the Holy Roman Emperor.

How big was the state? A little less than 34,000 square kilometres – as big as Moldova, or 50 percent more than Wales – and was inhabited by no more than 1,200,000 people. The Duchy of Savoy was 10,786 square kilometres in size and had around 300,000 inhabitants. The County of Nice was 3,600 square kilometres with 70,000 inhabitants, whilst Oneglia was 146 square kilometres, small and populated by some 15,000 people. The Duchy of Aosta was 3,260 square kilometres, but had no more than 5,000 inhabitants. Last, the Principality of Piedmont: it was far smaller than in the following centuries, for future wars reconquered, or added, some areas Victor Amadeus did not rule at the beginning of his reign, as the French-ruled Pinerolo, the Mantuan-owned Casale and Monferrato, and the Habsburg-ruled areas in

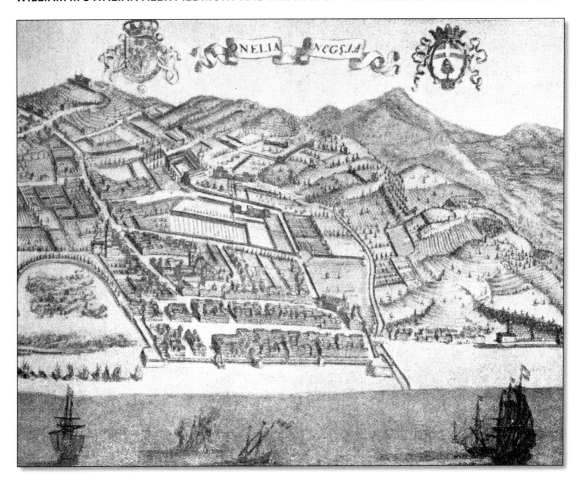

13. Oneglia

the east: the Langhe and Vercelli. At this time Piedmont was 16,000 square kilometres wide and populated by some 800,000 people.

The economy was not healthy. The annual global income of all the inhabitants was evaluated as 50,000,000 *liras* and heavily relied on agriculture. The Commons (towns) were poor, or at least could always resent of the result of a bad harvest. According to accurate studies, 4/5 – or 8/10 – of global incomes came from agriculture and only 1/10 originated from commerce and industry, the remaining tenth coming from real estate rents.

This complex situation also heavily influenced the policy of the Duchy. Every town and every Common had some privileges and kept them as firmly as possible, for a reduction of privileges could make the difference between survival and starvation, due to excessive tax pressure. In case the Commons were not happy with the ducal rule, they could, in theory, ask the Emperor for justice or, more concretely and quickly, revolt.

In such a doubtful situation the state relied upon only two pillars: the aristocracy and the army. But the regent Mary-Jane had basically put aside the army and substantially bribed both the aristocracy and the Commons. Security had been left to France, and in the third quarter of the 17th century the Savoyard army could be considered as a small auxiliary French force, to be used as, and where, the French wanted. Luckily the French did not need it, apart for a few regiments committed to Flanders during the wars against the Netherlands.

When Victor Amadeus took the power, his first problem was how to enforce his rule on his states. And the only way he had was fighting.

One thing must be made clear: no matter which theories or schemes historiography has suggested, especially in the 20th century; it is absolutely useless to try to plug the Savoyard State in any of them. Theories are recent, but people lived in that time long before theories, and did not act according to theories.

Victor Amadeus was an absolute monarch. He perceived and ran his state just as the owner of a private firm or of a big real estate property. Of course, he was not the owner of everything, but almost. Everything depended on him, and it was up to him, and only to him, to manage his state.

State management was centralised, and the decision-making process was firmly in the Duke's hands. He had to think of how each decision could influence, or affect, or dictate, every aspect of his state and his subjects' lives. Our contemporary perspective lets our minds think of ruling as a sort of process made by people acting with a certain degree of decisional autonomy, and later reporting to the chief of the state, who purposely delegated them an authority and a power to achieve some goals. For instance, in military terms, we think of an army as something commanded by a chief of staff, who is delegated by the chief of the state; and nobody expects the chief of a state to be the commander on the ground. But, also if in the 17th century it could be so – e.g. Louis XIV in France, the Emperor, or the Kings of Spain – Victor Amadeus did not act that way. He was the one who managed the foreign policy according to the means he had, or expected to have. He commanded his army on the field, and used it as a political tool. He decided how big the army could be according to the taxes and revenues he could get; and he imposed taxes and revenues according to the funds he supposed to be able to get from his subjects, or donors like Spain and the Maritime Powers during the Nine Years' War, or to borrow from bankers or commercial companies. Taxes and revenues had to be calculated according to the economic situation the Duchy was facing, and the Duke knew that he could not squeeze his subjects beyond a certain point, otherwise the result could be a total collapse. In other words: he knew how many golden eggs his goose could produce, and knew that he could not force her to go beyond that, otherwise she would die of exhaustion. This balance had to be kept day by day, compensating as much as possible the problems and lack due to unpredictable events. For instance, an excessively rainy period, or frost,

14. Victor Amadeus II Duke of Savoy portrayed when a teenager, probably at the age of 16

could affect agriculture, reducing the harvest. If so, the food and fodder price rose, and more money was needed to feed both the army and the subjects, who had to produce whatever the army needed, including manpower, that is to say recruits. Improving agriculture meant reducing recruits and weakening the army. A weaker army could be reinforced by enrolling or contracting foreign professionals, but this too needed more money, hence one had to find it, asking donors, or borrowing, or imposing new taxes. New taxes could cause reactions somewhere and somehow, and this could have a domino effect, which had to be carefully considered. So, Victor Amadeus had to think of waging war, managing foreign affairs, managing state affairs, thinking of how to get money, and taking care of all the mutual influences and interactions in order to keep all in balance, and let his state survive.

Clearly he could not be wherever he was needed whenever he was needed, so he relied on some ministers whom he deeply trusted. They were three: Carlo Giuseppe Vittorio Carron di San Tommaso, Count di Buttigliera and Marquess di Aigueblanche, who was the State Secretary until his death, in December 1696; Giovan Battista Gropello, later ennobled as the Count di Borgone, and Filiberto Sallier de la Tour, Baron de Bordeau, President of the Chamber of Accounts of Savoy and later his personal envoy to William III and the States General. They provided the facts, figures, and information Victor Amadeus needed. They acted according to his orders, but Victor Amadeus was the only one who evaluated, decided and commanded, and it was a very heavy burden, to be carried day by day.

2

Baroque – or Early Modern – Warfare in Italy and Abroad

What in English is known as the early modern era, and in Italy is simply known as the modern era, or Baroque Era, had some commonly shared military characters, but in other respects they were peculiar, due to some local influences and evolutions.

The battle of San Quentin, won by Victor Amadeus' great-great-grandfather, marked the triumph of regular fire, and that of manoeuvre and interaction between cavalry, artillery, and infantry, which prevailed on the static column formations. It was an actual but unconsidered turning point in Western military art. What happened on the ground on that 10 August determined a good portion of following century's warfare. A further improvement occurred when the Swedish troops entered Germany during the Thirty Years' War. Gustav Adolphus' systems became the new and more recent milestone of the art of war. They were imitated, developed, and also opposed by other very good commanders, the best of whom were mostly French and Italian, such as Turenne and Montecuccoli.

Here is a point we must immediately make clear. If we want to understand how and why the European generals, and the princes of the House of Savoy in particular, fought in a certain way, we must remember that, until Napoleon, there never was a military science as it was conceived since Austerlitz, and Clausewitz. There was a way of waging war, the background of which was mutual to all the European military leaders, and each commander later developed this background according to his personality and experience.

There were many texts of military art. There was a collection of examples and studies of how to organise the movements and the armies, and these books presented also tactical examples or strategic principles. But ignorance was so widespread that only a few officers cared to read them. At that time, apart for some schools for young gentlemen, providing also a sort of rudimental military training, the practice of arms was the only actual school. And the practical school educating the young and noble volunteers had at least a main, if not only one, common ground, the war against the Sublime Porte: the campaigns opposing Venice, the Empire and Christendom to the Ottoman advance in Eastern Europe.

French, German, Danish, Italian, Spanish, Portuguese, Polish, Bohemian, Hungarian, Swedish, Walloon, and Flemish volunteers systematically enlisted under the flags of Saint Mark and of the Habsburgs. They fought on land in Hungary and in the Balkans in the Imperial army, and at sea on Venetian ships and islands against the same enemy, using the same weapons and in the same way. They met, established contacts and made friends. Then they returned home and served in their respective sovereigns' armies. The common preparation they received in the Levant and the Balkans was completed by the European wars they were involved in. And often they found in the opposing camp some old comrades-in-arms from the campaigns against the Sublime Porte of Happiness.

It was during the wars between Europeans that they quickly learned the systems used by their respective armies: the employment of cavalry and infantry, siege techniques, how to advance and withdraw, the importance of foraging and of magazines, of reconnaissance to spot enemy supply lines, and the need for short marches. All these things, due to the different environment, had to be performed a little differently than how they had learned them against the Ottomans.

The young officers passed through some dozen campaigns, half a dozen wounds, some pillages and then were army-command ready. The most cultured among them could have learned as much Latin as needed to read Plutarch, Cesar, Livius, Tacitus, and Sallustius. Then they could try a comparison between the learned theory and the daily practice. If they were skill and lucky, they survived and their career went on, otherwise they simply died. The smartest among them had a good imagination, good practices and a certain knowledge of the enemy commander's mentality, an enemy commander they often met in their youth, when they fought together in the same army against the Ottomans.

Their commanding action was limited only by their sovereign's orders, but in Victor Amadeus' case, he was the sovereign, so he had no limit. Well, actually he too had some: supplies.

Every army relies on two basic things: firing and eating, and supplies are never plentiful for either of these things.

Let us start with food. Until the early 17th century, armies ate what they found in the countries they crossed or they stayed, and often that meant to starve. To avoid such a situation, during the last quarter of the 17th century armies established a supply service. It had to find, keep, and distribute food and forage, but it had to provide also uniforms – whose first use is documented in Italy since the last quarter of the 16th century – gunpowder, bullets and weapons.

Some civil contractors gathered all these materials from a widespread network of small producers, and poured it into the magazines. Then, the military administration or the contractor forwarded the supplies by water or by land to other magazines, closer to the troops in the war theatre. If the system did not work, or did not work as much as needed, the army raided the neighbouring area and pillaged whatever it could find: food, forage, carts, and animals, not disdaining money, of course, with some rapes and tortures here and there, just for the soldiers' amusement. If the supply system worked, the army could be fed without requisitions in the operational area, but depended almost entirely on the presence of magazines and on its link to them.

The maximum autonomy – and consequently the widest range of action – an army could have was dictated by the quantity of food the soldiers could carry. It was certainly not that much if the famous 'five-marches system' invented by Frederick the Great was greeted as brilliant. Since the mid 18th century that system allowed the troops with nine rations – three in their bags and six in the following wagons – to march ahead during three days and then return to the camp, whose stocks would provide the evening meal of the sixth day. But at the end of the 17th century this was still a dream.

Thus the generals tended much more to destroy enemy communication lines and magazines than the enemy army, for a field clash would cost, in men and weapons, much more than a raid against a supply centre. Moreover seizing a supply centre necessarily enforced the enemy to withdraw to his surviving stores, further but still intact, whilst a battle could not always force the enemy to withdraw. And that is why many generals said it was possible to win a war without fighting too much or, as the Marshal of Saxony said in the 18th century, with no fight at all.

Campaigns were therefore rather slow and the battles relatively scarce. On the other hand, there were a lot of marches.

Fighting occurred mostly in spring and summer. Autumn always slowed down war activity, for the first rains rendered the roads muddy, so the supplies needed for major operations could not be moved and this hindered the movement of troops. Thus, the armies left the theatre of war and lodged close to their magazines, getting so-called winter quarters. Winter quarters had to be paid for by the sovereign, but almost often he mostly graciously gave such a honour to the Commons, whilst the commanders-in-chief returned to the Court, reported about the just-finished campaign and prepared the next. Before the next spring the army was reassembled. Gaps due to dead, wounded, prisoners, sick and, in large part, deserters were filled and troopers were re-equipped and rested.

But only the major operations were suspended. At least in Italy small operations continued as long as possible. It was so, for instance, in Piedmont during winter 1690–91, when big units of the opposing cavalries continued to fight during all the poor-weather season, galloping up and down the roads in search of convoys or enemy troops, trying to inflict the greatest possible damage to the enemy.

A winter battle was an exception and a surprise, and there were very few before the War of Spanish Succession. This depended mainly on the lack of ammunition during the poor-weather season, due to the bad state of the roads, and to the great variety of firearms, and consequently of calibres and projectiles.

The problem affected infantry and, much more, artillery. Infantry had up to two or three different types of individual firearms. Since contemporary technology allowed only an approximate uniformity of the barrels and, therefore, of gauges, the soldier at the camp looked for bullets in a pile, chose some balls, tested to see if they entered the barrel and, more or less, he found always enough bullets to feed his weapon.

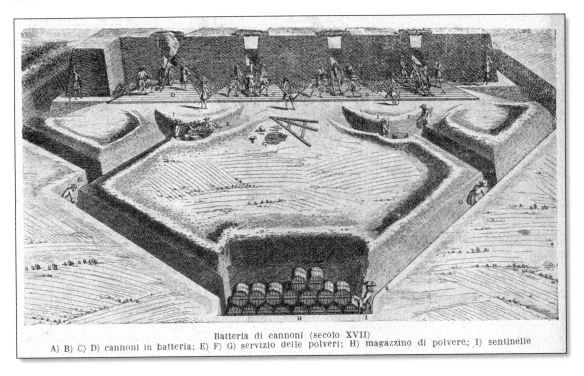

Batteria di cannoni (secolo XVII)
A) B) C) D) cannoni in batteria; E) F) G) servizio delle polveri; H) magazzino di polvere; I) sentinelle

15. Artillery – cannon battery

Artillery had a completely different and more complicated situation. Guns were classified according to the weight of the projectile – usually an iron ball – they shot. Thus their variety was wider than infantry weapons and changed according to the army. For instance, in 1713 there were 13 types of guns officially listed in the Imperial army, whilst the Piedmontese had a dozen and the French no more than seven or eight.

During the 17th century the technological evolution of the gun carriages led to their progressive lightening and consequently to a decrease of the horses, or oxen, needed for towing. Besides, at the end of the 17th century and the beginning of the 18th one still needed a dozen horses to tow a 33-pound gun, eight horses for a 24-pound gun, six for the 12-pounder, and so on.

The ordnance – ammunition, gunpowder, tools, and equipment – in the Piedmontese army were carried by the convoys of the so-called artillery train. It used four-horse wagons, whose loading capacity went from 500 up to 800 kilogrammes.

Each gunshot could need from two to 18 pounds of gunpowder, being a pound some one third of a kilogramme. The gunpowder, whose grain varied according to the type of firebox to which it was intended, was usually stored in barrels. A barrel's weight went from 100 kilogrammes – for the bigger guns – down to 50 kilogrammes for the smaller guns. Thus, a wagon could carry from five to eight big barrels, or from 10 to 16 small barrels. This allowed the firing of some 16 shots with a big gun, or around 50 with a small one.

A large-calibre gun could safely fire up to 50 shots a day, thus its gunpowder needed to be carried by three or four wagons, that is to say by 12 to 16 horses, and three or four coaches; and this was what the daily activity of a single gun needed only in gunpowder, not considering the balls.

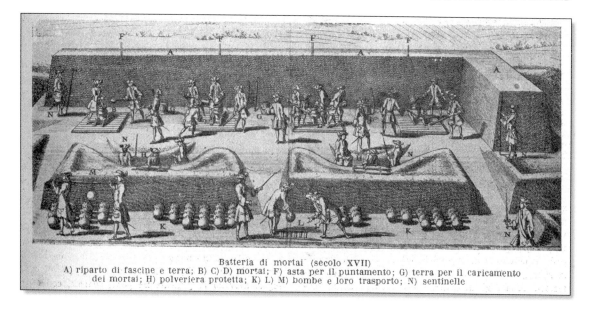

Batteria di mortai (secolo XVII)
A) riparto di fascine e terra; B) C) D) mortai; F) asta per il puntamento; G) terra per il caricamento dei mortai; H) polveriera protetta; K) L) M) bombe e loro trasporto; N) sentinelle

On the other hand, there were many different projectiles: free balls, enchained balls, shells, hollowed grenades, canisters and so on. They were carried by other wagons; and usually no wagon could load more than 30. Then it was necessary to provide the gunpowder for the fuses, which needed a finer grain. This kind of gunpowder was in 25 kilogramme boxes. And then the wagons had to carry the additional equipment: brushes, shovels, spoons, fuses, flints, and so on.

16. Artillery – mortar battery

In principle, we can therefore calculate at least six wagons needed for the daily and non-intensive activity of each big calibre gun. And that was just the minimum needed.

It is recorded that the 20 Piedmontese mortars battering Pinerolo during the 1693 siege required 10,000 bombs and 2,500 carts. And we are informed that, when the siege began, 100–150 wagons left Turin every day just to feed the mortars. If we calculate no less than four horses for each wagon, we have a total of 400–600 animals daily employed only for feeding siege batteries.

The horses needed to rest, thus they needed to be changed, and had to be fed. Their fodder had to be carried by further wagons, pulled by further horses, which also has to be fed. Then, food, ordnance, tools, and spare parts had to be provided to the soldiers; and the wounded had to be evacuated. And it was necessary to feed the cavalry; and the horses of the artillery in front of the city.

Moreover Pinerolo was a lucky case, because that city was very close to the main ordnance storage and Arsenal in Turin and there were no marches. Had it been a normal campaign, it would have been necessary to use between two and 10 times the number of animals, men and wagons, depending on the distance from the supply base.

The logistic problem caused by this large quantity of vehicles and animals was increased by other militarily useless people: the families of officers, non-commissioned officers and soldiers, with servants, clients, boys,

17. Pinerolo – the town

cellars, prostitutes, jugglers and receivers, who 'composed an army of almost innumerable rascals'.[1]

Reliable studies about the Imperial army in Italy during the following War of the Spanish Succession since 1701 until 1706, calculated these people to be as many as the fighting personnel. And, when considering the French, Piedmontese and Milanese (in Spanish service) armies in eastern Lombardy in 1701–1703, we find an army-related people to local population ratio from a maximum of three military-related to one local, to a standard minimum of two army-related to one local. All this mass of people had to move whenever the army moved. Hence, the marching unit had to carry its heavy quantity of baggage, plus the personal effects of officers, soldiers and their families; and that slowed the movements of the whole army. The situation in Piedmont in 1690–96 was basically the same. A remarkable city like Saluzzo had some 15,000 inhabitants when in summer 1690 it was stormed by some 10,000 French soldiers. We do not know how many additional people followed the French army in Piedmont, but, according to contemporary standards, it is reasonable to think them to have been at least half of the military personnel, if not as much as the military, which would give at least a 1:1 ratio to local population.

The army's overall figure and how it affected military movement was a serious problem, especially when considering how strategically important the march was. Generally a march was done in short stages, in daylight, sunshine to sunset. Security was impressive. Troops were detached ahead, on the flanks and to protect the back. Light cavalry was sent far ahead, along with the commissioners, who had to choose the camp location and find all, or at least a portion, of the supplies needed for the incoming army.

When on the spot, the chosen place was inspected, and if all was fine, cavalrymen went ahead to check if any enemy in sight. Meanwhile, commissioners requisitioned everything they could find, and demanded what was missing, sometimes threatening local people with pillaging. If people gave them what they asked for, the commissioners promised to pay, a promise they sometimes did not keep, especially if they were penniless Austrians.

1   Rossi, Anton Domenico, *Ristretto di storia patria ad uso de'Piacentini* (Plaisance, 1832), Tome 4, p. 272.

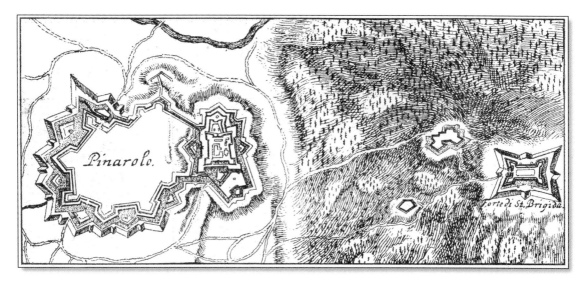

18. The French fortifications of Pinerolo in 1691

When the army arrived, usually a few hours later, the soldiers put up their tents where ordered.

During a march, every evening the camp had to be assembled, and every morning had to be dismantled. In between, soldiers had to think of getting dinner. Usually this meant that, if what the commissioners had found was not enough, the army had to send out infantry and cavalry detachments looking for food, water and fodder, losing additional time to be subtracted from the march.

All these operations did not leave that much time for marching from one place to another. Thus it is not surprising that until the Napoleonic era the standard march did not exceed a dozen kilometres per day (three leagues, or about seven miles). The troops marched in column, but generally not in order, on narrow roads. As a consequence, it was not rare to have an army whose head began setting up the arrival camp, whilst the rearguard was still disassembling the departed one.

Moreover, marches were short, but very fatiguing. Troopers had only one uniform, the winter one, but they marched and fought in summer, and used that same uniform. In that case, when marching and whilst in camp, they could remove their overcoat, but if we think of a poorly fed soldier, marching in summer, carrying 30 or 40 kilogrammes total weight, dressed in winter clothes, with an external temperature that, in Northern Italy and Southern France could easily be between 25 and 30, and perhaps 35 centigrade, we shall not be surprised to discover that the casualties due to marches were high. Reports and diaries between 1688 and 1748 give a bleak overview. The only exceptions appear to be Marlborough's supplies in 1702–1710, and the logistics organisation of Charles Emmanuel III of Sardinia, Victor Amadeus' youngest son and heir, in 1733–38 and 1741–48. Complaints of desperate generals and cries of pain by looted and mistreated civilians reported by diaries and chronicles arose to heaven everywhere. Therefore there was a harsh friction between the marching or encamped troops and the local population. Civilians reacted as they could. They concealed or consumed all the food and fodder they had. So, the army needed much more time for

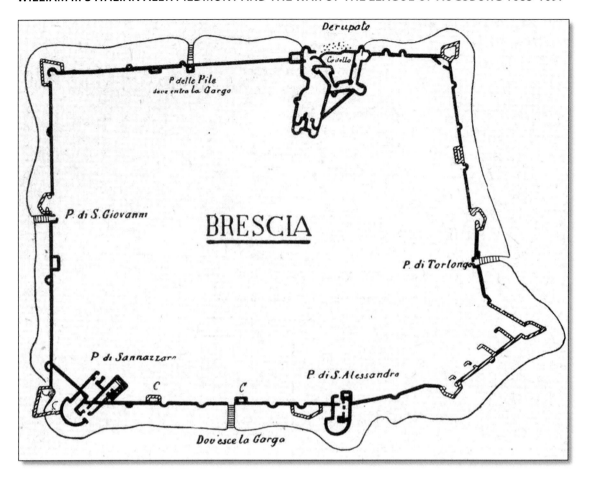

19. Brescia

finding food, and slowed down its movement. The other civilian reaction was violence. Peasants looked for isolated soldiers or small detachments, and attacked and massacred them without mercy.

This regularly happened in Piedmont when invaded by the French or by the Spaniards. At the beginning, in the 16th century, these were isolated initiatives, easily broken. But during the 17th century resistance became harsher and more organised, also thanks to the militia established by Emmanuel Philibert and enhanced by Charles Emmanuel I. Its military relevance increased so much that during the War of the Grand Alliance it became a relevant factor, also if its best performances were in the next century, against the French in 1702–1707, 1742–1748, and 1792–1796.

Military counter-reactions were as usual: looting, and then hanging – when the enemy was humane – all the people suspected of resisting, or to have resisted, a looting.

Local chronicles, especially from the period of the following War of Spanish Succession, provide plenty of details about these cases, and the results of those clashes filled the underground of the Po Valley, where, still in the late 19th century, at least in the Province of Brescia, it was possible to run into mass graves of Imperial soldiers massacred by the angry population between 1702 and 1706.

The major obstacles a 17th and 18th centuries army had, the hardest to overcome, were the cities, the walled ones, of course. If a city was not immediately seized, it had to be besieged; and this generally required a lot of time, because a ring of fortifications and siegeworks had to be built around its walls. And all these fieldworks had to be held by a substantial number of soldiers, which was very difficult to get in a period when 15,000 men composed a good army and the King of France's 200,000 men was considered an amazing figure, hard to be equalled and, above all, dramatically expensive.

It is true that the sieges could be planned well enough, but it is equally true that they only succeeded if the besieging army had safe and continuous supplies.

We must underline a problem here. The literature in English during the 20th century focused only on war theatres where the British fought, mostly Flanders. In some case this was due to a logical and reasonable interest on one's own country or culture. In other cases this happened because the authors read and understood only English, thus were unable to read diaries, journals and accounts written in languages other than English. No matter the reason, this left many people making two remarkable misunderstandings. The first was – and still is – to consider the valuable Geza Perjés' work[2] as absolutely valid, and a set of rules good for explaining logistics on every war theatre of every war prior to Napoleon, whilst Perjés himself clearly said he was speaking about the 17th century alone. A focus on different war theatres would provide evidence of differences between some aspects underlined by Perjés – mostly relying on sources concerning Hungarian campaigns – and the contemporary eyewitness accounts from other war theatres and other wars. The second misunderstanding was to consider sieges as the main kind of warfare of that period, and to think of the 17th and 18th century generals as focusing on sieges and thus relatively neglecting battles. This is a fallacy, a real mistake, bigger than blindly considering Perjés' work as always good despite the period, location, and circumstances. It comes, normally, from a wrongly overstressed application of the concept of 'reason'. Being the 18th century, the Age of Reason, that period's warfare was 'rational', hence logical, thus planned, and the best example of planning was siege warfare, thus siege warfare had to be, and was, the best loved and practised warfare of that period.

Actually, nobody would deny that the 17th and 18th centuries were marked by an enormous quantity of sieges, but due to a completely different reason. Logistics was the main issue, and logistics needs free and protected connections, that is to say, in that time, roads, waterways and related facilities. Cities commanded roads and waterways, hence they had to be seized and kept. If this could be done without a siege, it was the best option for all. Marlborough always did his best to cause a battle and to avoid sieges. Eugene of Savoy undertook only two sieges during his life, from 1690 to 1736 – Lille and Belgrade – and, at the end of the story, the first had no real consequence on a strategic level, whilst the result of the second was overthrown just one

---

2   Perjés, Geza, 'Army Provisioning, Logistics and Strategy in the Second Half of the 17th Century' in *Acta Historica Academiae Scientiarum Hungaricae*, T. 16, No. 1/2 (1970), pp. 1–52.

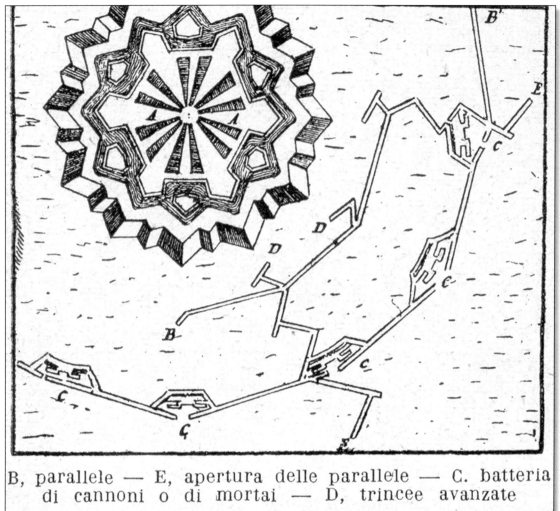

B, parallele — E, apertura delle parallele — C. batteria di cannoni o di mortai — D, trincee avanzate

20. The plan of a siege

year after Eugene's death. On the other hand, Eugene definitely swept out – and forever – the enemy from the theatre winning three battles: Zenta, Turin, and Oudenaarde, whilst Marlborough and he did the same at Blenheim.

Sieges worked well in the Rhineland and Flanders, where the plains, the dense network of canals and the wide range of rivers including the Rhine itself, allowed regular and copious amount of supplies. But if one looks at war reports from theatres other than Flanders and the Rhineland, finds the trend of the operations to worsen according to the roughness of the ground. In central Germany they did not go that well, and the more one proceeded eastward, the less sure the result of a siege became. In Italy, due to the Alps, there were two possible results. The besieger from across the Alps immediately won, in a very few days, or, and that was the most likely case, his siege took longer than expected, went very badly and often had to be interrupted. Thus, generals disliked cities – and sieges – just due to the risks involved. Every trick was good to seize a city: heavy shelling, mines, climbing, underground digging, underground fights with poisonous smoke,

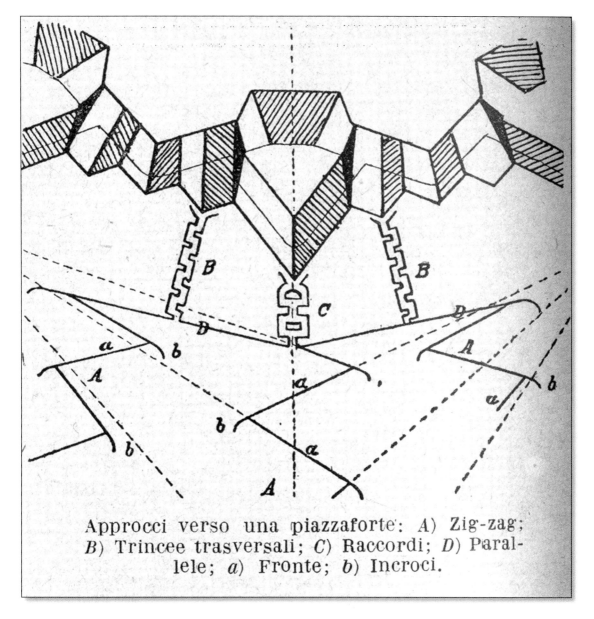

Approcci verso una piazzaforte: A) Zig-zag; B) Trincee trasversali; C) Raccordi; D) Parallele; a) Fronte; b) Incroci.

21. Siege – approach (1)

starvation, bribery, poisoning, and very favourable surrender conditions offered to the defenders. Everything was good to seize a fortified city, but no general of the late 17th and the 18th century really loved sieges, except Marshall de Saxe, who seemed to have found the secret to undertake and win whatever siege in a few days.

Sieges went always the same way. They began with the incoming army blockading the city, or the fortress, by distributing its troopers around it. Then, the besiegers' commander decided the main attack approach and its scheme, and gave the order to 'open the trench'. This meant the digging of the siege trenches. It could be carried out both by the soldiers of the besieging army and by ad hoc raked civilians. It was not a very long story, even if it was dangerous and complicated, and the duration of the siege was calculated

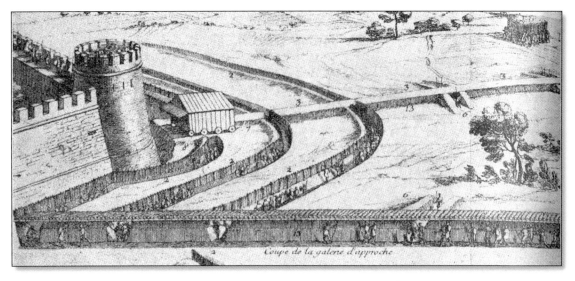

22. Siege – approach (2)

from the day they started opening the trenches, i.e. from the first day of the excavation, no matter how long the excavation could last.

Once the trench was made, the army could start the real siege. Its schedule was dictated by the structure of the fortress and by the practice.

First of all it was necessary to overcome the defensive positions out of the walls. This was not easy, as some European fortresses had a defensive mine system. Mines were fired and exploded under the feet of the besiegers, causing terrible casualties. Turin was one of the best-protected cities in Europe. Its underground network included tunnels and mine stoves and, after the improvements made by Victor Amadeus II, it was organised on three underground levels, totalling some 10 miles.

Besiegers had to neutralise mines with countermine works and, if all went well, they could then storm the external defensive positions facing 'only' the enemy artillery and riflemen.

Then there was the attack to the counter-scarpe and to the scarpe, that is to say, the seizure of the outer edge of the moat, the descent into the moat itself and, if possible, the attack on the walls. The next step was always considered so important that special messengers were chosen among the high-ranked or noblest officers to inform the sovereign. It was the conquest of the covered road. It had this name because it was 'covered', that is to say protected, by the fortress artillery. It was the internal road behind the defensive wall, allowing the defenders to move along the inner part of the walls; this seizure was actually anything but decisive.

Once the covered road taken, it was time to break through the fortifications with all available artillery. Assuming that the besieged troops did not dig mines under the siege cannons, making them blow, as the Piedmontese did in Turin against the French in 1706, and assuming that their sallies were always repulsed, the day came when a breach was opened in the walls. Its width was measured in 'men on front', that is to say the number of infantrymen who could enter it marching side by side.

Now, if it was a matter of a fortress, at this point the garrison received a demand to surrender. Usually, in order to complete that task, the besieging

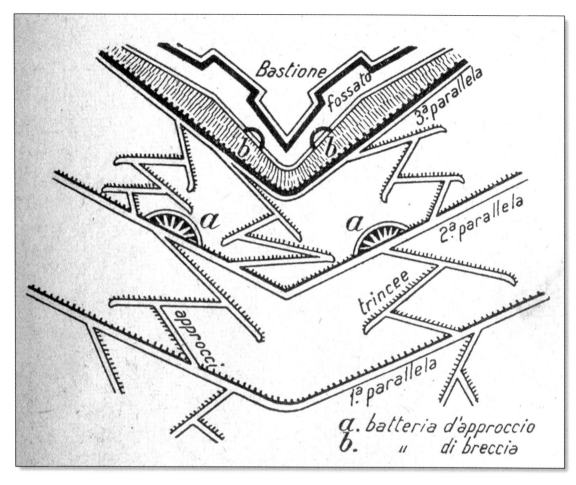

23. Siege – attack

commander granted to the besieged one not only the honour of arms, but even permission to withdraw with all his men, a small number of guns (usually no more than half a dozen of light guns), playing their fifes, rolling their drums, waving their flags and bringing their wagons along. The besieged had only to promise not to fight again before a certain term was up. The same could happen in battle, if an army surrounded so a big enemy unit that waging a negotiation seemed easier than a further bloody assault.

If he was – or was supposed to be – still strong enough to negotiate, the besieged commander discussed the capitulation, then ordered the drummers to 'roll the surrender',[3] lowered the flag and came out of the walls bringing what was permitted according to the capitulation, that is to say the written text listing the surrendering conditions.

But if a city was besieged, things went in a completely different and much more annoying way for the besiegers. A city always had its own fortified citadel, where the garrison withdrew every time they saw a breach opened in the walls. Then the besieged commander gave the city delegates the

---

3   If the besieged commander asked for surrender before being demanded to by the enemy, he ordered the drummers to 'roll the call'.

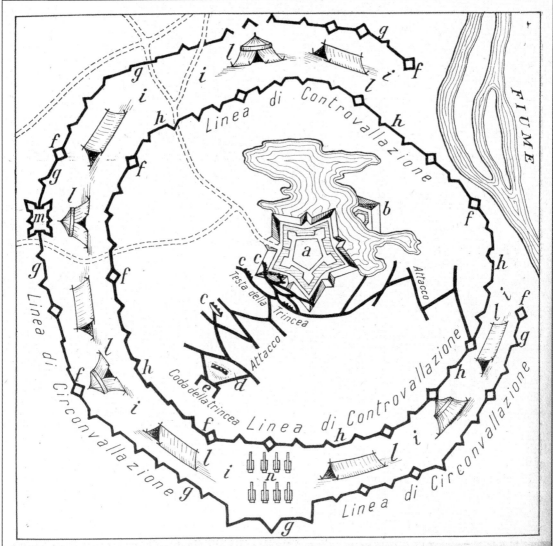

Linee di Circonvallazione e di Controvallazione intorno a una piazzaforte assediata (secolo XVII): *a*, piazzaforte; *b*, mezzaluna; *c*, batterie dell'attaccante; *d*, idem; *e*, *f*, ridotte; *g*, fossato della linea di Circonvallazione; *h*, fossato della linea di Controvallazione; *i*, campo; *l*, tende; *m*, deposito viveri; *n*, parco d'artiglieria.

24. Siege – circumvallation

permission to negotiate with the besiegers, whilst he retired into the citadel with the garrison and arranged to hold it. Hence the unlucky besieger had to start a new siege, for the capitulation often concerned only the city.

Meanwhile, a relief army could come. If so, it was rare to see a besieging army keeping the siege and, at the same time, turning against the relief army and defeating it. Eugene of Savoy destroyed the incoming Ottoman relief army whilst he was besieging Belgrade in 1717, but usually the besieger packed his tents and left swiftly, so as not to be surrounded and defeated in turn.

It could happen that every surrender demand was rejected. If so, the garrison could later surrender only 'at discretion' of the winner.[4] Thus if the garrison rejected any negotiation, it could not be sure to be taken prisoner of war when the city fell. If the city was seized, or, as they said, was 'taken by assault', that is to say stormed, looting and massacre were certain. This explains why until Napoleon so many cities surrendered after sieges so short that they looked like a pure formality.

In most cases the generals were much more willing to fight the enemy in the open field. They did not consider it as their best choice, but the battle could be regarded as a colossal duel. And if they were forced to do it, since no gentleman refused a duel, they deployed their respective troops and made them fight.

The armies clashed with remarkable ferocity and enormous difficulties. This was mostly due to the individual and corps weapons. Not all the armies of that time were organised in the three branches of infantry, cavalry, and artillery.

In the past, the battle of Saint Quentin had destroyed both France, and the myth of the infantry's invincibility by less well-considered corps as cavalry and artillery. To cope with the threatening preponderance of the former, based on speed and impact, European armies quickly and widely adopted portable firearms to damage the charging enemy cavalry before being engaged. On the other hand, they improved guns, looking to render them lighter and lighter, easier to handle, and capable of a firing high rate.

In the 17th century there were remarkable achievements. Troops abandoned the arquebus, which could be used only by putting it on a supporting fork due to its weight, and progressed first to the matchlock musket, then to the flintlock musket or the flintlock rifle. There was a difference in Italy between the two: the rifle had a longer barrel than the musket, thus infantry long-barrelled weapons were called rifles, whilst the cavalry's relatively short-barrelled weapons were muskets.

Technical improvements in infantry firearms made infantry white arms, especially pikes, decrease. Pikes first remained to protect musketeers; and then, in the last quarter of the 17th century, began disappearing. Initially bayonets were plugged into the rifle barrel, thus rendering the rifle a sort of short pike. However as such a tool prevented infantrymen reloading and firing again quickly, the French invented the socket bayonet, to be put on the barrel, thanks to a ring. According to French sources, it seems to have been used by the very first time at the battle of Marsaglia, in Piedmont, in 1693. Triangle-shaped, looking like a sort of mason's trowel, lighter and longer than the previous plug-in bayonet, the new bayonet allowed the rifle to shoot

---

4   Surrendering could be, 'with quarter', 'without quarter' and 'at discretion'. In the first case the winner promised to pay for the prisoners' lodging and food, and hoped to be repaid – with interest – when getting the ransom. 'Without quarter', or 'no quarter', meant simply that the prisoner had to pay for his own lodging and feeding once captured. 'Discretion' meant that the winner could do whatever he wanted to the prisoner. Troopers normally charged screaming: 'quarter', 'no quarter' and 'discretion' because, in a period of professional armies, professional soldiers on both sides found it correct to let the enemies know in advance what could they expect. It was just to let the enemy evaluate whether it was more convenient to fight or to surrender, the latter option being discarded in the case of the fourth and most feared of all the cries: 'no mercy'.

25. Pike drilling from Marzioli

and be reloaded. The firing rate was therefore higher, although its precision remained somewhat approximate.

The flintlock rifle, adopted by all the armies at the end of the 17th century, was smoothbore. Therefore it was neither accurate nor did it have a long range.

The first inconvenience could not be solved. The second was solved making rifle barrels longer. Thus rifles became as tall as their owners. But this was a new problem. Since the weapons of the time were almost all muzzle-loaded, infantrymen had to put the rifle's stock on the ground. Then, holding the barrel, the soldier had to put the gunpowder and the ball in. It was a long process, it took time, and during that time the soldier was at the enemy's mercy and could react only using his own white arms.

Therefore, to protect each other, to ensure an uninterrupted firing and to better withstand the attacks by the enemy cavalry, infantry manoeuvred on the battlefield in squared order, divided in several lines, one by one, moving relatively quickly also under the enemy fire. This meant that in a battle, whenever they were commanded, troopers advanced towards the enemy having the captains and lieutenants marching before them continually checking the ranks did not tumble into disorder. It was not a rare situation. Lines could be disordered by the ground, but the main risk was artillery fire.

There were too many unpredictable factors the commander had to face, and no theory, and often no plan, could be kept in an actual battle. Ground, fortifications, enemy cavalry and artillery, weather, time … everything had to be evaluated moment by moment, without prejudice. In fact every general, and every colonel decided on the spot how to manage the situation, according to the ground and according to the kind of units he had at hand and in front of him.

Regiments were the core of armies, and every regiment had a different kind of soldier. Fusileers had to hold the front. Grenadiers were used for attacks and protection whilst retreating. There was normally a grenadier company in each battalion, supported by the sappers. Sometimes, at least in the Piedmontese army and at least until the Napoleonic Wars, regimental grenadiers were gathered in occasional battalions or regiments, to be used during the fight.

Bandsmen were employed to play music on march and in battle – which gave the troopers the marching cadence and contributed to keep the lines in order – but were also employed for gathering the wounded and to bury the dead. The regimental provost and his soldiers, usually still called 'archers', were the military police, and were often supported by dragoons.

Weapons and clothes differed according to the soldier's specialisation. All dressed in a wide coat, basically an overcoat. During the Nine Years' War, fusileers already used the normal tricorn, and had a bayonet, a rifle, or musket, and a short sword to be used during a hand-to-hand fight.

Grenadiers had the same weaponry as the fusileers, but with a huge quantity of hand grenades, to be launched on the enemy from a short distance. This affected their hat and rifles. To launch their grenades, they had to put aside the rifle. This was dangerous, so they soon started applying a belt to the rifle, to hang it to their shoulders whilst throwing the grenades. Musket belts became the distinctive sign of grenadiers' weapons, but they had another problem. It was not easy to wear musket belts having on the head the wide tricorn of that time, hence the grenadiers started using in battle their free-time cap, the nightcap, which had to be worn only in the barracks or in camp. Then they added to the nightcap a cardboard frontal plaque, which became taller and taller, and in Continental European armies south of the Rhine was later covered by fur.

Sappers had to act as pioneers during attacks, digging, opening a way through enemy trenches, and quickly preparing field fortifications. Thus they were usually dressed like the grenadiers, but they had a big axe, no rifle, and a wide leather apron.

Piedmontese line infantry since the War of the League of Augsburg was flanked by irregular units, composed of Waldensians. We shall see later who the Waldensians were. Here we can say they were a useful mountain light infantry, and, in a certain sense, the ancestors of the Italian Alpine troops established in the last quarter of the 19th century.

The Waldensians fought in scattered order. Grenadiers attacked in column, opening their own way with hand grenades, whilst fusileers held the line and fought in line.

Cavalry was divided into heavy and light cavalry. There were dragoons too, but they were quite distinct. As in other armies, in Piedmont too dragoons were mounted infantry, and in the Piedmontese army they were an élite corps. Being infantry, they had their grenadiers, used rifles instead of muskets, and did not have boots. They used the so-called *bottine alla granadiera* ('grenadiers'gaiters'), made of leather.

During the War of the Grand Alliance, Piedmontese cavalry relied mostly on dragoons, and actually as later in the Italian army – it first four and oldest regiments were, and are, dragoon regiments.

There were also cuirassiers, briefly called 'armours', and the heavy cavalry, tasked to charge and crash the enemy lines.

Cavalry patrolled, performed long and short range reconnaissance, escorted convoys, raided, protected withdrawals, attacked by surprise, disturbed and opposed the advancing enemy, or pursued them when retreated.

Cavalry was employed in battle mainly to crush infantry. Artillery had not yet a long range fire, at least at the end of the 17th century. Cannons were used all at the same time against all the targets in sight. Fire was not concentrated, and the projectile was shot to a longer distance by simply increasing the launching charge. This made the barrel suffer a big strain and a quick overheating. There was no solution but to use the cannon until it broke, or exploded, and try to refresh it using buckets of water.

The most used firing technique was that used mainly by the French, and which had been used by the Portuguese navy at least since the 16th century. The cannons fired their balls at a relatively close range, in order to let them bounce many times – as flat stones on the water – until crashing against the enemy men and horses.

It was during the Nine Years' War that the howitzers appeared by the first time. Traditionally, they are said to have been used by the Anglo-Dutch troops in Flanders, to have been seized and copied by the French and then used by them on the Italian front too. Artillery usually included the military engineers corps.[5] At that time engineers dealt both with machines and civil construction, hence the officers composing the engineer corps were all military architects and, at the same time, able in dealing with every kind of machine, whilst weapons and ordnance were normally reserved to the artillery officers, whose scientific background was basically the same.

---

5   It must be underlined here that whilst in English the word engineer means both the man dealing with engines, and the person having a master degree in engineering or in architecture, in Italian – and in French – the man dealing with engines is called a *macchinista*, and the word 'engineer' means only the person who has a master degree in engineering.

Engineers had to draw maps, direct road and fortification works, and direct the sieges. Directing a siege meant planning the fire sector of each battery, planning and overseeing the excavation of trenches and mine galleries, and taking care of the technical side of the attacks on the besieged fortress.

Infantry, cavalry, and artillery too, had to keep their lines in battle, thus a strict discipline was enforced, and it had to be kept every time and everywhere. Penalties were hard. A Piedmontese soldier guilty of *lèse majesté*, betrayal, cowardice in front of the enemy, complaint or protest against a superior whilst in rank, atrocious blasphemy, aggression to members of the clergy, sorcery, desertion, blackmail, or insubordination was sentenced to death. Normal swearers and people acting against the Roman Catholic faith were sentenced to prison the first time; to the stocks the second time, and the third time to have their tongue pierced. Minor faults were punished by *strappados*, by the stake, by passing through the bars – in infantry – and through the sticks in cavalry.[6]

These punishments kept more or less in order a heterogeneous, mostly illiterate, and superstitious troop, largely composed of people released from prisons or sometimes who had been forced to enlist. Ruined peasants, dismissed servants, men with no family, artisans who lost all, people unemployed and looking for adventure, booty, or even daily food and a roof, both national and foreign subjects, were trained by corporal and non-commissioned officers, under the control of the officers, until their discipline and the habit of executing orders were so automatic to allow them to advance in open field, in close order, at a speed of about 80 steps per minute[7] without even attempting to shield themselves from enemy bullets.

Obviously, as soon as the opportunity came, many soldiers deserted. There was little chance for them: enlist in another army, or turn to brigandage, with the threat of the gallows for desertion and a reward on their head. The best opportunities generally came after a battle; but the battles were few due to supply problems.

But when there was no other solution and it was necessary to fight, armies faced each other in open field with remarkable ferocity. Movements were not very fast, at least compared to the wars of the following centuries, simply because ranks and close order had to be kept. It was not that easy, due to smoke. The first volley produced so thick and stagnant a curtain of smoke that nobody could see through it. Therefore, after an initial exchange of shots at a very close distance – usually some tens of steps – the armies engaged in the hand-to-hand fight.

An additional problem came now. Uniforms looked practically the same in all the armies, and since the most internationally used colour was grey – later, in the following century, different shades of white – it was very hard

---

6 'Passing through the rods' or 'through the bars', or 'through the sticks' meant that the punished soldier had to walk step by step between two rows of comrades – usually his whole company, or two companies – each of them armed with a rod, or with the rifle ramrod – which in some armies was wooden, but in others iron. Each of them had to hit the punished soldier when he passed In front of him. Some men died before the end of the punishment.

7 This is the ordinary and parade cadence of the Italian alpine troops even now.

to know who was the friend or who the enemy; nor could one succeed in hearing the enemy speak, because every commander enlisted foreigners, no matter whether they were single deserters or whole units of mercenaries, volunteers or prisoners. So it was very easy to find people of the same origin or nationality under opposing flags.

The only sure distinctive mark was a badge. In a short time it became the cockade, worn by each soldier at least in battle on the left side of his hat, and whose colour varied, but with little imagination, according to the sovereign.[8] Only, it was not always possible to see it in time. So it was better to hit first, and then make one's own deductions.

Casualties were huge. The number of dead was often very high and few wounded survived the clash. No medical service existed, for there were only a few surgeons. In general, only at the beginning of the campaign the military administration organised a field hospital by contract. The field hospital followed the army with ambulances, servants, nurses, surgeons and doctors, who were considered civilians in all respects.

Many of the wounded by a gunshot died within hours due to wound infection and blood loss. Moreover, given the size of the bullets of that time, if limbs were concerned, the physical damage was often so terrible that one could do nothing but amputate.

The biggest concern armies had was disease. Military physicians and surgeons[9] had good practical experience. They knew what happened, but did not know why. Studies were going on, but an additional and remarkable result appeared in 1700, when doctor Bernandino Ramazzini first published his *De morbis artificum diatriba* – debate on workers' diseases – a milestone in the history of medicine and the starting point of occupational medicine. Ramazzini examined in Chapter 11 of his book *de Morbis Castrensibus*[10] what he called, according to contemporary use, the 'camp diseases' whilst the term 'camp disease' is now a synonym of typhus. Ramazzini remarked how the lack of care during winter quarters weakened and sometimes definitely handicapped, or killed, the men wounded during the previous campaign. It was rare not to have battalions devastated by diseases, and the whole army stopped by an epidemic. According to Ramazzini, the worst was what were called 'camp fevers'. The first occurrence seems to have been in the Imperial army during the 1566 Hungarian campaign. It was a consequence of the rotten food and waste water, also if their effects were enhanced by concomitant causes as excessive labour, lack of sleep, rain, excessively cold or hot weather, fear,

---

8 Spaniards and Neapolitans had a red cockade; the Piedmontese and the Venetian had a blue one; the Papal troops used a yellow and red cockade, the French usually had white ones but sometimes also black. Black was used by Prussians, the British and, from a certain period, by the Austrians. The latter, however, when fighting as Imperial troops, that is to say always except for the 1741–1745 period, wore an oak twig on the hat: the badge of the Empire.

9 We must always remember that surgeons and physicians were two different kind of medical doctor, the latter often considering the former as culturally inferior because they were not doctors.

10 Ramazzini, Bernardino, *De morbis artificum diatriba* (first edition Modena, 1700); I used here the Venetian 1743 edition.

and 'a thousand further uncomfortable and noxious things'.[11] But, Ramazzini underlined, the worst came from how filthy camps were, and, he added, this was because people simply did not take care of where and how they left their faeces. Whilst the Hebrews – according to the Bible – and the Ottomans used latrines, that is to say holes dug in the soil far outside the camp, and covered them after use, European armies – as he saw in Imperial winter quarters in 1690–96 in Northern Italy – did not, and left everywhere within the camp their 'production', 'the work of the body', as the medieval Italian language said. The first consequence was a terrible stink, and if the results were terrible for men of the late 17th century, accustomed to living among stinks men of the 21st century simply don't imagine, we can easily understand how hard that had to be.[12] The result was dysentery, typhus, and 'evil fevers', which were probably mostly malaria,[13] normally spreading among the troops during the end of summer. Their symptoms were headaches, fevers, deliria, convulsions and diarrhoea, alone or all together. Suggested drugs and cures seemed to be not that useful, also if, when speaking of malaria in another part of his book, Ramazzini was among the first who suggested and supported the use of chinchona, a quinine-rich flowering plant from South America, no matter how toxic many contemporary physicians claimed it to be.

The sick and wounded were less fortunate than prisoners. Prisoners were robbed immediately after, if not already during, the battle. The same occurred to the dead, who were stripped of everything, and left literally naked on the ground. It was the fastest way to remedy the shortcomings of military supplies, and the eternal lack of money of the privates, although every camp had receivers who bought everything.

Moreover when losing their uniforms, the enemy suffered an economic loss, for his administration had to fully re-equip its own men once released due to an exchange of prisoners.

Last, another serious problem was the slowness and approximation of information. Normally a mounted messenger needed at least a quarter of hour to reach the army commander from a sector. Assuming that he got an immediate answer, he who had sent him asking for instructions received the answer not earlier than half a hour, or perhaps never if the messenger had been wounded or killed when going or coming back. This meant that usually most of the orders were issued according to outdated information, thus they were hopelessly useless, and the situation could be solved only thanks to the sector commander's experience and skill, and to how good in holding the line his regiments were.

Army commanders tried to solve this problem staying where they could see the whole battlefield, and delegated the command of the different sectors.

---

11 Ramazzini, Bernardino, *De morbis artificum diatriba* (Venice 1743), p. 231.

12 Ramazzini mentioned the works by Dutch physician Raymond Minderer (1570–1621) on military medicine, by Swiss physician Heinrich Screta (1637–1688), and by the Neapolitan physician Luca Antonio Porzio (1637–1715), but he got also much important information from the First Physician of the Duke of Hannover, Doctor Georg Heinrich Bernstorff, during the wintering of the Hannoverian troops in Modena.

13 Malaria is an Italian combined word, literally meaning 'evil air'.

More exactly: the army commander decided the battle plan, told it to his subordinates in a council of war, and assigned and explained to each of them what he had to do, and the respective tasks. Everyone had relative autonomy during the action and only the general direction and management of the battle remained in the commander's hands. Traditionally there were six subordinated commanders: one for each wing and for the centre on both the first and the second line. It was their ability, precision, smartness, skill, experience and constancy which dictated the result of the battle.

This was the European armies' warfare in the Baroque or early modern era, according to very precise rules and conventions. Such warfare was basically the same from the end of the Thirty Years' War until the early Napoleonic campaigns. And that was the way Victor Amadeus' army had to fight.

3

The Duke of Savoy's Army

I. The Enforced French Military Alliance

A treaty Mary-Jane of Savoy made with France on 24 November 1682 said that, in war, Savoy had to receive one third of all the mutually made conquests. But in exchange France established a real protectorate. In fact the treaty,[1] after an apparently friendly article, established a six year defensive and offensive alliance between France and Savoy. The Sun King promised to defend the Duke, and the Duke promised to commit his troops if the French garrisons in Pinerolo and Casale and in the places on the Rhône were attacked.

The worst was in article two. Seeing that Casale, according to the French, was not yet able to resist, and seeing that the few ducal troops were all committed in garrisoning their own places, but seeing also that some important places or fortresses could be 'surprised and seized, causing damage to His Majesty's or to Lord the Duke of Savoy's service if nothing was done in advance, His aforesaid Majesty proposed the lodging of three thousand men, as well light cavalry as of the Dragoons in Piedmont'[2] and all these troopers had to depend only on their own officers, that is to say on France.

According to Article 5, Victor Amadeus had to enrol and keep on active duty a further 1,000 light cavalrymen, or dragoons, regardless of the 800 he already had, and a further 500 foot, not considering the 6,700 he had on active duty. Louis promised to pay him an annual 300,000 *livres tournoises* subsidy, in monthly shares. As soon as these new troops were combat-ready, Louis would withdraw one third of the men he had in Piedmont when signing the Treaty. In other words: Victor Amadeus was compelled to a 20 percent increase of his troops, who had to remain scattered in their garrisons, whilst he had to host in the middle of his country a foreign, centralised, and not exactly friendly mass, not under his command and ready to intervene against any enemy of France, including him. Moreover, the increased force of his army would depend on French money, and in case that money was lacking, as happened just before the Grand Alliance, the situation would become difficult whenever the Duke's

---

1   *Traité d'alliance défensive entre Victor Amé Duc de Savoie et le Roi de France*, made in Turin on 24 November 1682, rep. in Solaro della Margarita, op. cit., vol. II, pp. 103–4.
2   *Traité d'alliance* cit., article II, op. cit., vol. II, p. 105.

policy differed from the French one. Lastly, in case of war, the French promised to give Piedmont a yearly 1.2 million *livres* funding, and that funding had to be used to implement Piedmontese disposal of up to 4,000 cavalry – dragoons included – and 8,500 foot. On their own side the French promised to commit 3,000 cavalry and 14,000 foot more than they already had in Piedmont, to be supported by an artillery train of no less than 15 and no more than 30 field guns. Clearly, the command had to be in French hands whenever the two armies operated jointly and their commanders' rank equalled. But of what form was the army we are speaking of?

II. Infantry

Victor Amadeus' father, Duke Charles Emmanuel II, reorganised his army between 1660 and 1664. In 1655 he introduced bayonets, to be plugged into the musket barrel, and, following the trend, in 1672 the Arsenal of Turin standardised some 18,000 muskets. In 1674 calibres were determined to be equal to a heavy lead bullet, whose weight was an ounce of Piedmont, that is to say 30.7 grammes, or 1.22 British ounces, and between 17.3 and 17.5 millimetres in size.[3]

Five years before, in 1669, Charles Emmanuel declared six infantry units to be 'order' regiments, that is to say six 'standing' regiments, called that way as they had to keep the 'order', or the ranks of the army's core in battle. However the army had standing units since long before. In 1619 was established the Savoyard Regiment du Cheyne, which later evolved into the Casale Infantry Regiment. In 1625 was raised the Fleury Regiment of Foot,[4] later known as the Catalano Alfieri Regiment, after its commander's name, and then as the Piemonte Infantry Regiment and last as the 3rd and 4th Piemonte Infantry Regiment. The Savoy Infantry Regiment – later 1st and 2nd Savoia Infantry Regiments in the Royal Sardinian army, and then 'Re' ['the King'] Infantry Regiment in the Royal Italian army – was originally raised in 1639. Prior to 1660 some more units were organised: the Guards,[5] and the Nice and Monferrato Infantry Regiments.

---

3   See Sterrantino, Francesco, 'L'esercito del Duca di Savoia', in *La guerra della Lega di Augusta fino alla battaglia di Orbassano* (Turin, 1993), p. 217.

4   In 1619 Charles Emanuel I appointed Jean Wilcardel – or Villecardel – de Fleury, Fresne e Sandreville, lieutenant in his son's – Prince Thomas of Savoy's – company of cuirassiers as the Marquess of Mortigliengo, and the new Marquess raised and commanded the regiment.

5   Officially the Guards are said to have been established as late as 1659, but I am rather doubtful. The year was decided in the 19th century due to a levy order issued on 18 April 1659, but I found different documentary evidence in Turin. The Turin State Archive has in Materie Militari, Ordini e Regolamenti, Mazzo 2, number 1, an order issued on 22 April 1617 by Duke Charles Emmanuel I, printed by Luigi Pizzamiglio 'ducal printer', and entitled *Ordine del Duca Carlo Emanuele I per la levata delle Compagnie di Soldatesca ivi espresse per il suo Reggimento delle Guardie* ('Order of the Duke Charles Emmanuel I for the levy of the companies of soldiers within expressed for his Regiment of the Guards'). The text provides evidence showing that it did not speak of the Duke's Household, but of a regular and normal infantry regiment.

Once power was only in his hands, Victor Amadeus kept the military organisation his father established, but enhanced it with a deep and progressive reorganisation.

In 1685 he established grenadier units after the French example. Meanwhile he slowly increased the quantity of infantry regiments up to 10, establishing Croce Bianca,[6] Saluzzo, della Marina,[7] and Chiablese, and in 1690 he ordered the troopers to abandon pikes, leave the musket and use the new flintlock rifle. So, by 1690 ducal infantry included 14 regiments, that is to say: Guardie (Guards), Savoia (Savoy), Monferrato, Piemonte (Piedmont), Aosta, Mondovì, Nizza, Croce Bianca, Saluzzo, La Marina, Chiablese, Fucilieri, La Trinità, and Artiglieria (Artillery), which included the whole artillery, listed within the infantry.

By the end of the 17th century the 'order' infantry regiments Guards and Savoy had two battalions, whilst the other regiments had only one. Each battalion was composed of 10 companies.[8] The Reggimento – literally meaning in ancient Italian 'the government', or 'the rule' – was also called *colonnello* – 'colonel' – or *colonnellato*, which could be translated as 'domain of the colonel', for it was supposed to compose a 'colonna' – a column – and that was why it was commanded by an officer called a 'colonel', which meant something like 'the columner'. The colonel commanded at the same time his regiment and a company, named after his rank as the *compagnia colonnella*, the 'colonel's company'.

In hierarchical order, under the colonel there was a lieutenant-colonel – literally meaning 'the one who keeps the colonel's place' – and the *capitano maggiore* – meaning the 'senior captain' and shortened to *maggiore,* hence the English spelling, 'major' – who respectively commanded the 'lieutenant-colonel's company' and the 'major's company'. All the remaining companies were commanded by normal captains. No matter how many battalions existed – one or two – all the captains depended directly on the colonel, and each of them was (or was supposed to be) supported in his company by a lieutenant – literally meaning 'the one who keeps the place' – an ensign, a lodging marshal and by the sergeants, who were the platoon commanders.

---

6   The Croce Bianca ['White Cross'] Regiment was so-called due to its officers being all Knights of Malta, whose coat of arms was a white cross. Actually the white cross on scarlet shield was also the coat of arms of the House of Savoy. Originally Savoy's coat of arms had been a black eagle on a golden shield, but when the Duke of Savoy was appointed Imperial Vicar of Italy, his House received the Imperial Vicar's coat of arms: a white cross in a red shield.

7   The Reggimento La Marina or della Marina – 'The Navy Regiment', or 'the Navy's Regiment' – belonged to the infantry and normally fought on land, for the navy included only three galleys based in Villafranca, but it was supposed to serve on board too. That is why it was later dressed in red and green, red coat and green cuffs and pants, also if during the Nine Years' War it was dressed in grey and green. Red was the distinctive colour of military personnel serving on galleys in all the Italian fleets (whilst who served on vessels was dressed in blue), and green was – and still is – the distinctive colour of the Order of the Saint Maurice and Lazarus, committed to the war against the Unfaithful – the Moslems – and hence responsible for the navy. No real marine corps existed in Italian independent Sates, because Venice used its infantry both on land and sea, as did Genoa, Tuscany and the Papal states; so, Savoy's La Marina Regiment was the only one specifically established to serve on ships.

8   Regiments hardly respected rules, hence they could have from 16 up to a maximum of 25 companies, depending on the cases and on the periods. Companies could differ depending on the case and the period, from 90–100 men in the Guards down to 40 in the Savoy Regiment.

Each platoon was divided into *squadre*, literally 'teams', and each team was commanded by a corporal.

The colonel had also a staff, including himself, the captain-major,[9] the adjutant-major, the quartermaster, the surgeon-major, the chaplain, the drum-major, the sergeant-major, the corporal-major, and the sergeant-provost.

The adjutant-major was an officer and in fact the colonel's secretary. The quartermaster – usually a lieutenant – was responsible for regimental lodging, feeding and managing materials. The surgeon-major, the *chirurgo maggiore*, was the surgeon and usually had some nurses, called in Latin *fratres* – 'brothers' – helped by the bandsmen, because, as said, the bandsmen had to gather the wounded after the battle. The drum-major was the chief of the bandsmen, and he was especially important because the drummers rolled the signals during the day, and above all in battle. The sergeant-provost was the Regiment's constabulary, and his soldiers – the archers – were the regimental military police and executioners. The sergeant-major, who was considered an officer whose rank equalled that of the captain-major,[10] was the chief of the sergeants. The corporal-major was the chief of the corporals, but was considered a corporal as all the others. Last, the staff could include also a carpenter and a *armaiuolo*, literally a gun-maker, who actually was a gun-repairer. He was always quite busy, because every Savoy's soldiers had firearms, whilst officers and sergeants still used sword, and, respectively, spontoon and halberd.

As all the Italian princes, the Duke of Savoy too kept foreign professional regiments in his pay, but this will be seen when speaking of the war. Besides, Swiss and German infantry units served practically under every colour in Italy from the 16th through to the 18th centuries.

III. Militia

As all the Italian States, the Duke of Savoy maintained local militias, which were employed as an additional military organisation to be called upon in case of war.

Militiamen were globally grouped into the so-called Battalion of Savoy and Battalion of Piedmont. Both the battalions could serve as reserve to the 'order' Regiments, but could also develop local units – battalions or regiments – named after the city they came from. Militiamen generally had to drill once per season using their own firearms, and only when called they could be organised into infantry regiments. Militiamen had some benefits and privileges. Emmanuel Philibert granted some when he established the militia. Victor Amadeus also did so during his reign, especially during the periods

---

9 Who successsively lost the command of a company and obtained that of the sole staff, which in Italian was and is called *Stato Maggiore*.

10 A comparison between the ransom to be paid for a sergeant-major in 1690 and those for the comparable ranks in infantry and cavalry provides evidence that the rank of a sergeant-major equalled that of infantry captains, for their ransom was far higher than a sergeant's, as it is showed in the *Traité d'échange, et rançons des prisonniers de guerre faits par les troupes de Sa Majesté Très-Chrétienne, et celles qui composent l'armée de S.A.R. monseigneur le Duc de Savoie, et de ses Alliés, tout en deçà que delà des monts*, in Solaro della Margarita, op. cit., vol. II, p. 132 and following.

of war. An exception was provided by the Waldensians, who composed relatively small and scattered bands, especially suitable for mountain warfare. This system proved quite useful and effective in both Savoy and in Piedmont, from the Grand Alliance onwards.

IV. Cavalry

Cavalry in Europe was generally divided in light and heavy regiments, and dragoons. The latter were actually mounted infantry also if they were often employed as cavalry instead of infantry.

In Piedmont cavalry included the *Guardie del Corpo*, literally 'the bodyguards', that is to say the Duke's household, and two cavalry regiments – Savoia and Piemonte Reale – resulting from grouping during the Nine Years' War pre-existing Gendarmerie companies, and three dragoon regiments, known as the Red, the Green and the Yellow Dragoons, due to their uniforms: the Red Dragoons were actually His Royal Highness' Dragoons, and wore a red coat with blue cuffs. The Dragoons of Genevois[11] – the County of Geneva, owned by the Dukes of Savoy before the Calvinist reformation – were originally dressed in green with red cuffs, whilst the Dragoons of Piedmont originally had a yellow uniform with black cuffs, changed to a red coat and pearl-white cuffs by their new colonel in 1691.[12] Cavalry regimental organisation was just like in the infantry with a few differences: trumpets instead of drums, brigadiers instead of sergeants, 'appointed', instead of corporals, swords and pistols instead of rifles, whilst the dragoons, being mounted infantry, had also grenadiers, drums, and hautbois instead of infantry fifes, which the cavalry did not.

Militia cavalry units existed until the Nine Years' War. They were grouped into companies, under the Squadron of Savoy and the Squadron of Piedmont.

V. Artillery and the Engineer Corps

Artillery was considered a civilian-composed corps under the control of military officers. The same happened for the engineer corps. Only in 1697 were artillerymen grouped into a regiment, included in the infantry. On the battleground artillery had to be protected, following the French example, by the purposely established Fusileers Regiment.

When the war began, in 1690, artillery still had a peculiar structure. It was divided into three different corps, the Artillery of Savoy, the Artillery of the County of Nice and the Artillery of Piedmont, and the whole was commanded

---

11   According to tradition, originally the regiment was raised by Giuseppe Maria Manfredo Scaglia Count di Verrua, who in 1689 levied a dragoon regiment of 400 men divided in eight companies, each 50 men strong.

12   During the war there was also a fourth regiment, known as Balthasar's Dragoons, but it was a small, professional, privately owned one, composed of French Huguenots in British pay and service, and in 1696 moved to Flanders.

by the Artillery Great Master – the General of the Artillery. The Great Master had under his direct orders two different branches and many lieutenants, including a 'lieutenant commanding the artillery'. The lieutenants were in fact lieutenant-colonels[13] and the lieutenant commanding the artillery, that is to say commanding the operational branch to be employed on the field, was the most important of them, and was supported by a *Maggiordomo dell'Artiglieria*, literally the 'the most senior man of the Artillery', who was basically the Major of the Artillery.

Lieutenants headed different branches of the artillery service and were more important than the captains, because they 'kept the place of the general'.

Three different captains commanded the bombers, the miners and the gunners, who were considered 'low officers', that is to say non-commissioned officers. Other six captains commanded the artillery of each garrison.[14] They were supported by 'gentlemen' and 'adjutants' whilst in smaller or less important garrisons artillery was headed by an 'ordnance-guardian'.

Engineers depended on the artillery. An engineer was more important than any of the three captains commanding the bombers, gunners and miners, but was less important than a lieutenant, and was helped by one or more adjutants.

All the artillery officers, as well as those of the engineer corps, could get their commission through an exam, no matter whether they had been educated and trained into the Royal Academy, established in 1667.

The artillery and ordnance administration were under the responsibility of the Artillery Council, chaired by the Great Master, and including the lieutenant-generals on active duty in the army, and also an 'auditor and accountant'. He had under him the 'entrepreneur of the artillery', who was responsible of the practical management of the artillery's factory. The council was responsible of the whole artillery administration, from the provision of wood – normally elms, to be used for gun carriages – and saltpetre, to be collected also in the interior of private houses, to the payment for lost cannonballs retraced in the fields and given back by people.

The artillery's needs determined a major change in Piedmontese army, as elsewhere, due to the increasing need of gunpowder, balls, and related materials and tools. Cannons and mortars in ducal fortresses were 449 in 1667, and a few more in 1690.

The increasing use of firearms – as said, Savoy's army was among the first, if not the first, to provide its soldiers exclusively with firearms – included an equally increasing need for gunpowder and balls. Artillery and its ammunition needed carriages and horses. Year after year, logistics became a growing concern and supply, march, and communication routes became more important too.

---

13 General Cesare Maria Montù, in his *Storia dell'Artiglieria Italiana* (Roma: Tipografia d'Artiglieria e Genio, 1934), volume 2, says the lieutenants to have been lieutenant-generals in 1697, but a comparison between the ransom to be paid for each of them in 1690 and those for the comparable ranks in infantry and cavalry provides evidence that their rank equalled that of infantry and cavalry lieutenant-colonels, for their ransom was far lower than a general's and just a little more expensive than an infantry or cavalry lieutenant-colonel's. Cf. See *Traité d'échange, et rançons des prisonniers de guerre* cit., in Solaro della Margarita, op. cit., vol. II, p. 132 and following.

14 City of Turin, Citadel of Turin, Vercelli, Cuneo, Nice, Montmélian.

4

A Key Issue: Piedmontese Logistics

As in the rest of Europe, operations in Italy began in early spring. Major operations were routinely conducted during summer and first months of autumn, generally until the end of October. Armies entered winter quarters in November as bad weather and mud caused by rain and snow made routes impracticable and often impassable, especially to heavy carts. The consequence could be a reduction, if not an interruption in supplying and each army halted operations until the following spring. Only limited operations made mostly by cavalry or, rarely, by some infantry companies, were carried out for purposes of foraging or reconnaissance. Foraging, that is to say supply on the field, was vital for every army.

The War of the Grand Alliance marked the culmination of a surge in the size of the armies, and this was especially right for Victor Amadeus' army. His father's army had been small. Its aims were those of a small client state enchained between two powerful neighbours, and watched by one of them from inside.

For an entire generation, nobody thought seriously of a war against France. One could think of waging some operations against the Spaniards in Milan, but, of course, with substantial French help, or, as happened during Charles Emanuel II's reign, against a small enemy such as the Republic of Genoa, but France was completely another issue. And now, in 1689, France was likely the enemy to be fought by Piedmont.

European standing armies had been relatively static in numbers, between 20,000 and 50,000 since the eve of the 17th century, also if sometimes, exceptionally, in Italy they could rise to bigger numbers, as it happened in 1629, when 100,000 men gathered around Mantua, or in the 1640s during the Castro War between the Pope, on one side, and Venice, Modena Tuscany and Parma on the other.

But now, on the eve of the War of the Grand Alliance the problem was different. France's strategic commitments increased and so increased the number of the enemies France had. Anti-French Coalitions started to be formed during the Franco-Dutch War in 1672–1678. The trend reached its

26. Map of Genoa in the 17th century

apogee during the War of the Spanish Succession, but the War of the Grand Alliance was just a step behind it in terms of figures.

Louis XIV's standing army was credited to be 200,000 strong. Nobody opposed it, or, rather, succeeded in opposing it, but now, in 1689, all the German States, no matter how small they could be, gave the Emperor money and men, as Britain, and the Netherlands, and also Spain did, and suddenly the armies on the field rose in size, and easily reached a 100,000-man force.

All these king's horses and all these king's men had to be dressed, be paid and be fed. The supply of these unexpectedly big armies by pre-industrial states caused real troubles. Provisioning had been a major concern of warfare, but now it became the major concern. Provisioning needed money, a lot of money, and now it needed much more money than in the past, and not that many states had it.

Leaving aside the general European situation, the Duke of Savoy had a problem. He had to hold out against the French. He needed money to do so, and money could be found, somehow. But he needed also men, many men. His military organisation in theory could allow him to field a consistent army, just calling the militia to arms. But there was a direct ratio between military and civil manpower he had to respect. The former could not exceed two percent of the latter, otherwise the lack of manpower would affect agriculture. In a pre-industrial age, the harvest depended on the weather and on the number of workers. You could have the best possible weather, the weather of your dreams, but if manpower was lacking, nobody worked the ground, and the result was no harvest, thus no food.

The Dukes of Savoy, and later their descendants, the kings of Sardinia, knew that in case of emergency they could call every man to arms, but they knew very well that this meant to win the war within a campaign, or to starve in the following year, hence they never declared a general levy.

What to do? Luckily for him, Victor Amadeus was considered a key ally by William III. In William's mind, Piedmont had to be secured, first, and then had to be used as the base for attacking southern France. William of Orange was too experienced a soldier to believe that such an action could solve the war. Everybody knew that the Spaniards invaded Provence from Italy in 16th century and it did not work. Paris was too far, and Provence too wide to be permanently occupied, but such an invasion would attract French troops from Flanders: an important result for the Allied armies there. Hence, Savoy had to be supported in men and money. William gave his orders, and Victor Amadeus received money, and infantry units directly funded by England.

Baroque Age armies were composed of professionals, hence they were quite expensive and hard to keep. As said, a 15,000 men army was decent, a 25,000 one was threatening, a 60,000 one was enormous and a 200,000 one – the maximum reached by Louis XIV's France – hard if not impossible to be equalled, won and paid, in the literal sense of the word. Victor Amadeus' problem was how to get a credible military result having only the money he had, or could be given.

Resource optimisation was the first step. In 1688 he reorganised military administration concentrating all into the *Contadoria Generale* – General Accountancy – and in 1692, to face the war problems, he created the First Secretary of War, who was responsible for general affairs, personnel and transmitting orders.

In order not to waste money, Victor Amadeus had to see how much did he spend for every soldier in terms of weapons, clothes, lodging, wage, equipment, recruitment, drilling, ordnance, general logistics and general administration. Hence he started from wages and regulated them differently,[1] depending on when they were paid, and on the rank of the man. It was during the War of the League of Augsburg that the ducal administration made comparisons between the food prices in different parts of the Duchy,[2] and between different cities, just to discover how much did troops' staying

---

1   E.g. see in the army Staff's Historical Service Archive in Rome (henceforth AUSSME) the *Paghe dell'artiglieria dal marzo 1699* [wages of the artillery from March 1699] ms., copy ex-Turin State Archive (henceforth AST) Ms. 129; then the *Paghe e spettanze dell'artiglieria*, del 1708, ms. in AUSSME, L 3, 8, Lavori svolti; *Paghe e spettanze di pace e di guerra*, del 1701–1713, in AUSSME, L 3, 8, Lavori svolti; *Parallele de la paye en temps de paix et de guerre*, ms AUSSME, ex-AST – Ufficio del Soldo, 1701–1713.

2   E.g. the *Raffronto fra i prezzi delle derrate ad Aosta e a Torino – Tassa del prezzo delle Vettovaglie che si vendono nella valle d'Aosta*, del 1691, [comparison between the prices of foods in Aosta and Turin – tax of the price of the foods sold in Aosta Valley, of 1691] ms. in AUSSME, L 3, 11, Stati Preunitari – Piemonte, showing that the same quantities of the same foods were cheaper in the Valley than in the city of Turin.

cost. As a consequence it was decided how much every Common had to pay in case soldiers were lodged within its limits.[3] Clearly all the Commons complained, especially if they suffered due to the war.[4]

Gathering all the available data, facts and figures, the Duchy produced a scheme showing that the annual cost of an infantry company[5] composed of three officers and 50 men equalled the cost of an artillery company, composed of 35 men, or of half a cavalry squadron three officers and 32 cavalrymen strong. Hence, the administration knew that a cavalryman's or a dragoon's cost was as much as 4.2 foot, or 2.1 artillerymen, and, knowing how much money was available, it was easy to know how many infantry, dragoons and artillery companies, and how many cavalry squadrons one could field keeping a certain ratio among them.

As last, Victor Amadeus kept the *deconto* – 'detraction' – that is to say the money the administration retained: 20 percent from each soldier's wage to pay his uniform, ordnance and equipment, according to an old decree issued by Emmanuel Philibert, who, when speaking about soldiers who enrolled and did not own weapons, had said: '…we shall provide to those who will not have weapons, with a two year time for paying them, and they must not miss it, for that is our mind.'[6]

Wages – more or less five *soldi* per day per foot, plus a daily bread allowance of 24 pounds in peacetime – were paid every five or every 10 days. There was a further 20 percent deduction by the captain commanding the company, to pay fo the goods whose distribution he was responsible for. Hence only three out of five *soldi* per day were received by the private. On the other hand, this money was traditionally increased by some fringe benefits, and, in wartime, by additional assets and food, such as meat and wine, and the Duke carefully regulated them too, as well as he deeply considered transport.

Armies spent most of their time in camp. In Piedmont, 'to camp' often meant to be in a fortress, a town, sometimes in a city. The armies encamped only in case of an expedition further than the standard marching range from their departure base.

As said, during the Baroque Era few camps were more than 12 to 16 kilometres – or seven to 10 miles – apart, because this was the most that an army could comfortably travel in daylight, also if there is evidence that in Italy this rule had very often remarkable exceptions. Anyway the Piedmontese army relied on an effective system established long ago. In 1591 Victor Amadeus' great-grandfather, Duke Charles Emmanuel I, issued a

---

3   E.g. the manifesto issued on 21 November 1691 starting with 'The continuation of the war brings with itself the need for supplying the Troops in Winter', signed by Victor Amadeus II, Bellegarde, Granerij, and Marelli, printed in Turin, by Antonio Valletta H.R.H.'s and of the Most Excellent Chamber's printer, 1691.

4   For instance the *Rimostranze della Città di Vercelli con sue risposte, toccante il quartier d'Inverno del 1695*, [Remostrations of the city of Vercelli with its answers, concerning the 1695 winter quarter] ms, in AST, Imprese Militari, Mazzo 8° d'addizione.

5   All included, a company needed a standard of 9,400 *liras* of Piedmont per year.

6   Rep. in Scala, Edoardo, 'Intendenti, commissari ed amministratori egli eserciti sabaudi', in Scala, Edoardo, *La guerra del 1866 e altri scritti* (Rome, 1981), p. 23

decree[7] and organised the marches. The standard *tappa* – 'the trip' – was, by decree, 10 miles long, no more and no less. The Common – the town – had to provide men, animals and four wagons to each company of the incoming troops when they entered the Common's limits, until they left it. Colonels and soldiers were strictly prevented from keeping animals and carts after 10 miles, the former 'under penalty of losing our favour', the latter under penalty 'of three strappados'.[8]

The Common was repaid by the ducal administration, according to the season and the kind of animals used. When no agricultural work was in progress, that is to say from 1 December until the end of February, the owners received 'four florins and half for each wagon with two oxen every 10 miles, during the whole other time seven florins and, where there will be four oxen, one third more'.[9]

The 1591 rule and the others issued by Charles Emanuel I were still used when Victor Amadeus became duke, and had no substantial change all along neither his reign nor the first part of his son's, that is to say until the 1730s.

Actually the *Ordine delli 13 agosto 1620* – 'Order of 13 August 1620' – by Charles Emanuel I confirmed the existing rules, simply reducing to only one per company the number of wagons to be used to carry sick and wounded.

On 18 February 1622 another order by Charles Emmanuel had divided Piedmont – 'the whole State on this side of the mountains' – into 12 trips,[10] that to them meant Provinces, declaring that all the troops' baggage and whatever military load had to be equally shared among the Commons of the Provinces according to the rules.[11] Lastly, in 1651 an additional rule ordered the Commons to provide to the General Ammunitioner as many carts and wagons as might be needed each time.[12]

This was valid only for a company's baggage, but in the case of war the army needed much more, and the State found one, or more, civil firms providing animals, wagons and coaches and guaranteeing their activity to

---

7   *Stabilimento delle Truppe, passaggi & Alloggiamenti, Ordine del 23 novembre 1591*, in AST, Materie Militari, Ordini e Regolamenti, Mazzo 2, *Ricavo d'ordini Militari per il buon regolamento delle Truppe de'duchi di Savoia dal 1591 al 1682* [List of military orders for the good rule of the Troops of the Dukes of Savoy from 1591 until 1682].

8   *Idem.*

9   *Idem.*

10   Actually the word used was *tappa*, whose translation is 'staging point', but, as we shall see, the word 'tappa' in fact meant – and still means also – the trip to be made from a staging point to the next, that is why the word 'trip' seems more appropriate.

11   *Ordine del sud.° Duca per cui ripartisce tutto lo Stato di qua da Monti in 12 Tappe, o sia Provincie; con dichiarazione che tutte le Moggiate della Soldatesca, ed ogni altro Carico Militare si debba frà tutte le terre d'esse Provincie ripartire egualmente, nel modo, e sotto le regole ivi espresse,* [Order of the aforesaid Duke for he shares all the State on this side of the Mounts in 12 Trips, that is to say Provinces, with a declaration that all the Burdens of the Troop and every other military load must be equally shared among all the Lands of those Provinces, in the way and under the rules there said], in AST, Materie Militari, *Ordini e Regolamenti*, Mazzo 2, n. 15.

12   *Obbligo alle Comunità di provvedere li carriaggi al Munitionero generale,* [Enforcement to the communities to provide carts to the General Ammunitioner] on 17 July 1651, in AST, Materie Militari, Ordini e Regolamenti, Mazzo 2, n. 22, *Ordini Militari dell'A.R. di Carlo Emanuele II dall'anno 1648 à l'anno 1674,* folio 17.

be continued also across the border, that is to say where subject Commons did not exist.

March routes in Piedmont had been quite well known for a couple of centuries, due to the long war periods between 1534 and 1544, again from 1592 until 1601, and, last, from 1613 to 1656. Every road, every bridge, every ford was in the officers' and soldiers' mind, as well as how many houses every village and every town had, and how much food, and which commodities could be offered. So marching in Piedmont was rather a simple affair, except for the threat provided by the enemy.

A good portion of supplies came, as we know, from contributions levied in the occupied area. Whilst in Flanders and Rhineland French and Allied commanders found an agreement about the quantity and quality of contributions, it seems that nothing similar happened in Piedmont. On the other hand, whilst on the northern front the armies did not take prisoners, whenever possible, in Piedmont it was not so. In Flanders prisoners were not welcome, because it was too expensive to keep them, and, in some cases, the captors looked for a ransom to be paid for a specific feature – a general, an important nobleman etc. – whilst in Piedmont since the very beginning the Savoyard and the French armies signed a formal agreement, whose attached table specified, rank by rank, the sum to be paid to free a prisoner.[13] Basically, the French and the Piedmontese – and their allies – promised to give back the prisoners, whenever taken, immediately or at most within eight days. The change had to be done one for one, exchanging prisoners of the same rank. In case ranks did not equal, the comparison between the ransom said how much money had to be paid to fill the gap.

A general's ransom was 500 *pistols* – and the treaty specified 'pistols evaluted eleven *liras* of France, or fifteen *liras* of Piedmont, each *lira* of Piedmont being evaluated fifteen *soldes* of France'[14] – whilst the privates paid two *scudi*, or a *double* of Savoy each.[15]

How did Piedmontese logistic organisation work before Victor Amadeus, and, above all, how did its transport system work? The former is an easy question: it worked quite well. The latter is harder, because contemporary

---

13 See *Traité d'échange, et rançons des prisonniers de guerre faits par les troupes de Sa Majesté Très-Chrétienne, et celles qui composent l'armée de S.A.R. monseigneur le Duc de Savoie, et de ses Alliés, tout en deçà que delà des monts*, in Solaro della Margarita, *Traités publics*, cit., vol. II., p. 132 and following.

14 *Idem*, ivi, p. 133.

15 The *pistol* was the common name of the golden 'old' Louis of France, whose legal change in Piedmont was 15 *liras* of Piedmont. The normal Piedmontese *scudo* was a half a *double* of Savoy. The *double* of Savoy was a golden coin minted since 1638; its weight was 6.69105 grams and contained 6.06376 grams of fine gold, title 906.25. The *scudo*, also known as *scudo bianco* (white *scudo*), was a silver coin, minted since 1658. Its weight was 27.32178 grams, and contained 25.04496 grams of 916.67/1000 silver; cf. Felloni, Giuseppe, *Il mercato monetario in Piemonte nel Secolo XVIII*, Milano, B.C.I., 1968, p. 28, tables 3 and 4. This pistol – which in 1697 increased to 12 French *liras* – was less than a contemporary British pound, for it equalled – in contemporary British currency – 17 shillings and 6 pence. By consequent, 15 *liras* of Piedmont equalled 17 shillings and 6 pence. A *double* of Savoy was 15 *liras* and 15 *soldi* and equalled roughly 18 shillings, and one needed 20 *soldi* to get a *lira* of Piedmont, and four *liras* and six *soldi* of Piedmont, or 86 *soldi*, to get a white *scudo*.

reports and thus successive accounts normally don't speak of transport, or make just a quick mention.

The 1672 war against Genoa provides an example. We know very well all the plans and movements of both the Sabaudian and Genoese troops; we know their casualties, but we know nothing about their transport, a part for some information scattered here and there about carts or mules, whose number is never mentioned. The same happens about the service organisation and effectiveness: we know nothing. Anyway, seeing the contemporary situation, in general we can say that the transports were organised relying on private contractors or on the Commons and we find no trace of complaint about lack of supplies. Thus we should presume that, thanks to the small size of the armies involved, transport performed well, in spite of the rough terrain of the mountain of the Ligurian Apennine, separating the Piedmontese operating army from their logistics bases.

What about the Nine Years' War? How did Piedmontese logistics work at that time? The Piedmontese army followed the French system, which included up to three carts and up to 40 pack animals available to each general and colonel. Several pack animals and two four-horse carts for the *vivandiere*, the food provider, of each infantry battalion and, ultimately, according to fairly reliable calculations, one could get to 1,000 wagons and some thousands of mules for an army of 50 battalions and 50 squadrons, that is to say for an army composed of about 25,000 foot and 2,500 cavalry. The whole organisation was called by the French a 'train', which in Italian was rendered with the phonetic spelling of *trèn*, hence the word *treno* simply meant and still means 'train'.

The transport system had to supply both ordnance – weapons, gunpowder and ammunition – and food supplies. The Piedmontese private of the Grand Alliance period received a two pound, equal to 738 grammes, daily ration of wheat bread and rye; a pound – i.e. 369 grammes – of meat, and a pint and a half – two litres and five centilitres – of wine.

The horses had to get not less than one *rubbo* – equal to 9.2 kilogrammes – of hay, and a measure – two litres and 87 – of oats a day, or, alternatively, two measures, i.e. five litres and 74, of *biada*, a dry fodder mixture composed of oats, rye, barley, farro, broad beans, and vetch.

It must be said that the rations did not always reach their destination, so the soldiers provided by themselves, requisitioning, that is to say often robbing the peasants. Apart from such, not a small detail, the General Intendant of the Army, Count Olivero, had to feed and supply about 20,000 men including foot, cavalry, artillerymen and sappers belonging to the field army and to the garrisons, no matter whether national or foreign professionals, and at least 10,000 horses. It meant preparing every day the movement of over 90 tons of hay, 28 tons of oats, seven and a half tons of bread, three or four of meat and more than 40 tons of wine, that is, as we shall see, about 160 tons of food, because the animals were moved to the troops and slaughtered on the spot. Then, tons of gunpowder and ammunition had to be carried in variable quantities, according to operational needs.

As we said when speaking of logistics in general, the average of a contemporary wagon was between half a ton and a maximum of 800 kilogrammes. Thus daily supply of only the troopers would have required at least 200 wagons, if not 300. But such a calculation however had several variables: the bread was not distributed every day, but usually every four, so the tons to be transported went up to 30, but to be moved only every four days. On the other hand it was necessary to transport flour and yeast to the ovens, where the *Munizionieri* – ammunitioneers,[16] that is to say the supply corps, composed of civilians – were preparing the bread. When baked, the bread was loaded onto the *provianda* – provision[17] – carts attached to the convoys of the ammunitions, or the artillery train. But even so, one cannot even make a calculation, because, in order to simplify and speed up the distribution, in May 1692 a bread-baking test was made using experimental mobile ovens. Their baked bread resulted in loaves as good as the usual ones, and Victor Amadeus ordered the army to go forward with that new system, hence there was a substantial reduction of carts used for bread.

The same problem affects the figures we can try to obtain about horse-related supplies: the figure of 10,000 horses needing hay and fodder rations is completely theoretical and certainly inaccurate. In fact we have to add the war horses owned by cavalry and dragoons, and the horses and oxen belonging to artillery, and *provianda* trains, also the animals used by the infantry, whose regiments had to get fodder and hay rations for the horses of their officers, ranging from 12 rations for the horses of the colonel commander of the Guards, to the single ration of the ensign.[18] That was still not that much, if one thinks that the colonel commanding His Royal Highness' Dragoons received 20 fodder or hay rations per day. Moreover, even if we want to consider annual budgets, we could not trust the calculations, due to the impressive and sudden variations in strength of men and animals. A battle could easily cause a 25 percent reduction of the fighting force and the loss of up to the whole train, as seems to have happened in 1690 at Staffarda.

Let us now have a look at the specific case of logistical problems for a siege. The 20 heavy Piedmontese mortars besieging Pinerolo in 1693 were expected to be fed with 10,000 bombs, needing 2,500 transport carts. When the siege began, 100–150 wagons left Turin every day to provide the daily ammunition consumption. Calculating at least four horses or oxen per wagon, we have a total of 400–600 animals used daily only for feeding the

---

16 The Italian verb *munire*, from which the Italian word *munizioni* and the English word 'ammunition' come, means simply 'to furnish', 'to provide', and hence also 'to fortify' or 'to protect'. When speaking of supplies, at that time it meant 'to furnish', and the *munizionieri* were not the people dealing with ordnance or fortifications, but just and only the furnisher of the food. That is why the bread they baked was officially called *Pane di munizione*, that is to say ammunition bread. Such a martial sounding couple of words meant simply 'the furnished bread', that is to say the bread furnished by the military administration to the soldiers. Cartridges and balls being furnished by the administration, they too were called ammunitions. The difference was marked by an additional word: *munizioni da guerra* – 'war ammunitions' – meant cartridges and balls, *munizioni da bocca* – 'mouth ammunitions' – meant food.

17 *Provianda* is a Latin verbal form meaning 'the things to be furnished' or 'the things to be provided', so the convoys of the *treno di provianda* were those of 'the train of the things to be furnished'.

18 The ensign was an officer whose rank was just below the second lieutenant. He was the regimental colour bearer.

siege batteries. Then we can attempt a calculation of the needs dictated by the changes of the horses to let them rest, by their casualties due to fatigue, illness, or death, by the transport and refilling of the fodder stocks needed for the train and cavalry animals, and by what the men needed, that is to say food, ammunitions, tools and spare parts. Result: the global weight to be moved every day exceeds the hundred tons of the metric decimal system. This increases the figure of the needed carriages and horses, and leads to a further and co-related increase of logistical problems due to the maintenance of the animals, of the vehicles and of the men in charge of them.

Almost all operations occurred in Piedmont, thus the logistical problems were relatively easy, due to the short distance between the troops and their supply bases. This 'almost' is due to the exception: the 1692 Allied raid into Dauphiny. As we shall see, crossing the mountains presented some sustainability problems due to distance, and to such a major obstacle between the magazines and the troops.

5

The 1686 Campaign Against the Waldensians

No matter how well organised it could be, the ducal army was scarcely engaged between 1660 and 1690. It happened twice during Victor Amadeus' reign before the Grand Alliance. The first engagement was a police operation in 1682 against riots in the town of Mondovì due to salt revenue enforcement. Victor Amadeus committed some regiments, commanded by his uncle Don Gabriel of Savoy,[1] in what was later known as 'the Salt War', along with militia, especially from the so-called Waldensian Valleys, and the army succeeded.

The second engagement was far more complicated, and had a domino effect influencing, if not somehow determining, Victor Amadeus' accession to the Grand Alliance.

In XII century a Frenchman named Peter Valdo, from Lyon, established a heretical movement whose members were called Waldensians after him. The movement was later recognised by the different Protestant churches and it survived also in some Piedmontese valleys. In the age of counter-reformation Duke Emmanuel Philibert did little and in fact almost nothing against the Waldensians; but Charles Emmanuel II organised in 1655 so terrible a persecution, that Cromwell himself urged him to stop.

Waldensians were left more or less in peace until 1685. When in October 1685 Louis XIV revoked the 1598 Edict of Nantes, which guaranteed freedom of religion to his Protestant subjects, troops were sent everywhere in France and in French-ruled territories to enforce the Protestants to convert or leave. This influenced Piedmont too, due to the French garrisons in Casale, Pinerolo and in the valleys commanded by Pinerolo, thus, on 12 October 1685, Louis signed a letter demanding Victor Amadeus act the same way. As the French ambassador Marquis d'Arcy told Victor Amadeus, the King ordered the French governor in Pinerolo to eradicate Protestantism from the Chisone Valley using the same systems as in France, that is to say, lodging his dragoons there, which meant looting, raping, and in one case killing.

---

1   Don Gabriel of Savoy was a natural son of Duke Charles Emanuel I, Victor Amadeus II's great-grandfather.

On 27 October d'Arcy wrote that Victor Amadeus told him he had received 'with respect and gratitude H.M.'s advices' but that he had to consider seriously the issue of the Waldensians' enforced conversion, for his ancestors already tried it without success. D'Arcy wrote that he had replied to Victor Amadeus that none of his ancestors had the facilities Louis XIV was offering him, and that he would not get any better offer for a long time in the future.

On 10 November Louis wrote that the Duke had to be convinced that he had to do it 'at any cost', and in case he lacked troops, d'Arcy could tell him that the French army was ready to support the Duke's. On 24 November d'Arcy reported about his last meeting. He met the Duke and his foreign affairs minister, the Marquess di San Tommaso separately, and told the latter that without the use of force nothing could be achieved. On 7 December Louis wrote again:

I see that your solicitations remain without effect … You must tell the Duke that until he will leave the Huguenots live on the borders of his States, his authority will not prevent my Calvinist subjects' desertion, and, for he can by himself realise that I will not suffer it, and that their insolence would give me displeasure, so it could happen that the sense of friendship I until now showed to him would alter. I have confidence that the Duke will have the most serious reflections on this issue.[2]

27. Carlo Emilio San Martino, Marquess di Parella

The threat was now clear and dangerous. No surprise if d'Arcy could report the Duke's promise to act accordingly. But in fact Victor Amadeus was trying to delay as much as possible, so on 12 January 1686 Louis wrote to d'Arcy to urge the Duke. And on 26 January d'Arcy answered:

Sire, they promised that on next Wednesday the Duke will let know his will … and I continue to proclaim so loudly Your Majesty's strong will of not tolerating such a refuge of heretics so close to his kingdom, that … I think the negotiation will end only at Your Majesty's satisfaction.[3]

On 31 January 1686, Victor Amadeus issued a decree. He started implicitly saying that it was due to Louis XIV's imposition and ordered the Waldensians to convert to Roman Catholicism. The Waldensians decided to resist. The Swiss Protestant cantons tried to convince the Duke to change his decree, but the best they could get was the permission for the 14,000 Waldensians to leave. But on 9 April Victor Amadeus issued a new decree with so many

---

2   Louis XIV to the Marquess d'Arcy, 7 December 1685, reported in Carutti, Domenico, *Storia del regno di Vittorio Amedeo II* (henceforth *History*) (Florence, 1863), p. 97.

3   D'Arcy to Louis XIV, 26 January 1686, reported in Carutti, *History*, p. 98.

28. General (later Marshal) Catinat

hard conditions that many Waldensians decided to resist in arms. On 22 April a French and a Piedmontese corps attacked the few hundred Waldensians in their valleys. The French concentrated 4,000 men near San Secondo, not far from Pinerolo, whilst 4,500 Piedmontese with 12 field guns gathered between Torre Pellice and Garzigliano. The two corps had to advance separately and then join towards Castelletto.

General Nicolas de Catinat commanded the French. He divided his troops in two columns, sent the first commanded by La Vieufville towards Perosa, and entered San Martino valley with the other. La Vieufville had a small success entering the village of San Germano, and crossed the River Chiusone, but, when he reached the village of Pramollo was repulsed and routed by 200 Waldensians after a 10-hour fight. Catinat moved to San Martino valley and pillaged it, massacring as many people as his troops could. At the same time all the 4,500 Piedmontese, commanded by Don Gabriel of Savoy and the Marquess di Parella, entered Luserna valley and reached San Giovanni with their field guns.

On 23 April at dawn the ducal troops coming from Bricherasio, Caffaro and San Giovanni were engaged by some 500 Waldensians in the Luserna valley and at the Angrogna hill. The grenadiers of the Guards headed the column and attacked. Supported by the fire of four cannons, they forced the defenders to withdraw to Ronçailles, at the foot of Mount Castello. The Waldensians had prepared trenches there, for the terrain was rough, and easy to defend. The troopers stopped out of Waldensians' fire range and waited for the guns. When the artillery arrived, it started shelling the trenches. The Waldensians did not move, hence the grenadiers attacked, but were repulsed.

Progressively the Piedmontese employed the Marina, Saluzzo and Savoy regiments, but with no result. At sunset Don Gabriel stopped the infantry and restarted the artillery fire, to keep the Waldensians there and give the French time to arrive. The next morning Don Gabriel organised a new attack, but the Waldensians silently retreated during the night, so on the 25th the Piedmontese could join the French in Pra del Torno to attack the Waldensians' last strongpoint in Villar and Bobbio, in the upper Luserna valley.

The Piedmontese attacked Bobbio, and deployed in front of the town all their artillery and all their foot but the Guards, who were tasked to encircle the town. As soon as they started their action, the Guards suffered heavy casualties due to stones rolled down by the Waldensians from the heights, nonetheless the mission was accomplished, the town seized, and the Waldensians moved back to the Vandalino. But they were engaged once more, defeated, and surrendered after some more hours, after receiving a promise to be allowed to go to Switzerland.

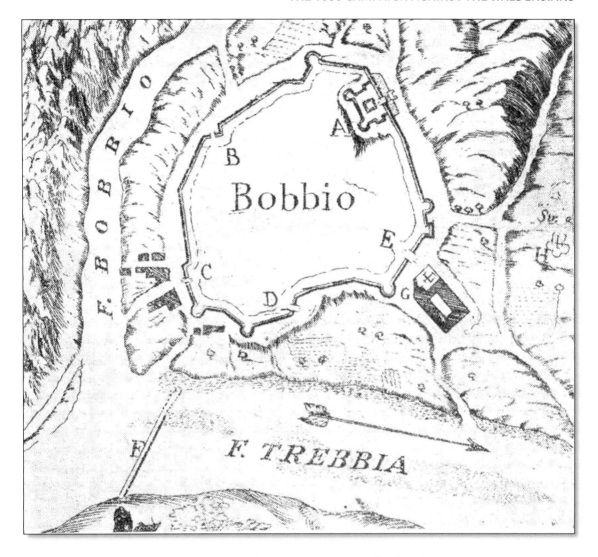

29. Bobbio

The Luserna valley was pillaged and devastated, especially by the militiamen from Mondovì, as payback for what the Waldensian militia in ducal service did in their town in 1682 during the Salt War. So at the end of the operation, on 28 April, there were no more Waldensians in the valleys: 2,000 had been killed, 3,000 escaped, 8,500 had been jailed and a huge number died in prison due to starvation, cold, or disease. Survivors were permitted to seek refuge in Switzerland.

There was a further consequence: Victor Amadeus decided his army had to abandon pikes, for they had proved useless in recent fights on the mountains, hence only firearms were used subsequently.

6

The European and the Italian Situation

I. Courtrai, Casale and Luxembourg

A major change in French policy occurred in 1690, when the Grand Alliance was established inaugurating the Nine Years' War. The main French strategic and political effort was in Germany. Italy was important as long as the Spanish Empire was the central enemy, but in the last years of the 17th century the Austrian Habsburgs gained greater strength and power, and Spain became a minor problem. As a consequence, French attention focused on the Rhine. The Christian victory under Vienna's walls in 1683 and the uninterrupted chain of Ottoman defeats in the Balkans weakened France's best ally, the Ottoman Empire, and made the Holy Emperor Leopold, stronger.

Louis XIV's policy in the decade following the Treaty of Nimegue was sneaky. Officially he was in peace, but in fact, on 30 September 1681, his troops seized Strasbourg and its outpost Kehl, commanding the passage of the Rhine. Then Louis purchased from the Duke of Mantua the city and fortress of Casale in Piedmont, thus threatening the western side of the Spanish Road in Italy. In November 1683 his army suddenly seized Courtrai, in Spanish Flanders. This caused a real war with Spain, the so-called War of the Reunions, and offered Louis a further opportunity for new conquests. He had wanted for a long time to take Luxembourg, 'for he had fair rights to become its master, besides that the conquest of that city protected the whole Champagne.'[1] He committed a strong army to besiege it, and, after a 38-day siege, Luxembourg surrendered on 3 June 1684. It was a big French military success, but, in perspective, it was also a diplomatic French defeat, because it enhanced William of Orange's plans, resulting in the League of Augsburg.

---

1   De Riencourt, Simon, *Histoire de Louis XIV* (Paris, 1695), Tome II, p. 98.

II. The League of Augsburg

30. Casale

The League of Augsburg was a William's idea, and he worked very hard to create it. France tried everything to prevent any kind of alliance planned by William, but, step by step, the stubborn and clever Dutch prince succeeded. Long ago, the French have been perceived as the protectors of German autonomies against the Emperor, but now they appeared more and more as a threatening growing shadow, whose forces were crossing the Rhine, and then?

This threat caused William's success and, on 9 July 1686, a defensive league was signed in the German city of Augsburg. The Alliance's task was simple: keeping the public peace, and the respect of the Treaties of Westphalia, Nimegue and Regensburg. The treaty was signed by Leopold I of Habsburg, as both the Emperor and the Archduke of Austria, by Charles II of Spain, as the owner of the Circle of Burgundy, and then by the King of Sweden for he was also the Duke of Zweibrücken; by the Elector of Bavaria and his relative

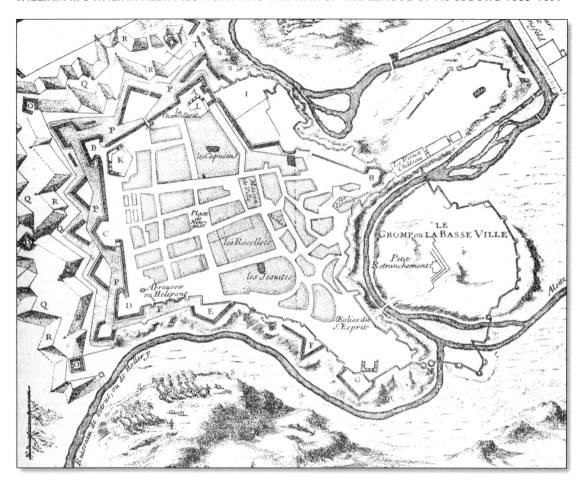

31. Luxembourg besieged by the French in 1684

the Elector of Palatinate, as well as the Elector of Saxony and the princes of the House of Brunswick. The Republic of United Provinces did not join. They feared too much Louis XIV's rage, knew how easy it was to be invaded by the French and perfectly remembered how terrible the last invasion had been, thus their Stadtholder William of Orange, although the promoter of the Alliance, did not try to involve the United Provinces, better known as the Netherlands, in the League, no matter how defensive it could officially be.

Actually, that defensive league could very promptly turn into an offensive one. The princes detailed in the treaty the forces each of them could field against France, and they all promised to back the Emperor's rights against the Dauphin's pretensions to the throne of Madrid in case the King of Spain died with no direct heir.

It would be useless to follow all the diplomatic clashes between France and the League, the former being firmly decided to let the League vanish, and the latter trying to widen its membership as much as possible.

Having to face the overwhelming French troops in Flanders and Germany, the Allies tried to gather as many forces as possible and included Savoy among their contacts. They secretly offered Victor Amadeus II inclusion, but he did not accept. In early 1687 he purposely and unofficially went to Venice to meet his cousins Max Emanuel, Prince Elector of Bavaria, Eugene of Savoy, and

Abbot Grimani, a Venetian clergyman serving as an Imperial diplomatic agent.

Talks were secret, seemed to have no consequence and left no written trace. But Louis XIV was informed by his spies and the French ambassador in Turin protested: how did the Duke dare to move to Venice without telling the King in advance, that is to say without asking for Louis' permission? Victor Amadeus protested: he simply went to enjoy the Venice Carnival and met his first cousin, the son of the sister of his father, and they spent time together, as relatives usually do. What was wrong with that? And why did the King complain so much? The late Duke Charles Emanuel II – his father – did the same: he went to Padua, and met his brother-in-law, the late Elector of Bavaria, and the King did not criticise him, why did he do so now?

The small diplomatic storm passed over, but the 1687 political situation deeply differed from his father's time and Victor Amadeus knew it perfectly, as well as he was perfectly aware of Louis XIV's increasing suspicion about him, Piedmont, and their links to the Emperor.

Guilielmus Henricus D. G. Princeps Auriacus

32. William III when Prince of Orange

III. The Dawn in the East

As the Holy Roman Emperor, Leopold's immediate task consisted of re-establishing Habsburg power in Germany, instead of holding theoretical Imperial power. A strong Germany was the French nightmare since the time of Richelieu. The French intervention in the Thirty Years' War had succeeded in keeping Germany divided and weak. The long Ottoman Wars had forced the Emperor to fight in south-east for his own security, first, and whenever a Ottoman victory occurred, France improved her power, and widened her influence in Germany. The Empire had been kept by the Habsburg thanks to the victories of Count Raimondo Montecuccoli both against the French in the west and the Ottomans in south-east, but, after his death, the Ottomans had reached and besieged Vienna in 1683. The city had been rescued by the army led by Jan Sobieski, King of Poland, and then, after the victory of Vienna, Pope Innocent XI proclaimed a Crusade. The European princes raised thousands of volunteers across Europe, from Sweden to Italy, to fight against the Ottomans. The Pope also negotiated a military agreement between himself, the Emperor, the King of Poland, Venice, the Knights of Malta and the Grand Duke of Tuscany, and on 19 January 1684, a 'Holy League' was forged.

Venice was given charge of the maritime campaign and of land operations in Dalmatia and Bosnia, supported by Papal, Maltese and Tuscan squadrons.

33. (above): Venice – Saint Mark's Square and Ducal Palace

34 (below): Map of Venice

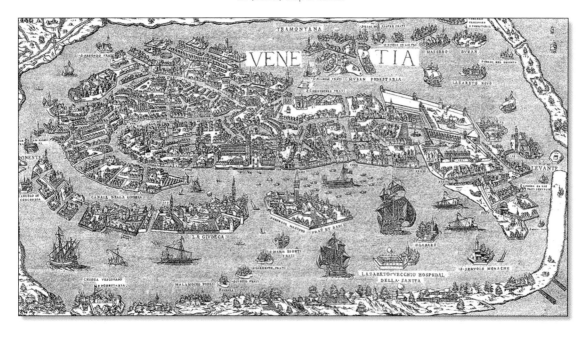

35 (top, left): Raimondo, Count Montecuccoli
36 (above): Francesco Morosini, Doge of Venice
37 (below, left): Holy Roman Emperor Leopold I

The Venetian naval Captain-General Francesco Morosini left Venice on 10 June 1684. Three months later he swept the Ottomans from the Greek coast. The following year the Ottoman fleet practically disappeared, whilst Venetian troops conquered the entire Peloponnesian peninsula, the Morea.

In 1686 Buda was liberated after a 145-year Ottoman occupation. Urged by the situation in the west, Leopold in that same summer accessed the League of Augsburg to defend Germany in case of a further French threat, but did not move troops from the east.

On 12 August 1687, an Ottoman army was dramatically defeated in Mohacs by the Imperialists. At the same time general Cornaro extended Venetian possessions in Dalmatia, and the Venetian fleet under Morosini besieged and seized Athens. An uprising occurred in Constantinople. The Sultan fell, and a new one, Suleiman III, was chosen by the army, and offered peace talks with Emperor Leopold. As soon as he knew of it, William of Orange advised Leopold to accept, for a peace in the Balkans could allow Imperial troops to move to the Rhine. However Leopold decided to reject the talks, and to go on with the war. On 7 August 1688 the Imperial army crossed the Sava and approached Belgrade. The city was besieged on 12 August and stormed on 6 September 1688. Meanwhile, other Imperial armies widened the Habsburg-owned territory in Hungary and the Balkans.

In less than four years the Ottomans had lost more than half of their European possessions. And that is why Louis XIV decided to invade Germany. No matter the excuses he found about keeping his sister-in-law's heritage – the Palatinate – after the death of her father and her brother. It was the desire, if not the necessity, to help the Ottomans which pushed France to war, or, in this case, the will to establish a foothold in Germany before it was too late.

IV. Philippsburg

The Rhine was the next step. Being an unfordable river, the Rhine could be commanded only when controlling its few main crossings. Louis had already seized Strasbourg and Kehl, he now wanted Philippsburg. Originally a small village called Udenheim, it had been fortified in the 14th century by the Bishop of Spira. Fortifications had been added in the following centuries, and, in 1615 they were once more enhanced by Philip Christopher von Zothern, Prince-Bishop of Trier, who gave the city his name.

Now, in 1688, Louis decided to seize it. He wanted to 'no longer leave Philippsburg in the hands of the Emperor, for he could exploit it against France after having made the peace with the Ottoman Empire.'[2] If I quote De Riencourt's words, it is not by chance. He is one of the strongest supporters of Louis XIV's actions. His work sounds to 21st-century ears like a sequence of unreliable praises to the Sun King. Whatever is French is right, whatever France does is right and whatever is not in favour of France is wrong. So, if such an author had to admit that Louis feared an Imperial intervention as

---

2   De Riencourt, op. cit., p. 136.

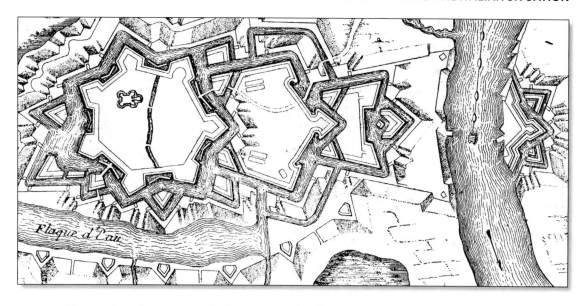

Flaque d'Eau

38. Phillippsburg

soon as Vienna signed a peace with Constantinople, this was clearly true and under the eyes of everybody at that time, also if it seemed to have been forgiven in the following centuries.

So in 1688 French troops crossed the Rhine. It was a sudden decision. Louis did not plan it in advance. As a matter of fact, he expected a still longer peace period, but the Ottoman collapse was so sudden and remarkable that any further delay could be fatal. Belgrade was taken on 6 September and Louis published his demands in a manifesto issued on 24 September. Had the League of Augsburg and the Pope accepted it, the Archbishop of Cologne had to be Wilhelm Egon von Fürstenberg, the candidate supported by the French, and the whole Palatinate had to be given to the sister of the late duke. There were two details: Cologne commanded one of the few crossings of the Rhine, and the sister of the late Palatine duke was the wife of the Duke of Orléans, Louis XIV's younger and only brother; thus, accepting Louis' demands meant to let the French firmly establish themselves on the right bank of the Rhine, that is to say in Germany.

Why did France act so quickly? According to Saint-Simon it happened because Louis XIV had a quarrel with Louvois about how a window in the Trianon Palace was designed. Thus Louvois, fearing a loss of his importance, started the war to let the King no longer remember the quarrel.[3] That could be a good additional and incidental reason. Nonetheless the main one was the Ottoman collapse, and a second good reason was what was going on in England. William of Orange, Louis XIV's worst enemy, was going to land there. His intentions to invade England were public knowledge by September 1688, although he landed only in November. But this was enough to act quickly in Germany. So, Louis ordered the besieging of Philippsburg. On 29

---

3   Saint-Simon, Louis de Rouvroy duc de, *Mémoires*, published in Italy as *Il Re Sole* (Milan, 1977), pp. 10–11.

September the Baron de Montclar crossed the Rhine at Kehl and started the siege of Philippsburg and in fact the War of the Grand Alliance.

As said, it was a sudden decision, so sudden that France started the war in spite of the bad condition of her infantry. Louis XIV had needed manpower to be used for the works related to the fountains of Versailles:

> … the water was scarce, and the fountains were dry … Who could believe it? That problem became the ruin of the infantry … Louvois planned to detour the river Eure between Cartres and Maintenon to bring it completely to Versailles. Who will be able to tell the quantity of money, and of men that stubborn attempt lost during so many years. Into the camp, which was organised and stood a long time, it was prohibited under penalty of terrible punishments to speak of the sick, and above all of the dead, who were killed by the very heavy work, and, more, by the miasma of the moved earth … in 1686 at last the war stopped those works.[4]

Thus, according to Saint-Simon, French infantry started the war weaker than it had to be according to the rules. One may wonder what if its strength was the regular one, for the League of Augsburg tried to organise the defence of the Empire, but with no success. Philippsburg capitulated on 30 October. The French kept 124 cannons, 22,000 cannonballs, and 16,000 sacks of flour. The 1,800 men composing the garrison were allowed to leave.

V. The War Begins

On 26 November 1688, Louis XIV declared war on the Republic of the United Provinces. The French navy seized two Dutch ships in the Mediterranean, between Messina and Leghorn: a man-of-war, and a merchantman from Alexandretta, whose load was estimated at four million livres.

Winter passed in a turmoil of diplomatic contacts and attempts. Louis supported James II and gave him an army, shipped to Ireland by the French Navy. At the same time, the Spanish governor of the Low Countries ensured the Dutch of his military help and started recruiting, On 11 February 1689 the Diet of the Empire declared war on France. Twelve days later William and Mary officially became King William III and Queen Mary II of England.[5] The possibility of a peace, if any, vanished very soon, and after March 1689 the French army stormed, pillaged and sacked the Palatinate. No less than 20 major cities and many towns and villages were sacked and purposely burnt. Violence, murder and rapes were carried out everywhere under explicit orders from Louvois.

Louis XIV still hoped Spain would join France in supporting James II, and tried what he could to let the conflict appear as a religious war of Catholics

---

4   Saint-Simon, cit., ivi.
5   England still used the old Julian calendar; but it being that the Gregorian calendar is used by us now, as well as being used by the whole Grand Alliance at that time, every date here will follow the Gregorian calendar, and the reader must simply remember that the English calendar of that time was 10 days late.

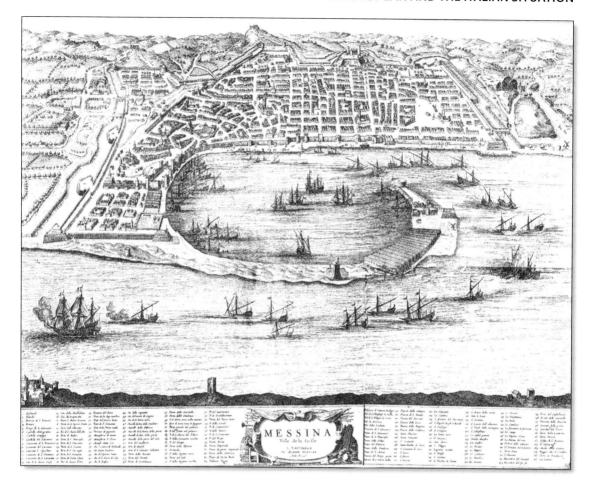

39. Messina

against Protestants. The Spanish help – if obtained – meant on a military level to weaken the Dutch, depriving them of the military help from the Spanish Low Countries, and, on a diplomatic and propagandistic level, to claim the existence of a Catholic front. If so, the expected result could be to charge the Emperor of felony, for how could a Catholic sovereign fight on the Protestant side against the Catholics? This was just what France did in the Thirty Years' War, when her support let the Protestants prevail, but this did not seem relevant to Louis XIV. Unfortunately for him, he suffered two severe defections. Charles II King of Spain refused to join him, and thus Louis declared war on Spain on 15 April 1689. It was a further mistake: a war on Spain meant an invasion of the Spanish-ruled lands constituting a buffer state between France and the Netherlands; it was a direct threat to the United Provinces, whose Stadtholder was now also the King of England. Thus on 12 May 1689, the Republic of the United Provinces signed in Vienna their alliance to the Emperor, and joined the League of Augsburg. Spain accessed on 17 June 1689; Britain on 20 December,1689. The whole of Europe was raising in arms against France, and the Pope too did not support Louis, and this meant that no Catholic front existed or could exist in the future. Worst of all, the Pope appeared in fact clearly supportive of William III!

VI. The Anti-French Papal Posture

It may sound strange or absurd, but Rome favoured William III because it had much to complain of about France. In 1662, the Pope had been forced to disband his Corsican companies, the police of the city of Rome, due to a harsh argument involving the French ambassador.

In 1676 Innocent XI was elected pope, and decided to deprive the foreign ambassadors of their jurisdictional privileges after the end of the appointments of the ambassadors he found there.

As a retaliation, Spain left her embassy without an ambassador. Venice recalled hers. Louis XIV ordered his ambassador, d'Estrées, to serve for life. But when d'Estrées died, the Pope did not accept any kind of arrangement, and caused a crisis. Moreover in 1682 the Roman Catholic Church in France – also known as the Gallican Church – proclaimed a limitation of Roman authority in France, which was neither recognised nor accepted by the Pope. Meanwhile, Louis chose some people to be consecrated as new bishops, but Rome did not accept them, for they were 'Gallican'. An additional clash happened over the use of the incomes from the French bishoprics, and, in the midst of this religious storm the Marquess de Lavardin was appointed as the new French ambassador to Rome. Louis ordered him to enter Rome with a big military escort of more than 400 former French officers-in-arms, followed by a good quantity of officers and soldiers from the Vessels Regiment – the French naval infantry – landed by the squadron which sailed him to Italy.

Seeing such a threatening attitude, the Pope did not receive him, also because de Lavardin had been ordered not to accept renunciation of the ancient privileges. In short, he was excommunicated. Louis then spoke of a naval expedition against Rome. The Pope did not change his attitude, and the French troops seized the Papal city of Avignon, in southern France. A negotiation ended the clash. The Pope won: he got back Avignon, and Lavardin was ordered to go back to France, but the clergy's memory was as long as an elephant's. And when in 1688 Rome faced the double crisis of the succession of the Electoral Archbishopric of Cologne and of the Glorious Revolution in England, the Pope had no doubt. On 20 September 1688, four days after Louis XIV's Manifesto, Joseph Clement von Wittelsbach was appointed by the Pope as the new Prince Elector and Archbishop of Cologne. He had opposed the French candidate, and four days later the French troops seized the city.

Meanwhile, the Pope had to decide what to do about James II and William of Orange. Seeing that Rome perceived James as close and very similar to Louis XIV, the Pope simply did not support him. But there was one step more, and it was made in Turin.

7

Victor Amadeus Versus Louis XIV

I. Premise

Now, as Germany was the main theatre of war, the French maintained a defensive posture in Italy. Catinat had started operations in Germany but was later moved back to Italy and in 1690 commanded[1] the French troops in Piedmont and watched all the passes. No offensive was foreseen and no French attempt was made to seize Spanish-held Milan or expand French military influence. Moreover, the most important French task was to stop any possible Allied offensive north-west across the Alps into Franche Comté – that is to say to the Rhine – or south-west, against Toulon, to destroy the French fleet and its main Mediterranean base.

Food shortages affected the French and this played a critical role. The limitation of military resources meant no French action in Italy. But what about Piedmont and its Duke?

We have seen how threatened Victor Amadeus had been when going to Venice in 1687. But two years later, in 1689, things were rather different. England was among the Allies. A good quantity of money could be provided by both the Netherlands and Britain, and the Emperor was far less engaged in Eastern Europe and far more in Western Europe than in 1687.

Victor Amadeus wanted to be a real ruler and to eliminate any possible political interference from inside and outside. Since he fully took power, his problem was mainly a matter of external interference from France. The main pillars of French power in Piedmont and more generally in Italy were the garrisons in Casale and Pinerolo.

In the 1720s Montesquieu properly resumed the situation in his *Journey to Italy*. He wrote:

Louvois demanded the establishment of a mail station in Turin and that a wagon free of inspection could pass through. It was accepted. This wagon, filled by French

---

1 Broglie, Emmanuel duc de, *Catinat, l'homme et la vie 1637–1712* (Paris, 1902).

40. Louvois

goods, was a very serious unfairness to the customs, and, for the consumption of those goods was really huge in the Duke's states, Louvois, who got his profit in that trick, demanded the wagons to be two. The Duke refused. The Sieur de Rebenac[2] asked for a meeting, the Duke allowed it also if he did not like it; he was in a room of his palace, from which the castle of Pinerolo could be seen in the distance.

The Sieur de Rebenac said to him: 'How is it possible that you refuse anything to a Prince who owns the castle you see over there?' As soon as he left, the Duke of Savoy said: 'So, I'll lose my States – he threatened me from the castle of Pinerolo!' and he let it be razed.[3]

II. Tricks and Counter-Tricks

Louis XIV had previously demanded of Piedmont 3,000 men, organised into three foot regiments 1,000-strong each. Victor Amadeus had answered he could give only 1,200 men, for his regiments were only 400 strong each. No matter, Louvois, the French War Minister, knew that Piedmont had 6,000 men, and could double them in case of war. So, Victor Amadeus was informed that he had to release what the Sun King had asked him for. But they could not be employed against the Emperor, being Piedmont a portion of the Holy Empire, the Duke said: and what about the Waldensians? They were plotting just across the border and how could it be possible to stop them if they decided to return and the army was weak?

Louvois wrote to the French ambassador in Turin: 'H.M. has seen the extravagant way the Duke and his ministers had in the negotiation; but he had no surprise, for he knows long ago that in this Court the way to do things in a civil manner was lost.'[4]

In other words, what Victor Amadeus asked for, was purposely and arrogantly perceived by Louis XIV as an offence: the Duke dared not to immediately acquiesce to the Sun King's wish! Nevertheless Versailles agreed not to deploy the Piedmontese regiments against the Emperor, but their strength had to be enhanced. Victor objected. Louis replied he no longer needed those units; and this was a threat. Victor Amadeus realised it, and

---

2 François Féuquières, Count de Rébenac was the French ambassador in Turin in 1690; see note 71 also.

3 Montesquieu, Charles Louis de Secondat baron de la Brede et de, *Viaggio in Italia* (Bari, 1971), p. 91.

4 Louvois to d'Arcy, rep. in Carutti, Domenico, *Storia della diplomazia della Corte di Savoia* (henceforth *Diplomacy*), 7 volumes (Turin, 1879), vol. 3, book IX, p. 170.

asked Louis to accept them. At last the King accepted and told the Duke that the three regiments – Aosta, Nizza and della Marina – will remain in France during the war, unless the Duke absolutely needed them back before the peace.[5]

III. The Absent Eugene, the Present Grimani and an Interesting Negotiation

According to some authors, in summer 1689 Victor Amadeus was informed that his cousin, the smart and brilliant Eugene of Savoy, serving as a general in the Imperial army, intended to pay him a visit. The visit was accepted and that was the first contact to accede to the Grand Alliance.

This is not correct. In April 1689 Eugene was in Vienna and it seems that he stayed there until August, when he left for Germany. On the eve of the war Eugene was in Germany, and participated in the siege of Mainz. The city surrendered on 8 September 1689, and Eugene followed the army. In the last week of October he wrote a letter to Victor Amadeus from Döppinger. He told his cousin that he sent a report to the Marquess di San Tommaso, praised the Duke for his operations against the Waldensians, and added that he was going to join the Court in Augsburg and stay there during winter quarters. Then he sent Victor Amadeus his New Year wishes from Augsburg and at the end of the winter he went to Vienna.[6]

Actually we know from Eugene's letters that in December 1689 he previously volunteered to help Victor Amadeus, but Victor Amadeus did not ask him. Why? We indirectly know it from the instruction the Duke gave to his ambassador in Vienna 10 years later: because Eugene was so natural a link between him and the Emperor, that one had to expect the ducal correspondence to Eugene to be spied upon, thus the link had to be different and less evident. So, Eugene was not exploited, or at least was not directly exploited. But we know that he gave the Piedmontese diplomat Count Tarino a letter to Victor Amadeus, and wrote: 'Monseigneur, whilst sending Count Tarino to Turin due to the business related to my abbeys, I committed him to report to Your Royal Highness about some other affairs, and I shall act fully according to what you'll tell him.'[7]

Had Tarino to speak about the Duke's accession to the Grand Alliance? We do not know and we shall never know, but we know that the real agent came, and remained in the shadows: Abbot Grimani reached Turin. Grimani explained the offers by the League, for he was its official representative. The

---

5   Victor Amadeus sent the three regiments, but, as soon as he joined the Grand Alliance, the French disbanded them and inserted their troopers into the French army. When President de la Tour in 1690 reached The Hague, he was contacted by the Cavalier di San Giorgio, the major of La Marina Regiment. They tried to organise the escape and repatriation of Piedmontese and Savoyard officers and soldiers who wanted to desert from the French army, and lacked money to go back home. By the end of April 1691 one hundred had been sent to Piedmont via Cologne, Frankfurt, Switzerland and Milan – the Spanish road in reverse – and some more tens of men came along that same route in the following years.

6   See all in detail in Paoletti, Ciro, *Il principe Eugenio di Savoia* (Rome, 2001), pp. 91–94.

7   Rep. in Paoletti, *Il principe Eugenio di Savoia*, cit., p. 93.

41. Prince Eugene, or his Most Serene Highness Prince Eugene Francis of Savoy-Carignan-Soissons

offers sounded very interesting, for they could allow Victor Amadeus to restart the traditional policy of his House: the expansion towards Italy.

There were many issues. Victor Amadeus wanted to eject the foreign troops from his lands. This meant not only to eject the French from Pinerolo and Casale, but also to prevent any other power – Spain or Empire – to put its soldiers in. Then it was necessary to get Casale from the Duke of Mantua, if possible. More: the Cisalpine domain, the states on the eastern side, the Italian side, of the Alps had to be stronger and wider, in order to have more subjects, hence to get more taxes and soldiers. A further task was to have natural borders easy to defend, and this meant getting back the complete control of the alpine crossings, and an expansion in the Po valley towards, and possibly across, the River Ticino, a natural border with Lombardy.

All this had to be supported by a diplomatic parity to the other powers. In other words, the rank of the House of Savoy had to be rendered equal to that of other European ruling houses. This was necessary because the importance of a diplomat in a negotiation was a direct consequence of that of his master's, but it was important also because if Victor Amadeus increased his prestige, he could be the most important among the Italian rulers and a reference in other European states' foreign policies.

Hence, it was not by chance that the Duke submitted his accession to the League to some conditions. He wanted back Pinerolo and the Chisone Valley, to eliminate French control and partially consolidate the western border. He demanded to widen his borders in Monferrato and asked to be allowed to purchase the Imperial fiefs of the Langhe, to widen his states. Lastly: he asked to get at least by the House of Habsburg the 'Royal Treatment', that his to say the same treatment due to a king, to himself and to his representatives and envoys, also if he was not a king.[8]

The Duke's accession to the Grand Alliance had to be signed as soon as a good opportunity came. Someone wrote that it had to occur in August 1690, after a Protestant upraising in Dauphiny. In fact it all happened sooner and – as usual in real life – in a completely different way than planned.

---

8   Charles II of England had already given Victor Amadeus the 'Royal Treatment' in 1682. Victor Amadeus wrote in a memoir in 1684, during his first months as a full ruler: 'About the Princes of the North, they are so far that they can do neither good nor bad. I do except the King of Great Britain who has accorded at last the royal treatement to my ambassador and whose friendship can be very useful to me', reported in Manno, Antonio, 'Un mémoire autographe de Victor Amédé II', in *Revue Internationale*, vol. I, 1884, p. 101, and also in Moscati, Ruggero, *Direttive della politica estera sabauda* (Milan, 1940), p. 32.

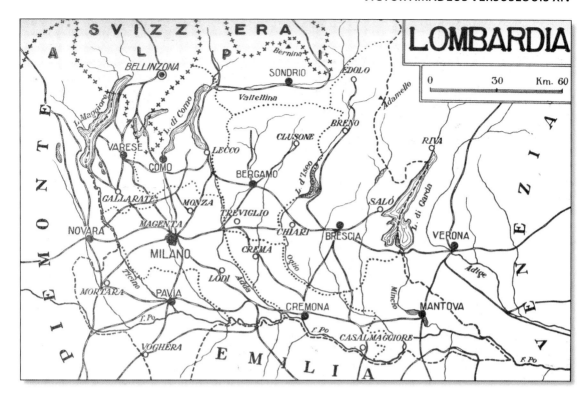

42. Lombardy

At the end of summer 1689 Victor Amadeus began recruiting men, but Louis prevented him and enforced him to reduce the army to a mere 2,000 men. At the same time Louis kept the three Piedmontese regiments within the French army and offered Victor Amadeus his troops. In fact France intended to keep Savoy weak, sending a real occupation army. Louis wrote to d'Arcy on 9 September 1689 that, had the Duke made a bigger recruitment, he would have 'a right suspicion about his plans; in a word, I could not accept him doing that.'[9]

But, just as this letter was going to Turin, Versailles received appalling news: the Waldensians had re-entered Piedmont!

IV. The Waldensians' 'Glorious Return'

In summer 1689 the Waldensian refugees in Switzerland organised an expedition to go back home. In August, 900 men entered Savoy, crossed the Moncenisio pass and entered Piedmont bound for the city of Susa.

As soon as he was informed, the Duke committed 250 dragoons from the garrison of Exilles to stop them. The Waldensians were intercepted and engaged. Both the groups fired, then the Waldensians rearguard – 100 men

---

9   Louis XIV to d'Arcy, Versailles, 9 September 1689, rep. in Carutti, *Diplomacy*, vol. 3, book IX, p.170.

– abandoned their luggage. The dragoons rushed on it, and the Waldensians escaped. No casualties on either side.

The Waldensians reached Salbertrand, and stormed the French garrison during the night. This time there were casualties on both the sides. The Waldensians lost 15 dead and 12 wounded, the French lost more and were defeated and disbanded, and the Waldensians passed by, reached their valleys and organised a stronghold.

The French declared it to be a comedy organised by the Piedmontese, the Dutch and the British. Victor Amadeus ordered General Marquess di Parella, colonel commanding the Guards, to enter the Waldensian Valleys and clear them using the Guards, and the Piemonte, Saluzzo, Monferrato, Chiablese, and Croce Bianca Infantry Regiments, that is to say almost all the ducal infantry.

It was a peculiar and odd fight, probably the most peculiar Italian history ever saw. Parella sent the Duke mountains of battle reports, but casualties seemed not to exist. When, two centuries later, military operations were re-examined by military historians, it was clear that the ducal troops went up the valleys where no Waldensian was, whilst the Waldensians went down the valleys where not a sole ducal private was. As far as we know, the ducal troops suffered no casualties during this 'war', and the worst damage the Waldensians suffered was when Parella's army seized the town of Bobbio on 23 October 1689, and took 'much cattle, flour, cheese, bread and lot of dry chestnuts', but killed no men. By December, Parella told the Duke the war was over; Waldensians were no longer in that area and he praised all the troops, especially the Guards, even if it is unclear what they did as fighters.

Meanwhile, d'Arcy loudly berated the Savoyard government: it had been and still was careless. Why did the Duke stop the boat patrols on the lake of Geneva and why did he recall his regiments from Chablais? That gave the Waldensians free passage!

Victor Amadeus replied that, when the French enforced him to reduce his army to only 2,000 men, he warned them about that risk. Now he committed his forces to the Waldensian valleys, but it was not enough and he wanted his three regiments back. 'Justice and reason want us not to leave in other's hands what we need' he said, and added that a prince deprived of his decisional autonomy, politically enforced and neither trusted nor considered, was an unhappy one, for a prince had to keep the respect due to his own glory and to his own state.

D'Arcy reported this to Versailles, and when his report arrived, Louis and his ministers puzzled about what to do. It was December 1689 and the situation was not as good as one year ago. The war was not going as well as hoped. The League of Augsburg had now been implemented and became the Grand Alliance, including also Spain, the United Provinces, and – just that month – Britain.

V. A Strategic Problem

France had a remarkable problem in Italy. Two months previously, in October 1689, the Spanish troops from Milan had seized the small town of Guastalla and razed the fortifications the Duke of Mantua made there. Officially it was a support to Vincent Gonzaga Duke of Guastalla,[10] a good ally to Spain, whose capital had been occupied and fortified by his cousin Ferdinand Charles Gonzaga Duke of Mantua, who, as we know, was of French descent and a French ally. In fact Spain was cutting the French strategic line across the Alps, through Casale to Mantua, because the Spaniards demanded Ferdinand Charles leave Guastalla, Correggio and Viadana, and those towns commanded the River Po upstream of Mantua.

It was a relevant strategic loss. The Spanish troops could not follow their traditional route from Naples to Flanders, because maritime travel from Naples was not safe, due to the French fleet commanding the Mediterranean. Hence the traditional Spanish Road was cut at its root, and also its land section was threatened by French-held Casale. But now, having Guastalla, Correggio, and Viadana in their hands, the Spanish troops could march from Naples, cross the Po and enter Milan. In other words, the alternative route to the Spanish Road was open again, and reinforcements from Naples could proceed on land towards the German war theatre. And this happened just when French business on the Rhine were not going as successfully as hoped.

43. Guastalla – fortress

Moreover the Spanish action could be perceived as a military demonstration to the Duchy of Modena, another pro-French State. Hence there were two good reasons why France had to intervene in the Po valley: a strategic reason due to the lost command on the Po, and a reason of prestige due to the French protection expected by her local allies. But now the Waldensians were acting where French supply and reinforcements had to pass. Thus, the Waldensians had to be crushed, because they were both a challenge to Louis' authority and a threat to French military communications. Moreover the French governor of Casale, the Count de Crenan was urging Versailles to send an army of 20,000 foot and 6,000 horses to Casale, and, from there into the Duchy of Milan, for it was poorly protected by its fortified system.

---

10   Vincent's branch is the only surviving one of the House Gonzaga, and now is known as the Most Serene princely House Gonzaga del Vodice.

44 (top): Naples at the end of the 17th century

45 (below): Naples in 1713

Could Louis commit so big an army to Piedmont? It was unlikely. The French garrison in the Dauphiny was not strong enough for such a detachment, and the French had been repulsed from the siege of Mainz and lost the battle of Valcourt, near the Marne. Nonetheless an army, no matter how strong, had to be sent. But alpine passes had to be cleared first. Could France commit Savoy to do the dirty job of cleaning and keep safe the French rear and supply line threatened by the Waldensians? That would be a help. On the other hand Louis knew Victor Amadeus to be poor and weak, because Louvois got by Mary-Jane of Savoy-Soissons in person a copy of that year's Piedmontese budget. It showed an eight million *lira* income and the army strength not exceeding 9–10,000 men. Last, according to French spies, the Duke was unpopular and probably very hated. What could he do, especially without the three regiments he was claiming back?

Thus Louis XIV refused to give him back the three regiments, and tricked him once more. He offered the Duke some 5,000 or 6,000 French dragoons. Supposedly it was a help, for 6,000 French were a better deterrent than 1,200 Piedmontese against, let us say, the Spaniards from Milan. Then he decided

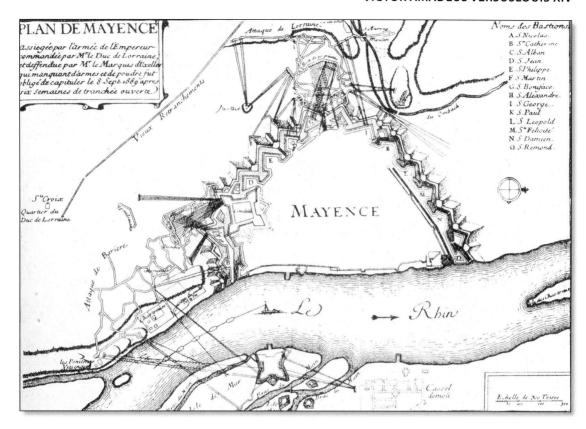

Plan de Mayence — text within map:

PLAN DE MAYENCE
(assiegée par l'armée de l'Empereur, commandée par M.r le Duc de Lorraine, et deffendue par M.r le Marquis d'Ixelles qui manquant d'armes et de poudre fut obligé de capituler le 8 Sept. 1689 après six Semaines de tranchée ouverte)

MAYENCE

Le Rhin

Noms des Bastions.
A. S.t Nicolas.
B. S.te Catherine.
C. S. Alban.
D. S. Jean.
E. S. Philippe.
F. S. Martin.
G. S. Boniface.
H. S. Alexandre.
I. S. George.
K. S. Paul.
L. S. Leopold.
M. S.te Felicité.
N. S. Damien.
O. S. Remond.

46. Mainz besieged in 1689

d'Arcy had been too rude, recalled him, and appointed François de Pas de Féuquières, Count de Rébenac as his new ambassador in Turin.[11]

Rébenac was milder and supposedly also more clever than d'Arcy. His arrival was supposed to be a change, but in fact it was not, for his instructions were too rigid and because very soon the diplomatic negotiation, if any, passed in fact into Louvois' and Marshal Catinat's hands.

Louis wanted the Duke to start again, from the next spring, the operations against the Waldensians. It had to be the first step on the path towards the invasion of Milan. On 26 January 1690, Charles Colbert, Marquess de Croissy and French foreign minister wrote a letter to the new Savoyard ambassador, Ludovico Solaro, Marquess di Dogliani. The letter was hard: Parella – Croissy wrote – did nothing, and his staying in winter quarters in Luserna Valley was useless. Parella had to pursue the heretics, otherwise it would have been up to the French troops.[12]

---

11 François de Pas de Féuquières, was a son of the French diplomat Isaac de Féuquières. He became Count de Rébenac when Jeanne d'Esquille, heir of that landlordship, married him. He was a diplomat. His eldest brother Antoine de Pas de Féuquières, who inherited the title of Marquis de Féuquières, was in the French army, and at the eve of the Nine Years' War, served in Rhineland. In 1690 he was sent to Italy to serve under Catinat. The two brothers have sometimes been confused.

12 Letter by French foreign minister Croissy to the Marquess di Dogliani, on 26 January 1690: 'His Majesty ordered me to write to you that the troops of the Duke of Savoy are at present very useless in the valleys of Luserne, and that it is necessary to let them advance, and even in

Then Louis XIV declared to have been informed that a good number of Protestant French refugees were going to Switzerland and to Milan, because they wanted to enter Piedmont and then Dauphiny. Thus he committed Catinat to stop them and decided to attack the Spaniards in Lombardy passing through Piedmont, with or without the Duke's consent.

Victor Amadeus knew it. He had a correspondence with the Emperor and the Spanish governor of Milan, and recently started to write also to William III. In fact contacts with England started as soon as William and Mary were crowned, because the Duchess Anne of Savoy, as a first cousin of the new queen, now came immediately after Anne Stuart in the line of succession to the British throne. In other words Victor Amadeus, as the husband of his wife, became a possible king of England.

Actually this was a possibility, whilst the reality was the nasty situation he had with France. Thus in 1689 Victor Amadeus was step by step preparing to join the Grand Alliance, but he could not do it so easily without immediate military support, for he had the French practically no longer in the backyard, but already in the kitchen.

Meanwhile, the Emperor and the League had accepted Victor Amadeus' conditions and, on 8 February 1690, Leopold I issued the Imperial diplomas about the Royal Treatment and the Fiefs of the Langhe. The Emperor prudently did not say if and how much Victor Amadeus paid. Actually Turin paid one million to Vienna to purchase those fiefs of the Langhe. Officially, as the Emperor said, it was a 100,000 *doubles* – which meant more than one million and half[13] – contribution paid by Victor Amadeus as a prince of the Empire supporting the war against the Ottomans in the Balkans, and that is why the Duke deserved those diplomas. But Louis disliked it and wrote a threatening letter, telling Victor Amadeus that he considered as an anti-French action any money given to the Emperor, no matter the reason.

---

a greater number, to the valleys of St. Martin, to act in concert with those of H.M., to jointly enforce the retreats of these rebels, so that this affair ends rather fast, without which, H.M. could not be exempted to let a considerable corps of troops march immediately in the aforesaid lands of His Highness to expel these seditious, not being prudent of him to let them establish there to attract a greater number of them', rep. in Carutti *Diplomacy*, vol. 3, book IX, p. 173.

13 As said, the double of Savoy equalled 15 *liras* and 15 *soldi* in 1706, but, as Felloni warns in op. cit. p. 28, table 3, note 4, it is not known how much its value could be before that year. Likely, its change in *liras* in 1690 had to be the same, thus a double equalled 315 *soldi* (one *lira* was composed of 20 *soldi*), thus actually 100,000 doubles equalled 1,575,000 *liras*.

8

Tricks, Troubles, Errors, and Delays

Luckily the French had trouble with the Waldensians. After Louis' proud declaration about the French troops' decisive commitment against them, Victor Amadeus in fact simply did not react, but sat down and saw, and what he saw was really remarkable. The still active 300 Waldensian fighters, in December 1689, established their strongpoint at the Balziglia, not far from the town of Perrero. Catinat and Féuquières blockaded and then besieged it with 4,000 men and five cannons from December until halfway through May, and suffered huge casualties. On 23 May they demanded the Waldensians surrender, otherwise their position would be stormed the next day. But, during the night, the Waldensians silently escaped, leaving behind them the bodies of the 370 prisoners they killed before leaving. Victor Amadeus was in a difficult position. Had he constantly agreed to Louis XIV's demands, the end of the Duchy was sure, for it would be absorbed; had he not, the end was sure too, for the Duchy would be occupied. He needed to be stronger, to establish the alliance with the League and get as much time as he needed to get Allied reinforcements, if any.

The first step was to get stronger. Louis XIV's prohibition to exceed a 2,000 men strength was clear and definitive. What to do? The Duke decided to turn around that imposition. On 28 March 1690, he issued a decree reducing the number of the members of the Battalion of Piedmont to no more than six percent of the men fit for military service and aged from 20 to 40, and ordered them to drill once every 15 days. The contingents were hence called and dismissed one by one during two weeks, so, thanks to this uninterrupted circular turnover, his army drilled as much as needed, but never exceeded the 2,000 men figure Louis imposed.

Meanwhile, the quarrel about the Langhe payment was still on. The Duke answered to Rébenac that he promised the Emperor the money to support the war in Hungary; but things went farer and faster than expected, for the bankers, after their own initiative, paid the Emperor the whole sum in advance (including a remarkable bribe to the Emperor's ministers, as it was usual in Vienna) before he could stop them, so he had felt obliged to give them back the money. The storm was now approaching. Louis decided there was no doubt: Piedmont had an agreement with the Grand Alliance.

The Marquess di Dogliani realised what was in the wind and wrote from Paris on 3 May that it was better not to oppose France and its overwhelming force.[1] The wind arrived in Piedmont on 6 May, when Catinat informed the Marquess di San Tommaso that he needed quarters and food for 10,000 men, because he had to march towards Milan. Victor Amadeus sent him Count Gazzelli, and Catinat told Gazzelli he had been ordered to enter the Duke's states immediately and that he would add more details very soon.

Then Catinat received an instruction from Louvois. This letter had been written on 2 May, but here destiny placed its finger, and changed many things. The secretary who wrote that letter made a mistake, and wrote 'or' instead of 'and', Louvois did not realise, and signed.[2]

The letter ordered Catinat to march to Turin and demand of the Duke of Savoy that citadel and to send 2,000 foot and three mounted regiments to France, to be quartered in the suburbs of Lyon, immediately. Had the Duke agreed, all was fine: Catinat had to proceed to Milan. Had the Duke disagreed, Catinat had to start operations against him.

But, due to the mistake, the letter actually told Catinat to demand the Duke the citadel 'or' the troops, not the citadel 'and' the troops. So, Catinat thought there was an alternative, which, according to Louvois, did not exist and had not to exist.

According to the misleading letter he received, on 9 May Catinat arrived in Avigliana, not far from Turin, along with 7,000 men and asked for a meeting with a ducal minister to inform him of the King's will. The day after, Victor Amadeus sent Marquess Ferrero, the former ambassador to France. Catinat told him that the King supposed the Duke to have had negotiations with the enemies of France, thus the King disliked what happened and asked for evidence of Victor's goodwill: the Duke was asked to send France two

---

1 The Marquess di Dogliani to the Duke on 3 May 1690: 'I know how hard it is for a sovereign like Y.R.H. not to be able to profit from a favourable opportunity to acquire such great advantages, but when in order to succeed, one must risk all his States, for one breaks links with so a powerful and formidable neighbour as the King is, prudence and good policy do not allow one to expose himself to such a danger. I am even sure that none of your good subjects will advise you to do it, for even when the Emperor and the Spaniards will have promised to you whatever kind of help, you will see the Savoy lost and Piedmont invaded and perhaps reduced to ashes like the Palatinate before they could give you any sort of help', rep. in Carutti, *Diplomacy*, cit., vol. 3, book IX, p. 178.

2 As Carutti too reports, Camille Rousset, in his *Histoire de Louvois*, vol. IV, explained this mistake. Louvois' orders to Catinat issued on 2 May said: 'Rien ne doit vous détourner de la ponctuelle exécution de ce que cette lettre contient de l'intention du roi, que la soumission de M. le duc de Savoye, c'est à dire la marche de ses troupes dans les faubourgs de Lyon, OU l'entrée des troupes du roi dans la cittadelle de Turin.' ['Nothing must deter you from the punctual execution of what this letter contains about the intention of the King, other than the submission of the Duke of Savoy, that is to say the march of his troops to the suburbs of Lyons, OR the entrance of the King's troops into the cittadel of Turin.'] But Louvois actually meant : 'Rien ne doit vous détourner, etc., que la soumission de M. le duc de Savoie, c'est à dire la marche de ses troupes dans les faubourgs de Lyon ET l'entrée des troupes du roi dans la citadelle de Turin.' This *ou* – 'or' – instead of *et* – 'and' – let Catinat think there was an alternative. Once the mistake was discovered, Catinat demanded the fortresses too. But the letter dated on 2 May spoke only of Turin, and did not mention Verrua, which was added in the following letter dated on 10 May whilst the demand for the Piedmontese troops to join the French against the Spaniards was made later, in a letter dated 18 May 1690.

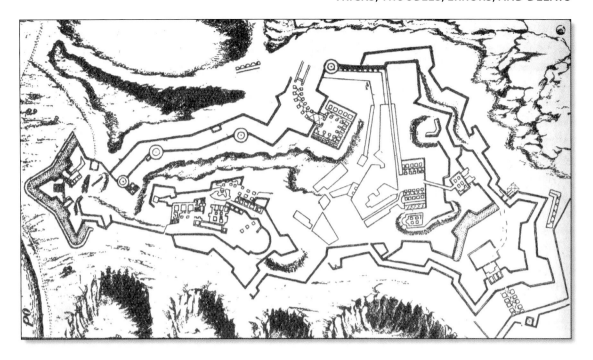

47. Verrua

infantry and two dragoon regiments, and had to answer within 48 hours: yes or no, and 'no' meant war.[3]

Victor Amadeus was in trouble. He had planned to join the Grand Alliance in August, when there would be no more time for a campaign in northern Italy due to the forthcoming poor-weather season. This could give him the entire following winter to prepare, but May was not August, and to reveal his position now meant to fight one year in advance. He needed time, thus feigned to accept and told Catinat that he was going to send to his ambassador in Versailles instructions about a treaty on this matter. Meanwhile he started war preparations, for he knew the crisis to have been delayed, but not cancelled.

Catinat informed Louvois. Louvois realised the misunderstanding and on 10 May sent new instructions, demanding more:

> You must only receive the citadels of Turin and of Verrua, if he gives you them, without engaging yourself to anything but to report to His Majesty about the obedience of the Lord Duke of Savoy. Having been the behaviour of this prince so disloyal and his project so noxious, the consequence is that he will be punished in

---

3   On 17 May the papal nuncio – The nuncio of Savoy Mosti to Cardinal Rubini Secretary of State, Turin, 17 May 1690, in the Archivio Segreto Vaticano (henceforth ASV), Nunziatura di Savoia, anno 1690 – wrote that Ferrero came back to Turin by midnight and reported to the Duke that he told Catinat that the term 'twice 24 hours', as Catinat said, was too short, for it would be night once he was back to Turin and the Duke would be gone to bed and it would be not polite to wake him up. Then 'il Signor di Cattinat had a look at the third sheet of a letter he took out of his pocket and replied to the Marquess that he gave him [up to] the whole Saturday to let him [Catinat] know the last resolutions of Lord the Duke, otherwise, in case no other convenient proposals were made to answer his [Catinat's] demand, he would execute the hostilities commanded to him against this State.'

a way he will remember all his life long, and will learn on his own cost the respect a Duke of Savoy owes to a King of France.

Once he received this letter, Catinat moved to Orbassano – six miles from Turin – and on 27 May told the Piedmontese he had further news for them.

Victor sent Catinat the Abbot di Verrua, another former ambassador to Versailles. At the same time Victor was claiming to be sincere, and appealed the Pope, asking for his mediation. Then he protested he could not work out how his small and weak state could further disarm in favour of a friendly major power as France. All he got from Catinat was a very vague answer: the King was much more displeased – that is to say irritated. In Louis XIV's concealed terms, the threat was clear and serious, for there was nothing worst than making the King displeased. Negotiation advanced, and at the end Catinat grumbled that, perhaps, the King could accept to consider as an evidence of friendship the cession of the citadels of Turin and Verrua, the last two major fortresses still owned by Victor Amadeus. It meant to give France the complete military control of Piedmont and of the Duchy. It must now be underlined that, later, French propaganda presented an entirely different situation, claiming that Louis offered Victor Amadeus Pinerolo, Casale, Geneva, a portion of Dauphiny and of Provence, and, lastly, the Royal Treatment.[4] But as things were, by mid May 1690 all these promises simply did not exist, no promise existed, at all; there were only threats.

Victor Amadeus realised the war to be only a matter of weeks, or days, and tried to get more time. He was rendering Turin's walls stronger, providing gunpowder and balls, preparing mobilisation and having contacts with the Spaniards in Milan for quick support, but he needed time. So, he sent the Abbot di Verrua back to Catinat along with Marquess Ferrero. Through them, he protested his innocence and proposed to release Turin and Verrua to a neutral power, such as Venice or the Swiss. The neutral power had to release both the fortresses to the Sun King if and when any evidence of Victor Amadeus' alliance to the League may appear.

Catinat answered that he had no room for a negotiation. Also the Papal nuncio Monsignor Mosti went to the French camp in Orbassano. Officially he wanted to be sure that, in case of war, the French would not damage the Holy Seat's fiefs and properties in Piedmont. In fact he had an active part in talks with both Catinat and Piedmontese envoys. He tried to negotiate in favour of Savoy, but got no result.

Catinat moved his army to Carignano, where on 20 May he received a letter from Victor Amadeus to Louis XIV. The Duke accepted giving both Turin and Verrua, but asked the King to choose two different fortresses, and for the matter to be arranged according to a formal treaty. Louis was asked not to forget their family links, for Victor Amadeus was his nephew, and to listen graciously to the special ambassador Victor was sending him, the Count di Provana, who had to submit some proposals concerning the aforesaid treaty.

---

4   De Riencourt, op. cit., vol. II, p. 182

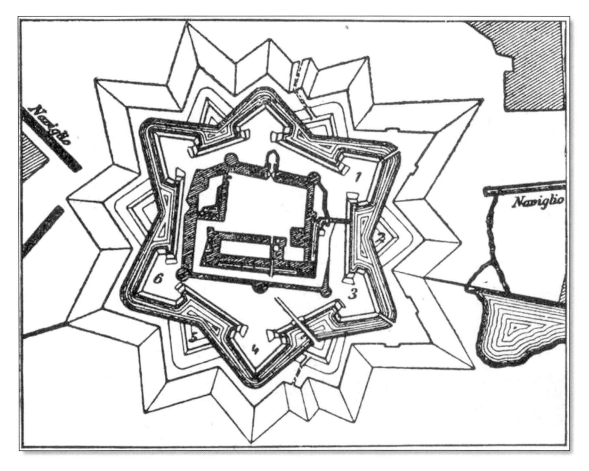

Catinat forwarded the letter to the King and stood. With that, the Duke, at the very last moment, avoided his state being devastated by the French troops – 9,000 men, including 5,330 cavalry and dragoons – who were already on the move from Orbassano.

48. Milan – citadel and castle

Meanwhile, Louvois had sent an additional letter, dated 18 May 1690, demanding the Piedmontese troops to join the French against the Spaniards. In fact, seeing the letter from Piedmont dated 20 May, the King answered he was happy to know that the Duke gave him the fortresses. He added that he would be glad to listen the Count di Provana as soon as he came, but, meanwhile, his troops would enter Turin and Verrua.[5]

When this answer reached Turin, Victor Amadeus realised he had no more room for further attempts. On the last day of May San Tommaso and Ferrero went once more to Carignano. They told Catinat that the Duke protested to

---

5   On 24 May 1690, Wednesday, the *Avvisi di Foligno*, a weekly newspaper published in the city of Foligno, Umbria, Papal States, published that ''on Thursday it was published [implicitly: 'in Milan'] that at last the Lord Duke of Savoy declared himself as (belonging) to the Austrian party, thus the Governor of Milan sent him 6.thousand foot and 3.thousand horses.' It is unclear whether Catinat or some French agent were informed of it. Anyway it is remarkable how the press, in this case a small local newspaper from a small and all but relevant city, far from the concerned area, succeeded in getting and publishing a real scoop 10 days in advance of the actual Piedmontese declaration of war.

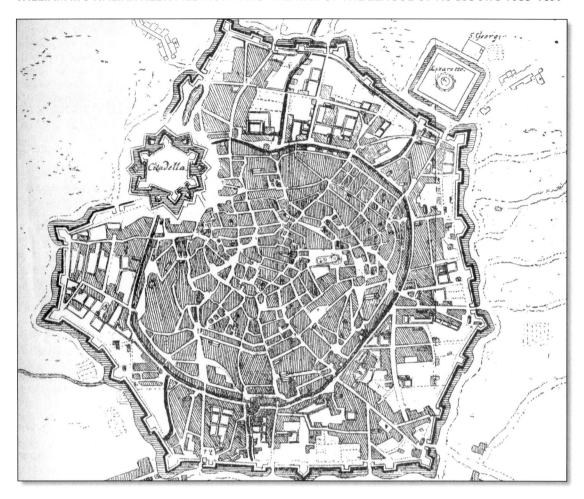

49. Milan in the 17th century

have been purposely misunderstood. He promised to release the fortresses only if a treaty was made about it, and there was no treaty, for his ambassador was not yet at Versailles. Catinat replied to have no possibility but obey his master's orders: the Duke had promised to release the fortresses, thus had to keep his word now. Then, Catinat added, according to the letter Louvois sent him on 18 May, that the King was not to receive the Piedmontese troops in France and demanded they join Catinat's army in Italy to act against the Spaniards in Milan.

That was new. Ferrero and San Tommaso protested. This demand was against the Duke's interest and honour. Catinat replied it was an imperative condition, no further discussion was possible. So, they told him they had to report to the Duke and would come back on the next day.

On 2 June, two days later, it was the Great Chancellor, Count Janus de Bellegarde along with Marquess Morozzo who came to Carignano. They tried all they could, but in the end Catinat stopped the discussion: Savoy had to accept the French conditions, or, within 48 hours, on 4 June, he would act with his army.

9

Joining the Grand Alliance

Victor Amadeus gained an entire month since the beginning of the diplomatic duel. The capital was now safe and ready to hold any kind of attempt, siege or storm. Ordnance and supply had been provided and stored. The cavalry, recalled from Savoy, was at Turin. The militia had been called to arms. Time was running out. Victor accelerated the negotiations with the League, for he knew he had no more than 10 days: the time the couriers needed from Turin to Versailles and back. He summoned Abbot Grimani, to sign on 4 June 1690, the alliance to the Emperor.[1]

Meanwhile, he had sent to Milan Count Brandizzo, who on the previous day, 3 June 1690, concluded the defensive alliance with the King of Spain.[2] Accordingly, the Count de Fuensalida would commit from the Duchy of Milan an army corps composed of no less than 8,000 foot, 3,000 cavalry and 12 field guns, entering Piedmont from Vercelli. Victor Amadeus promised to field four regiments of foot and two dragoons regiments, having the command of the whole Allied army. In case of a French attack directly to the Duchy of Milan, the Piedmontese army would be committed there to support the Spaniards, always under Victor Amadeus' supreme command. Pinerolo and Casale had to be taken. The former had to be given back to Savoy, the latter to the King of Spain. Any further conquest would be shared.

On the next day, 4 June 1690:

> Having the Caesarian Majesty of the Most August Emperor Leopold heard with outmost and benign forbearance the serious threat by the King of France against the Royal Highness of the Most Serene Duke of Savoy [caused] by the hate against the obsequent and most faithful zeal he professes to the Most August Person and service of His Caesarian Majesty, and that therefore a French army entered His

---

1 All these information come from the letters sent by monsignor Mosti to Cardinal Rubini. Mosti's account is particularly reliable because, as said, Victor Amadeus asked him for the Papal help, and also for acting personally as an intermediary to Catinat.

2 The treaty with Spain, signed in Milan on 3 June and ratified in Madrid by Charles II on 8 July, was written in Italian, as well as the treaty with the Empire, signed in Turin on 4 June and ratified by Emperor Leopold on 17 June. The accession to the treaty of Vienna of 12 May, 1689, that is to say to the Grand Alliance, signed in The Hague on 20 October, included the alliance to the United Provinces and Britain and was written in French, whilst the original Treaty of Vienna was in Latin.

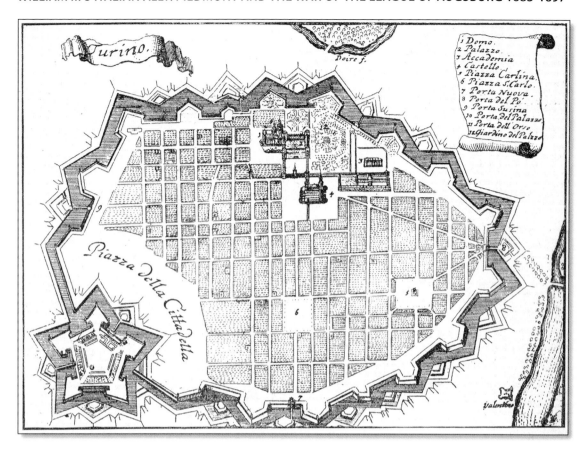

50. Turin as it looked in 1690

Royal Highness' States, trying to force him to release two of his main Places and two thousand infantrymen and two Regiments of dragoons, with the engagement to join them to the said army, to proceed damaging the State of Milan, the great soul of His Caesarian Majesty was excited to give his Imperial protection to a Prince of the Holy Empire … and he promises he will send a corps of five to six thousand of his best troops to join His Royal Highness, giving them the wage by His Caesarian Majesty without demanding winter quarters in Piedmont, and His Caesarian Majesty will let the Barbets, and French Religionaries, and other eight thousand men who the Lord Marquess of Borgomeinero ambassador of Spain says have to join them, act accordingly and depend on the orders by His Royal Highness…[3]

The Emperor too promised to give the Duke of Savoy Pinerolo.

On the razor's edge, Victor Amadeus managed to juggle as long as possible to give his soldiers time to concentrate under Turin, and the Spanish reinforcements time to arrive, whilst very close to Turin, between Orbassano and Carignano, commanded by Catinat, the French army was ready to assail him.

On 4 June 1690, once he had signed the agreement with the Empire and informed about the signature of that with Spain, Victor Amadeus ordered

---

3   *Trattato d'alleanza offensiva e difensiva fra Vittorio Amedeo Duca di Savoia e l'Imperatore Leopoldo contro la Corona di Francia*, rep. in Solaro della Margarita, op. cit., vol. II, pp. 129–131.

51. Turin's Castello Square at the end of the 17th century

the Count di San Tommaso to summon Rébenac, the French ambassador, and formally announce to him the final Piedmontese position and the war. As Rébenac was told, the extremity the Duke had been reduced to by France now enforced him to accept the help the Spaniards offered many time in the past, and he always rejected.

At last Victor Amadeus summoned the generals, dignitaries and nobles. In the throne hall, he told them what he had done. He underlined Louis XIV's intolerable pretensions, demands, urges and pressures, then he added he had tried whatever was possible to avoid the clash, with no result; hence – he said – he signed the alliance to the Emperor and the King of Spain, and ended saying: 'The Allied armies come to my rescue, but, more than on their strength, I rely on the value and the devotion of my nobility and my people. To this bravery, to this devotion the Royal House of Savoy has never appealed in vain', to which all, taken by the enthusiasm, began to shout 'Long live the Duke'.[4]

'The news spread in the city and was welcomed with equal exultation and the clergy offered the gold and silver of the churches to provide for the urgent necessities of the war.'[5] The people of Mondovì put aside whatever resentment they held due to the Salt War and immediately volunteered for war. It was no different in the rest of Italy and the Sabaudian resident in Rome reported that at the Papal Court 'since the liberation of Vienna [of 1683] there has never seen a similar joy.'[6]

As they had been managed by Catinat, due to the misleading and arrogant letters and instructions from Louvois, the diplomatic negotiation between France and Piedmont made everybody assess the King's mind to have been disloyal, and the Duke to have been fully persecuted and right: the troop issue

---

4   Solaro di Moretta, *Trattati e gesta di Vittorio Amedeo II*, rip, in Carutti, *History*, p. 124.
5   Rep. in Carutti, *History*, p. 124.
6   Rep. in Carutti, *idem*.

first; eight days later the demand for fortresses; after 12 days, the demand to declare war on Spain; how could France not to appear in the worst light?

Louis XIV too, when he knew the result of the letters, thought it to have gone a bit too far, but did not realise what a disaster he had actually caused. Thus on 12 June he naively and arrogantly wrote to Catinat that, if the Duke really released Turin, Verrua and the three regiments within two days once the letter received, the just-started hostilities would cease. Had the Duke persisted in refusing the release of the citadel of Turin as a serious disfigurement of a sovereign, the King could accept in turn Montmélian in Savoy, Susa, Verrua, Carmagnola and Mirabocco in Piedmont, and the Pope and the Venetians would be the granters of the peace.

One-hundred-and-fifty years later, the Piedmontese official historian, Baron Carutti di Cantogno, commented: 'It was a great result; the King of France, Louis XIV, retreated, offered his hand to a Duke of Savoy, who not only had disrespected him, but took the weapons against him.'[7] He was wrong. Louis was simply trying to turn around the obstacle, for he repeated his demands, with a sole difference: he left Turin to the Duke, but asked for five fortresses instead of two, and two of them, Montmélian and Susa, gave him an alternative passage across the Alps, safer than that bound to Pinerolo permanently harassed by the Waldensians.

Attached to the letter, Catinat also had a circular letter sent to each Italian sovereign, saying that the King of France was not looking for war, and desired only to ensure peace on his borders. Once that peace was achieved, no more problems would appear. If Louis thought Victor Amadeus to be so naive as to trust him, he was wrong.

As soon as the King's letter to Victor Amadeus arrived, on 15 June in the evening Catinat forwarded it by a trumpeter and asked for meeting a Piedmontese representative. By that day the Spaniards had already arrived and the Duke 'wanted to open the letter at the presence of the Spanish generals,'[8] then he replied:

> Monsieur de Catinat, you have as many witnesses as you have soldiers of what I have tolerated to demonstrate my respectful deference to the King your master. I consented to the request of my troops, and you showed particular satisfaction to Marquess Ferrero, as if that was the only aim of your commissions; and you answered affirmatively to his question whether, from then on, he could look at H.M.'s troops as at friends. Nonetheless, a few days later you insisted on having some of my fortresses in your hands; afterwards you demanded, contrary to your first mind, that my soldiers did not proceed to France any more, but would join yours to act against the State of Milan. After all this you see how I must desire that your questions come written to me, so that I can answer in the same way. I need to tell you this as an answer to your letter of yesterday; and that I shall always keep for you the sentiments of esteem, with which I am, etc.[9]

---

7   Carutti, *Diplomacy*, Book IX, p. 188.

8   The nuncio of Savoy Mosti to Cardinal Rubini Secretary of State, Turin, 17 June 1690, in ASV, Nunziatura di Savoia, anno 1690.

9   Carutti, 'Diplomacy', cit., Book IX, p. 188

Victor Amadeus took two more steps: peace with the Waldensians and agreement with the Maritime Powers. The former were granted to safely return their homes, have back their properties, and have their religion respected and officially allowed. The result went far beyond any possible good hope: since then on, the Waldensians always loyally served and obeyed the Duke and his successors, as, by the way, they did in the past.

The Duke chose Philibert Sallier de la Tour Baron de Bordeau as his personal envoy to William III. De la Tour, a 47-year-old official in the financial administration in Turin and the president of the Auditing Chamber of Savoy, had been Victor Amadeus' tutor and teacher. The Duke fully trusted him and gave him two different patents: one, dated on 14 July, to the States General, the other, dated on the following day, to William III. Another reason why de la Tour was chosen was his financial experience. In fact he had to obtain, manage and forward time after time the subsidies promised by the Maritime Powers, and the future would reveal it to be not an easy task.

De la Tour went to The Hague and met the Dutch and British plenipotentiaries. There was one British plenipotentiary, Lord Charles Viscount Dursley,[10] but there were eight Dutch, that is to say the Grand Pensionary and a representative from each of the seven United Provinces. On 20 October Britain and the Netherlands promised 30,000 *scudi* monthly funding – 20,000 from Britain and 10,000 from the United Provinces – following the signing of the Treaty during at least the next six months. Victor Amadeus could use half as he liked, whilst the other half had to be used to pay military units composed of Waldensians or by *Religionari* – which could be rendered as 'Religionaries', that is to say the French Protestant refugees[11] – to be employed against the French army.

Treaty between England and the States General, and the Duke of Savoy.
Dated at The Hague, 20th October, 1690:

Whereas His Royal Highness of Savoy, after having declared himself for the common cause, desires nothing more ardently than to enter into the Alliance with the King of Great Britain, and the Lords the States General of the United Provinces of the Low Countries, and that his Britannic Majesty and their High Mightinesses are willingly disposed to concur with the generous wish of a Prince whom they esteem so particularly, their under-named Plenipotentiaries, after having conferred together, thought it best to make this Alliance conducive to the greatest union of the confederate Powers to aggregate and associate His Royal Highness to the Treaty concluded between his Imperial Majesty and the Lords the States General, the 12th of May, 1689, into which his said Majesty of Great Britain is also entered; to the end that has there ought to be but one and the same mind, and one and the same interest among the allies, so there may be but one and the same Treaty, and one and the same alliance to unite

---

10   Lord Dursely, the son of the Earl of Berkeley, had been appointed British plenipotentiary since February 1690, that is to say three and a half months before Victor Amadeus started the war on France and exactly eight months before de la Tour signed the Treaty.

11   In exchange for this support, Victor Amadeus in a secret article promised the abolition of his 1688 decree against the Waldensians, as well as all the other decrees existing against them, freeing all who were still in jail, giving them their children, and leaving them their whole religious liberty.

them; and for the attaining to a design so advantageous to the common cause they have agreed to make the following declarations in virtue of their respective powers inserted at the end of these presents.

I

My Lord Dursley, Envoy Extraordinary from His Majesty of Great Britain, and the Sieurs Walrave, Baron of Hekeren, Lord of Netelhorst, Great Bailiff of the County of Zutphen; James Baron of Wassenaar and Duvenvoird, Lord of Duven voird Voorschoten Veur, &c., Great Bailiff and Great Master of the Dykes of Rhynland, one of the body of Nobles of the Province of Holland and of West Frize; Anthony Heinsius, Councillor, Pensionary, Keeper of the Seal, and Intendant of the Fiefs of the same Province; William of Nassau, Lord of Odyk, Cortgene, &c., First Noble and Representative of the Order of Nobility in the States, and in the Council of the County of Zealand; John Vander Does, Lord of Bergestein, Deputy from the Order of Noblesse to the States of Utrecht; John Abraham de Schurman, Burgomaster or Ylst, and Deputy to the States of Frise; Gaspar Henry de Lemker Burgomaster of Campen; and John Viglius Van Heek, Senator of Groninghen and Omland: Deputies from the Lords the States General of the United Provinces of the Low Countries do aggregate, associate, and admit His Royal Highness of Savoy to the Treaty which was concluded and signed the 12th of May, 1689, between his Imperial Majesty, and the Lords the States General of the tenor following:

Be it known and declared that though the Treaty concluded at Hague a few years ago, between his Sacred Majesty and the High and Mighty Lords the States General of the United Provinces for their mutual defence, remains yet in its full vigour; nevertheless, as well his Sacred Majesty as the said Lords the States General, considering the greatness of the common danger that threatens all Christendom since the last French invasion, and the bad faith of the French in observance of the aforesaid Treaty, have thought it necessary to strengthen the same and the former union, by stricter and firmer bands, and also at the same time to consider of more effectual ways as well for restoring as preserving the public peace and safety, and therefore the Plenipotentiaries for that purpose constituted by both parties, namely, on the part of his Imperial Majesty by his Privy Councillors of State, Leopold William Count of Konigsegg, Vice-Chancellor of the Holy Roman Empire, Knight of the Golden Fleece; and Theodore Althete Henry Count Stratman, Chancellor of the Court; and on the part of the High and Mighty Lords the States General by James Hop, Councillor and Syndic of the city of Amsterdam and Deputy for Holland & Westfrise in the Assembly of the States General, after mutual exchange of their powers, have agreed as follows:—

1.

There shall be and remain for ever between his Sacred Imperial Majesty and the States General of the United Provinces a constant, perpetual, and inviolable friendship and correspondence, each of them shall be obliged to promote diligently the other's interests, and to do as much as in them lies to prevent all damages and inconveniences thereto.

2.

And as the French King has lately attacked, without any legitimate cause or pretext, as well his Sacred Imperial Majesty as the Lords the States General, by a most grievous and unjust war, there shall be between the contracting parties not only a defensive but an offensive alliance, by virtue where of both of them shall act in hostile manner against the said French King with all their forces by sea and by land, and against such of his allies as upon warning to be given for that purpose shall refuse to separate from him; and they shall also communicate one to the other their advices for the better carrying on the operations of the war either jointly or severally for the destruction of the common enemy.

3.

It shall not be lawful for either party to withdraw from the war against France, or to enter separately upon any convention, treaty of peace, or armistice with France, or its allies, upon any pretext whatever, without the consent and concurrence of the other party.

4.

There shall by no means be any peace concluded before the Peace of Westphalia and those of Osnaburgh, Münster, and the Pyrenees have by common force and the aid of God been vindicated, and all things both in Church and State restored to their former condition, according to the tenor of the same.

5.

And if any negotiations of peace or truce shall by common consent be entered into, all things treated on shall on both sides be communicated bona fide, nor shall one party conclude anything without the consent and satisfaction of the other.

6.

After the present war shall by common consent be ended and a peace concluded, there shall remain between his Sacred Imperial Majesty, his heirs and successors and the States General of the United Provinces a perpetual defensive alliance against the often mentioned crown of France, and its adherents; by force whereof the contracting parties shall use their best endeavours that the peace to be made may remain firm and perpetual.

7

That if it shall happen the crown of France shall again attack one or other of the contracting parties, contrary to the said peace, at what time soever the same shall be done, they shall be obliged faithfully to assist each other with all their forces the same as now both by sea and by land, and to resist all hostility and violence, and not to desist until all things are restored to their former state according to the aforesaid peace, and satisfaction given to the party injured.

8.

Furthermore, his Sacred Imperial Majesty shall at all times protect and defend the rights of the States General, and they the rights of his Imperial Majesty, against the crown of France and its adherents, by all the ways and means in their power, nor shall they do any prejudice to each other in their said rights.

9.

And if between the contracting parties any controversies shall be as to the limits of their dominions, or that any such should arise hereafter, they shall be discussed and composed in a friendly manner, either by commission or deputies on both sides, without any manner of force, and nothing in the meantime shall be innovated therein.

10.

There shall be invited into the society of this present alliance on the part of his Imperial Majesty, the crown of Spain; and on the part of the Lords the States General of the United Provinces, the crown of England; and there shall be in a similar manner admitted into the same all the allies of either party who shall think fit to enter into the same. The most Serene Duke of Lorraine is also included in this Treaty, and the allies shall use all their powers that he shall be; reinstated in the Duchy, dominions, states, and rights of his Ancestors.

This Treaty shall be ratified, on both sides, within the space of four weeks, or sooner if it may be.

In witness whereof, and for confirmation of the credit and sincerity hereof, two instruments of the same tenor are made, signed, and sealed by the Plenipotentiaries of both parties, and are reciprocally exchanged.

Done at Vienna, the 12th of May, 1689.
L. S. Leopold William, Count of Kinigsegg.
L. S. T. A. Henr. Count of Stratman.
L. S. J. Hop.

And in the name of the King of Great Britain, and of the Lords the States General, we enter, with regard to His Royal Highness, into all those engagements, without any reserve or exception, into which they are entered with his Imperial Majesty, obliging, as by the present act they do oblige, his Britannic Majesty and their High Mightinesses to the entire and inviolable observation of the said Treaty according to its form and tenor towards His Royal Highness, as if they had over again hereby stipulated and contracted it with his said Royal Highness.

II

The Sieur de la Tour, Baron de Bourdeaux, Councillor of State to His Royal Highness, President of his Finances in Savoy, Intendant of his Household, and his Envoy Extraordinary, having seen and examined the treaty aforesaid, approves and ratifies it, and receives and accepts the said association and aggregation in the name of His Royal Highness; obliging him, as by the present act he does oblige him, to observe and cause to be inviolably observed the same conditions, guaranties, and obligations as are therein contained, and which shall have the same force as if they were hereby over again stipulated between the parties.

III.

His Britannic Majesty and their High Mightinesses being willing to give His Royal Highness effectual marks of their affection, and of the interest which they take for his preservation, do establish and promise him an aid of thirty thousand crowns a month, to commence on the day of the signing of the present Treaty, and to continue during six months to come; the moiety of which sum to be employed by his said Royal Highness where it shall be most convenient for repelling the enemy who has invaded his dominions, and which moiety shall therefore be presently advanced to him for that purpose; and the other moiety to be employed as well for subsisting his troops as for maintenance of the Vaudois and French refugees who have been armed at the expense, and by the care, of his Britannic Majesty and of their High Mightinesses: of the which sum of thirty thousand crowns[12] a month the King of Great Britain shall furnish 20,000 and the States General 10,000, which they shall regularly and punctually cause to be paid.

IV

And whereas his Imperial Majesty, by the treaty he made with His Royal Highness, the 4th of June, last passed, stipulated an express article, touching the restitution of Pignerol, of the tenor following:

His Sacred Imperial Majesty and the Confederates shall do all in their power, that Pignerol shall be restored to His Royal Highness, either by treaty or force of arms, but without prejudice to the rights and possessions ceded to and acquired by his Highness in the territory of Montferrat by virtue of the Treaty of Cherasco:

V

His Britannic Majesty and their High Mightinesses, entering into the whole intention of the obligation imposed by that article, will observe all its contents, and cause it to be punctually executed.

The above-mentioned Plenipotentiaries promise the entire and inviolable observation of the foregoing articles, and oblige themselves to return the ratifications thereof in due form in two months, or sooner if possible. In witness whereof, they have signed the present act, and have thereto affixed the seal of their arms.

Done at The Hague, the 20th October, 1690.
L. S. (Signed) PH. DE LA Tour.[13]

The alliance contained a:

SECRET ARTICLE concerning the Vaudois, concluded at The Hague, between the Ministers of his Britannic Majesty and their High Mightinesses the States General

---

12 The original, in French, says *écus scudi*, not crowns as it appears in the English translation I used here; see the Treaty in Solaro della Margarita, op. cit., Vol. II.

13 English translation reported in Blackly, W., *The diplomatic correspondence of the Right Hon. Richard Hill (L.L.D., F.R.S., &c., &c.), envoy extraordinary from the Court of St. James to the Duke of Savoy, in the reign of Queen Anne: from July 1703, to May 1706* (London, 1845), Part II, Translations, pp. 914–919. 'L.S.' means *Locum sigilli*, that is to say 'place of the seal', because, before signing, the official representatives had to press their seal on a few drops of still-liquid sealing-wax, that is to say the upper part of the ring they had, on which their family coat of arms was carved.

of the United Provinces of the Netherlands, on the one part, and the President de la Tour, Envoy of his Royal Highness the Duke of Savoy, on the other part.

His Royal Highness, who has already taken those of his subjects who profess the religion of the Waldenses into favour, and received them under his Royal protection, and who every day obtains fresh proofs of their fidelity and attachment to his service, declares by the present Article, which shall have the same force and validity as if it were inserted in the treaty, or in its annexes, concluded this day between the King of Great Britain and the States General of the United Provinces of the Netherlands, on the one part, and His Royal Highness on the other, that at the instance and in consideration of his Britannic Majesty and of their High Mightinesses, His Royal Highness has revoked, and hereby does revoke the decree is sued against the said Vaudois, dated the 31st January 1686, and all other edicts or orders whatsoever given for the execution of the above decree; has exempted, and does exempt them from the consequences of all contraventions of those ordinances, and grants them for this purpose, as long as it is or shall be necessary, full and entire pardon for them, so that it shall not be lawful to sue, generally or separately, in any manner whatsoever, either themselves or any others that may have assisted or abetted them. That His Royal Highness desires all prisoners to be set at liberty, and that all children of both sexes and of all ages, and in whatsoever place they may be, shall be restored without paying any costs or expenses, and shall be left at full liberty to return with their parents, and to profess their religion; nor shall it be lawful to disturb or prosecute either them or others, on account of any abjuration which they have made. That His Royal Highness preserves and replaces them, their children and their posterity, in the possession of all and of each of their ancient rights, edicts, usages and privileges, as well in regard to their abodes, their trade, and the exercise of their religion, as to every other purpose; re-establishes them in, and restores them to all their property, estates, houses, inheritances, claims interests, and actions, and in and to all other objects in being, and which they may be able to substantiate by any proof to have belonged to them previous to the said Order of January 31, 1686. That immediately after the ratification of the principal Treaty, and of the present Article, His Royal Highness will, in conformity with the present Article, cause to be promulgated letters patent, in the shape of an Edict, in favour of the said Vaudois his subjects, and of other persons of that religion, who shall be willing to settle in the said Valleys, on taking the accustomed oath of fidelity as loyal subjects of His Royal Highness, which letters patent his said Royal Highness will cause to be entered and authenticated by the Senate and by the Board of Accounts at Turin, and wherever it shall be necessary; and finally, the Ministers of her Britannic Majesty, and of their High Mightinesses, shall be instructed and authorised to regulate, according to the ancient edicts, rights and concessions, with the Ministers of His Royal Highness, the particulars of things, and whatever may have been left out and omitted, in order to provide for the security of the said Vaudois under this Article, as also for the execution of the same in respect of matters concerning their religion, and relative to their property, rights, and all other objects. The said Plenipotentiaries just mentioned have promised, and do promise respectively, in the name of their masters and principals, to cause the contents of the present Article to be inviolably observed, and to procure ratifications of them, in good and due form, within two months or sooner, if possible. In faith of which they have signed the present Article, and affixed to it the seals of their arms.

Done at The Hague, the 20th of October, 1690.

L. S. Ph. DE LA Tour[14]

Some days later, de la Tour moved to London, was officially admitted to William III's presence by mid November – the beginning of November according to the Julian calendar still used in England and in Russia, 10 days late on the 'papist' one used in the rest of Europe – and pronounced a brief speech of salute.[15] Then showed his credentials:

> Victor Amedeus the Second, by the grace of God, Duke of Savoy, Prince of Piedmont, King of Cyprus, &c. The goodness with which the King of England has been pleased to assure us of his Royal protection gives us hope that His Majesty will also be pleased to grant to us the honour of entering into alliance with him. For this end we have given the President de la Tour, as by virtue of these presents, signed with our hand, we do give him full power to treat and conclude with his Britannic Majesty, or with such as shall be deputed by His Majesty, a treaty of alliance with such covenants, conditions, and promises as he shall judge proper, though the same be such things as might require a more ample and special authority than the present power. Promising on the faith and word of a Prince inviolably to observe, and punctually to execute, all that the said President de la Tour shall treat, conclude, perform and promise, and to hold the same always firm, stable and irrevocable, and to ratify it, as we do ratify it by these presents. In witness whereof we have signed this present power, caused it to be countersigned by our Chief Secretary of State, and caused our Privy seal to be affixed thereto.
>
> Given at the Camp at Carignan, this 15th of July, 1690.
>
> (Signed) V. AMEDEO.[16]

William accepted the plenipotentiary and ratified the Treaty on 14 March 1691, whilst Victor Amadeus had already done it on 20 November 1690, and the States General on 8 February 1691.

The money could come, the war could be fed.

---

14 English translation reported in *Hill – letters*, Part II, Translations, pp. 923–924.

15 The speech was published as, *THE SPEECH OF THE President de la Tour, Envoy Extraordinary from his ROYAL HIGHNESS the Duke of SAVOY, To His MAJESTY, At his First Publick Audience, Novemb. 2. 1690,* re-printed by the Heir of *Andrew Anderson,* Printer to Their Majesties, Edinburgh, 1690.

16 English translation reported in *Hill – letters*, part II, translations, p. 922.

Part II: The War

10

The Spanish Endorsement

We must now spend time speaking of a neglected military effort, that by the Spanish military system in Italy. When saying neglected, I mean that nobody seemed to care very much of it in the three centuries following the conflict, but the Spaniards made a huge commitment in both men and money an all fronts of the Nine Years' War, and their direct commitment on the Italian front and from their Italian possessions to feed the Italian, Catalan, and Flemish fronts was as much remarkable as forgotten.

As said, Spain had one of her two major arsenals in Naples, and carefully kept the Spanish Road open. To this aim, every year, often in the last days of April, 12 galleys left Naples to land in Orbetello and the *Stato dei Presidii* – the State of the Garrisons – 18 infantry companies tasked to relieve the local troops achieving their year-long garrison duty.

In April 1687 the Spaniards were committing ships and infantry to join the Holy League forces restarting fights against the Ottomans in Levant and Greece, when they realised they had to start thinking of a possible forthcoming war against France too. A first signal occurred in July that year. When the French galleys which had just shipped the new French ambassador to Rome asked Neapolitan administration for the permission for a pit stop in Pozzuoli and Baia, simply to rest and get supplies, the viceroy of Naples, Marquess Del Carpio, allowed them, but reinforced the two concerned local garrisons with eight additional companies of Spanish and Italian infantry.[1]

In the autumn, the governor of Milan, Count de Fuensalida, cancelled the foreseen reduction of Milanese troops, and was ordered from Madrid to inspect all the fortresses of the Duchy on the western border and along the Spanish Road. The next signal of an approaching storm was in January 1688, when the Italian infantry units in Spanish service in Pozzuoli and Gaeta were gathered back to Naples, ready to be shipped to Milan.

---

1   *Avvisi di Napoli*, July 1687.

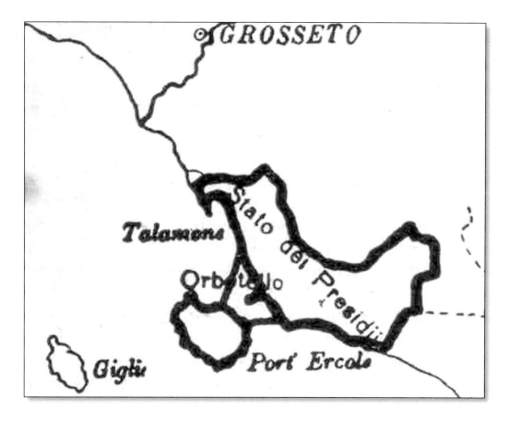

54. (above): *Stato dei Presidii* – the State of the Garrisons
55. (below): Porto Longone – a town of the State of the Garrisons

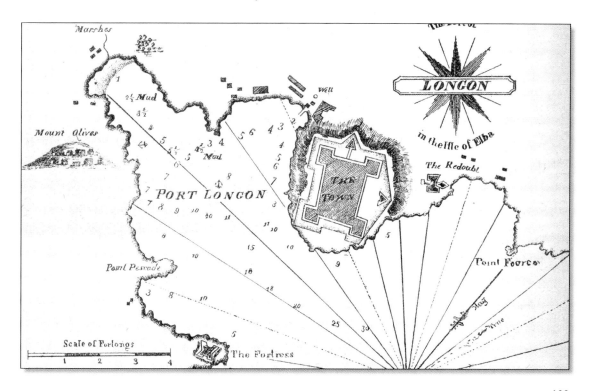

56. Orbetello – the main town of the State of the Garrisons

In spring 1688 the new viceroy of Naples, Don Francisco Benavides y Avila Count de San Esteban, sent the relieving troops to the *Presidii* almost a month and a half earlier than the previous year,[2] using Genoese galleys, whilst the pro-French Duke of Mantua was enrolling a dragoon and a foot regiment in Monferrato.

In July doubts about a forthcoming war spread when people were informed of a fight between two Spanish vessels, sailing from Naples to Spain, and four French men-of-war. But all doubts disappeared in October, when a plot was discovered in Orbetello. French agents promised a considerable amount of money to the Flemish governor of Orbetello – whose wife was French – if he delivered them the fortress. For had the sum to be paid in Leghorn, the Grand Duke was informed by his police, and warned the Spanish vicar of the *Presidii*. The governor was immediately jailed and some of the involved officers were arrested and executed. As soon as the news was known in Naples, the viceroy sent a new garrison to Orbetello, and, in spite of the bad weather at sea, on 24 November 1688 four Genoese galleys left Naples and shipped 300 men to the *Presidii*.

During 1689 war preparation increased in both Milan and Naples. Troops left Milan to Genoa to be shipped to Barcelona and the Catalan front against the French. Meanwhile, new regiments were organised in Spain and Italy to

---

2   In 1687 the *Presidii* new garrison left Naples on 29 April. In 1688 they left on 4 March; see Confuorto, Domenico, *Giornali di Napoli dal MDCLXXIX al MDCIC*, [Newspapers of Naples since 1679 until 1699], 2 vols., edited by F. Nicolini (Naples, 1930–1931).

be sent to Milan, and German regiments were hired. As soon as the war was declared by France, in the first half of May 1689, seven galleys[3] shipped 17 additional infantry companies to the *Presidii*, and a month later 15 galleys left Naples to Finale. There they took on board 2,000 men and proceeded to Spain.

Now, leaving aside the Italians in Spanish service fighting on fronts other than Italy, and focusing on Italy alone, the Spanish troops were quickly increased especially in Milan.

The Count de Fuensalida wanted to have a 15,000-man-strong army as soon as possible. In January 1690 Milanese reorganisation went ahead. Spanish and German infantry companies reached the Duchy. Cavalry companies were ordered to be increased by 25 more men each, and in February money was sent to Vienna to pay new local recruits in Milanese service.

In March it was clear that a clash between France and Spain in Italy was only a matter of time. Fuensalida sped up recruitment, whilst the French reinforced Casale. On 15 March Fuensalida summoned a council of war in Milan. On the 20th, newly enrolled German soldiers entered the Duchy. On the 21st Spanish troops in Milan were further incremented by 12 new companies: six of infantry 70 men strong each, and five of dragoons 50-men strong. The governor ordered payment of 100,000 *liras* for newly made artillery bombs and shells, and 1,000 *scudi* to each Swiss Grison company serving in the State of Milan. In April, Fuensalida decided to further increase his army to 18,000 and possibly 20,000 and committed officers to Germany to organise two new horse regiments. During that month, news about the establishment of new units in Milan appeared almost day by day. A new council of war met on 24 April, whilst news about the French in Piedmont announced the incoming storm. The Spanish troops were slowly concentrating on the western border and Fuensalida demanded the Senate of Milan organise a corps of Milanese country militia 6,000 men strong, to be paid and lodged by the Commons. The Senate disagreed, but no matter: on 24 May Fuensalida gave orders to organise it.[4] Then the Governor ordered the baking of 180,000 bread rations

55. The Viceroy of Naples, Don Francisco de Benavides, Marquess de San Esteban

---

3   Apart from vessels, Spanish naval organisation relied on the Galley squadrons of Naples, Sicily and Sardinia, and was supported by that of the Republic of Genoa, and by a privately owned galley squadron, the *Squadra de'particolari o del duca di Tursi* – the 'private men's or the Duke of Tursi's squadron' – contracted whenever it was needed. It was just this squadron that shipped the reinforcements to Orbetello in May 1689, as it had done in November 1688 also.

4   This great activity in Milan was supported by a similarly intensive activity in Naples and by a naval shuttle. Just on 12 April the Neapolitan and Tursi galleys shipped three companies, ordnance, food and supplies from Naples to the Presidii. Then they went back to Naples and, along with the Sicilian squadron, on 24 April reached Genoa, and the troops they carried, bound to Milan,

in Pavia, near the soon-to-be front, and chose the contractor for the artillery and supply train. On 9 May, whilst on that day in Piedmont Catinat arrived in Avigliana, with 7,000 men and asked for meeting a ducal minister to inform him the King's pretension of getting from Victor Amadeus men, and, or – as Catinat thought – Turin and Verrua, in Milan orders were issued for further 2,000 men to be enrolled in Switzerland, and for concentrating all the cavalry on the western border. At the same time Fuensalida urged the viceroy in Naples for men and money, but his requests were fulfilled only when the galleys came back from the *Presidii* and from Spain. Thus, on 24 May 1,200 Italian and 800 Spanish foot could embark in Naples bound to Finale and Milan, whilst on the 27th 310 more Spaniards landed in Voltri, near Genoa, to proceed to Milan. On 31 May, 50 sappers with 100 wagons loaded with shovels and other tools arrived in Pavia, completing the concentration of Spanish forces on the defensive line: the River Ticino.

---

were shuttled to Finale by boat. Back again to Naples, in the early days of May the galleys left to Barcelona shipping 1,000 men to the Catalan front. In Naples on 25 May was published the King's order for enlisting 2,000 men to be committed to Flanders. On 11 June near Genoa, Sicilian galleys landed the Spanish Tercio of Sicily, composed of 450 men, mostly sick and weak, probably due to the long travel. Six days later, on the 17th, nine galleys – seven Neapolitan and two Tursi – followed by six boats reached Genoa from Naples and landed 1,800 Spanish and Italian soldiers bound to Milan. During the first week of July 120 more men bound for Milan were shipped to Genoa. By the end of August, after a pause due to the time needed for gathering new recruits, the Sicilian, Neapolitan and Tursi galleys shipped from Naples to Genoa and Finale 400 new recruits, 200 professional foot and 250 cavalry with their horses, all bound for Milan. On 18 September 13 Spanish galleys landed four companies of foot in Voltri, near Genoa. Five days later, on the 23rd further companies of foot from Naples and bound for Milan landed in Genoa. On 21 October six Spanish and two Tursi galleys reached Vado and landed 800 Spaniards bound to Piedmont.

Garde du Corps, Campaign Dress, 1685–90
(Illustration by Bruno Mugnai, © Helion & Company)
See Colour Plate Commentaries for further information.

Garde du Corps, 1689

(Illustration by Bruno Mugnai, © Helion & Company)

See Colour Plate Commentaries for further information.

Plate C

Left: Regiment of the *Guardie a Piedi,* senior officer, 1690–94
Right: Infantry Regiment *Monferrato,* private fusilier, 1690

(Illustration by Bruno Mugnai, © Helion & Company)

See Colour Plate Commentaries for further information.

Left: Regiment of the *Guardie a Piedi*, grenadier, 1690–95
Right: Infantry Regiment *La Marina,* 1695

(Illustration by Bruno Mugnai, © Helion & Company)

See Colour Plate Commentaries for further information.

Cavalry Regiment *Savoia Cavalleria*, 1695–99, trooper and trumpeter

(Illustration by Bruno Mugnai, © Helion & Company)

See Colour Plate Commentaries for further information.

Infantry Regiment *Croce Bianca*, drummer, 1695–97
Infantry Regiment *Schulenburg* (German), NCO, 1695–99

(Illustration by Bruno Mugnai, © Helion & Company)

See Colour Plate Commentaries for further information.

Dragoon Regiment *Genevois*, dragoon in foot service, 1695
Dragoon Regiment of *Sua Altezza Reale*, dragoon, 1695–99
(Illustration by Bruno Mugnai, © Helion & Company)
See Colour Plate Commentaries for further information.

Artillery: gunner and miner, 1697–99

(Illustration by Bruno Mugnai, © Helion & Company)

See Colour Plate Commentaries for further information.

Plate I

Ordinanza flags, 1690

(Illustration by Bruno Mugnai, © Helion & Company)

See Colour Plate Commentaries for further information.

Above: Infantry Regiment *Piemonte, Ordinanza* flag, 1697–99
Below: Infantry Regiment *Savoye, Ordinanza* flag, 1699
(Illustration by Bruno Mugnai, © Helion & Company)
See Colour Plate Commentaries for further information.

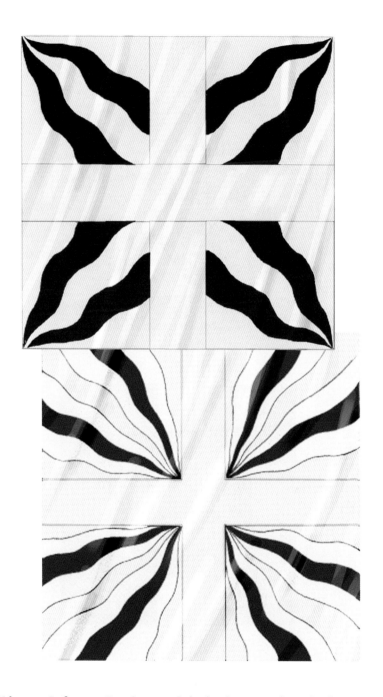

**Above: Infantry Regiment *Schulenburg,* Colonel's flag, 1694
Below: unknown infantry regiment (possibly the *Religionari
Miremont* or *Montauban* Regiment), *Ordinanza* flag, 1694**

(Illustration by Bruno Mugnai, © Helion & Company)

See Colour Plate Commentaries for further information.

Plate L

**Infantry Regiment *De Losche* (*Religionari*),
Ordinanza flag (above) and Colonel's flag (below), 1694**

(Illustration by Bruno Mugnai, © Helion & Company)

See Colour Plate Commentaries for further information.

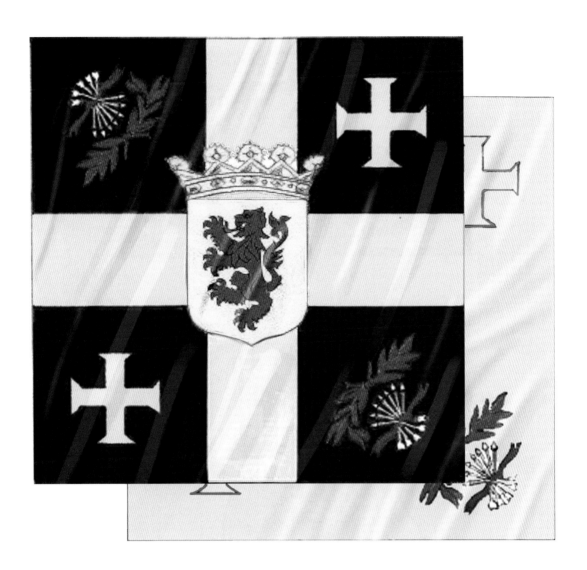

**Infantry Regiment *Lislemarais* (*Religionari*),
Colonel's flag (above) and *Ordinanza* flag (below), 1694–95**

(Illustration by Bruno Mugnai, © Helion & Company)

See Colour Plate Commentaries for further information.

***Ordinanz*a attributed to the German regiment *Heydelac*,
lost at the Battle of La Marsaglia on 4 October 1693**

(Illustration by Bruno Mugnai, © Helion & Company)

See Colour Plate Commentaries for further information.

Standards of the three companies of the *Garde du Corps*

(Illustration by Bruno Mugnai, © Helion & Company)

Detail, *Vittorio Amedeo II in maestà* (Victor Amadeus II in majesty)
by Martin van Mytens (1695–1770). Dated 1728.
(Public domain)

11

The First Campaign

I. The Situation on the Eve of the Campaign

The Grand Alliance's – that is to say William III's – strategy foresaw a grandiose pincer movement against France, an invasion from Flanders, the Rhineland, the Pyrenees, and the Alps.

As for the Alpine front, it was obvious that, before crossing the mountains, one had to eliminate or at least neutralise the French strongholds in Italy – that is to say Pinerolo and Casale – first. The tasked Allied army had to include all the Piedmontese forces, an Imperial contingent commanded by Prince Eugene of Savoy, a Spanish contingent and some units paid by Britain and the Netherlands.

In the early days of 1690 Victor Amadeus's army officially totalled 8,670 men, divided into 7,250 foot, and 1,420 cavalrymen and dragoons, who had to obey the newly issued rules of war.[1] Figures of course are only indicative, for the actual situation changed day by day, as was usual in professional armies of the Baroque/early modern era. The budgeted military expenditure – before June 1690 – was 3,233,900 *liras*. It seemed huge, but it soon appeared to be a pleasant dream, when compared to the growing military expenditure year by year affecting the Duchy of Savoy and its budget. Moreover, the funding did not arrive regularly, thus the expenditure was often a matter of choosing the major priority among the existing ones.

Some money could be spent directly abroad – for instance to pay a German-levied regiment – and some could be spent in Piedmont; but the problem was always the same: Victor Amadeus could never get all the promised money on the spot, at the beginning of the period that the money was expected to fund.

It was a continual plug of relatively little money into huge gaps to be filled. For instance during the first winter, in 1690–91, Victor Amadeus could pay his soldiers their arrears, their winter quarters and the recruitment for the next campaign only because he got from Spain a letter of change for 25,000

---

1   *Regolamento da osservarsi nel Servizio Militare dalle Truppe di Fanteria, e Cavalleria nell'Armata,* [Rules to be observed in the Military Service by the Troops of Infantry, and Cavalry in the army] issued on 12 July 1690, in AST, Materie Militari, Ordini e Regolamenti, Mazzo 4, n. 15.

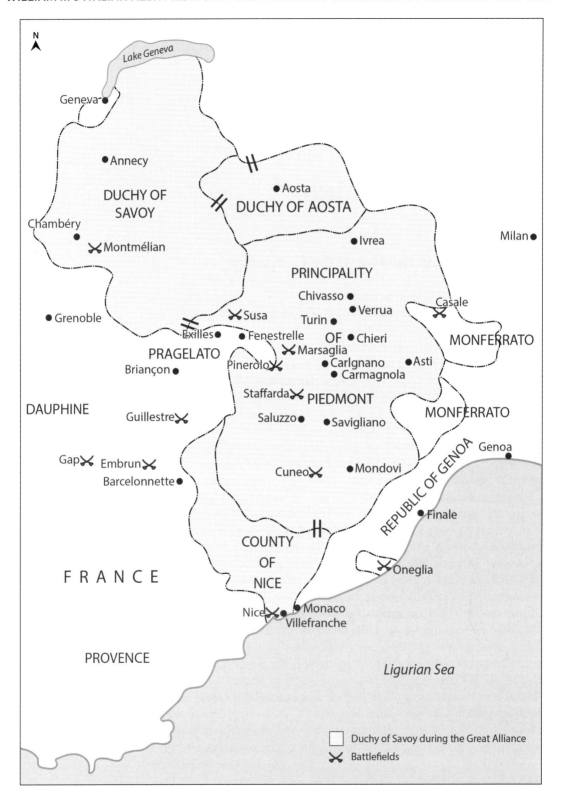

Map 3. The Duchy of Savoy during the Great Alliance, showing the most important battlefields.

pistoles, and a 100,000 *pistoles* funding on the revenues of the Kingdom of Naples. Just a year later, the Duke got a portion of what he had been promised by Charles II of Spain and used it to pay the recruiting price promised to the newly enrolled Protestant soldiers, who were supposed to be on British pay, that is to say paid by the money of the not-yet-arrived British funding.

When the 1690 campaign started, in terms of money Victor Amadeus was not well off but was not badly off. Normally he could rely on a roughly 7.5–8 million *liras* net yearly income. A good 75–78 percent of these revenues came from Piedmont. Savoy gave the remaining 22–25 percent whilst Nice normally provided a 0.20 percent only, In 1689 one third of the revenues was used for the army, and the State had a 16 million long-term debt. It was not a paradise, but the funding promised by Britain and the Netherlands could support the State and its army in the expected long clash for life or death.

Funding from the Maritime Powers was not that easy to get. Their governments did not assume direct responsibility for paying Piedmont. The British Treasury negotiated in Britain with merchants and bankers, who remitted letters of change equalling the subsidy of an entire year, from October to October the next year, because the Treaty came into effect from October 1690. In return the merchants and bankers received assignments on funds the government did not have yet, and sometimes these funds were expected to be redeemable after months or years, thus were not exactly welcome by the bankers.

The Dutch paid directly in The Hague, but normally they gave de la Tour a relatively small amount of money. Then de la Tour used it to purchase letters of change in Amsterdam bourse, and sent them to Turin, or used the money on the spot for the Duke's needs. This was a further problem, because it was possible that not enough letters of change were available. Letters of change had their market. Their price could have variations, and above all, there was a cost, that is to say: the total amount was affected and diminished by the price of the money transfer operation. So, a letter of change could be more or less expensive depending on when and where it was purchased and on when and where was it payable. Normally letters of change to Piedmont were payable in Leghorn, Genoa, Geneva, or Venice, but they were not always available in England, and their price and the annexed costs of the money could heavily affect the global amount of the final payment.[2] More, sometimes the local British and perhaps Dutch officials could be happier and feel more helpful if they were gratified with a relatively little present in cash, a present to be

---

2   A letter of change was a document issued by banker who received a payment from a customer and ordered another banker, acting in another city, to pay a certain sum to a certain beneficiary. It relied on the credit the issuing banker could have there, that is to say on how trusted he was in the place where the payment had to be made. Thus, the letter of change worked only among bankers, or merchants, with a mutual business relationship. That is why, due to the scanty foreign trade of Piedmont towards non-Italian countries other than France, British or Dutch letters of change could be paid in Italian mercantile cities as Genoa, Venice, or Leghorn, but very rarely in Turin, because of its lack of direct commercial links to the Maritime Powers. The letters of change paid in an Italian city out of Piedmont had to be converted into a further letter of change issued to be paid in Turin, thus there were at least two stages before Victor Amadeus got the subsidy, and each was charged with fees.

subtracted to the global amount of the transaction due to Piedmont, as de la Tour had to inform both San Tommaso and the Duke in December 1690 from London.[3]

Lastly, the most remarkable problem was that the subsidy was always late. The first letter of exchange was remitted by de la Tour in December. It covered the first part of the subsidy, and one could hope it was two months late because it was the first and the system as a whole took its time to start, but it was not so. The funding was always late during the war, and Victor Amadeus had to take such a delay in consideration regarding whenever and whatever planning he did.

II. The Problematic French Offensive

If Victor Amadeus had troubles, Catinat had more. His plans originally foresaw a march towards Milan. Once Savoy turned to the Allied side, Catinat's problem became really complex.

Piedmont and Milan are in the Po valley. Piedmont is in the west, Milan in the east. Piedmont is separated from France by the semicircle of the Alps, lies in its centre and is cut in two by the Po river, streaming west to east, from the Alps towards the Duchy of Milan and Venice. The Duchy of Milan at that time included some provinces which later became part of Piedmont, nonetheless it had a very good strategic defensive line in depth, along the Ticino, a river streaming north to south, from Switzerland – actually from the mostly Italian owned Lake Maggiore – to the Po, entering the latter at Pavia. Basically, the Piedmontese war theatre was a rectangle divided in four just as the English flag, with the Po acting as the horizontal red bar, the Ticino as the vertical one in the upper half of the flag. Piedmont was in the half on the observer's left, with Turin lying in the upper quarter, and Milan in the upper quarter right. Catinat was near Turin, and had to reach Milan. In other words, had Savoy kept its alliance to France, he had simply to cross the Ticino, but it was no longer so.

Before marching on Milan he had now to secure Piedmont, and securing Piedmont meant seizing the main fortresses commanding roads and fords. This could be made only relying on time and huge supplies in food and ordnance. And here came another major problem: the French logistic system was inadequate: Catinat had no magazines.

Louis XIV had planned to invade the Duchy of Milan relying on Savoy as an ally. In the King's, his ministers' and marshals' minds, this meant not to worry about supplies, because they intended to demand them of Savoy. That is why Catinat in May asked the Piedmontese government for food and wagons for 10,000 men: because he had to move to Milan, and had practically no magazines. In fact, there were supplies stored in Pinerolo and in Casale. But Casale was out of range, in the quarter down on the left, on the other side

---

3   See de la Tour to Victor Amadeus, on 15 December 1690, from London, in AST, Lettere Ministri, Inghilterra, n. 8.

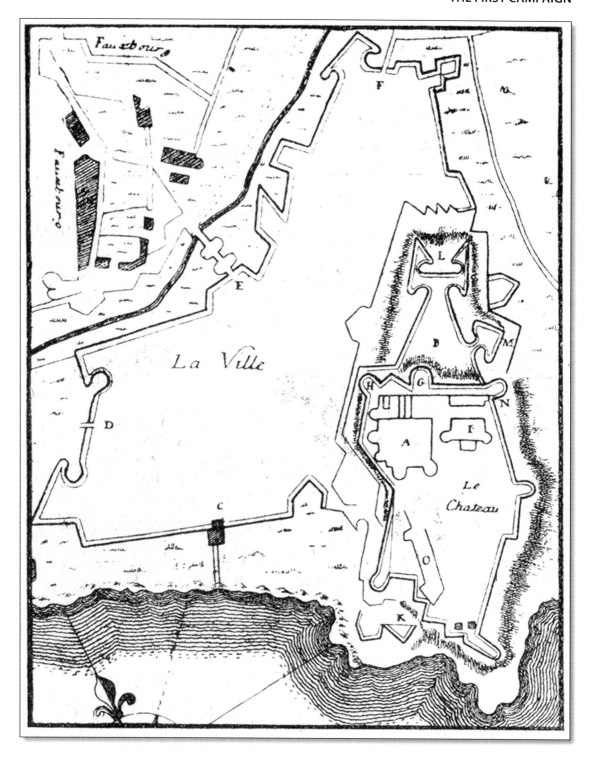

56. The Citadel of Nice in 1690

of the Po, because it was downstream of Turin on the right bank of the Po river, whilst Catinat was on the left side and upstream of Turin.

The Po was not fordable. It could be crossed on bridges only at Carignano, that is to say under the eyes of the Piedmontese just outside Turin, or in the city of Turin, because there were no other fords or bridges downstream of Turin until Pavia, deep in Spanish-held Lombardy.

Catinat could not reach the Casale area by remaining on the left bank of the river, marching along it, and crossing the Po in front of Casale, because he had to pass Turin, and he had neither enough men nor enough supplies to besiege it. An alternative could be to go around Turin and march to Casale downstream on the Po, but this meant the risk to be attacked on the right flank during the march, or, worst, on the rear by the Piedmontese, and, perhaps, engaged by the additional Spanish forces from their line along the Ticino when starting crossing the river in front of Casale. So Catinat had not that much choice. Food was his major and most immediate concern. Thus he had to look for food in the territory nearby, and in Pinerolo, on the other side of the Po. He could reach Pinerolo fording the Po near its springs, when it was still a sort of creek, not far from the Abbey of Santa Maria di Staffarda. When on the opposite bank, the right bank, he could march to Pinerolo, where he could at least rely on local supplies, and then move to Casale, simply marching along the same Po embankment of Casale.

But here another problem came. Pinerolo had such bad connections to France across the mountains, that its magazines emptied quickly and could not be refilled. In past times, Pinerolo got its supplies simply purchasing them from the towns nearby. The system worked until the war began. Then, Victor Amadeus formally forbade people to sell anything in Pinerolo or to people from Pinerolo. The armed peasants, i.e. the militia, enforced his orders, and the city had to rely on its provisions, day by day smaller and smaller. By mid June, Pinerolo had only 24 days supply of flour and wheat left and, worse, its garrison had become weaker than expected, because many Swiss companies of its and Casale's garrisons abandoned their weapons, refusing to serve against the Duke of Savoy. However, smaller and smaller was better than nothing, so Catinat decided to avoid contact with the enemy, and to move to Pinerolo to be close to the supplies and also to improve somehow its garrison weakened by the Swiss refusals. On the other hand, the lack of supplies dictated keeping the supply routes open. Thus the enemy positions across the Alps, Savoy, and Nice, had to be occupied.

III. First Operations in Piedmont

Catinat did not act fast against either Savoy nor Nice, and focused on Piedmont. He seemed willing to allow Victor Amadeus anything but surrender, but in fact he had troubles.

He began with looting and violence on the population, as hard as in the Palatinate. But things did not go exactly like in Germany. The militia-trained civilians fought just as ferociously as the French:

Here nobody is afraid of this army being all the country armed and resolute to defend itself, all the evil that they[4] can do will be between Carignano and Pinerolo, whilst nobody believes that they can advance this so much, expecting by this evening in the lands near the Stura a thousand horses of the State of Milan, which will then be followed by another 2,000, with 6,000 infantrymen and 12 pieces of cannon under the command of Count Lovigny, who this week is believed to be in condition to act against the French – having to join 3,000 infantry of Lord the Duke and 1,500 between horses and dragoons, besides a quantity of volunteering Nobility that will follow His Highness, who yesterday declared to want to get out at the head of the aforesaid army…

Meanwhile the Regiment of Monferrato, which is in the valleys, joined the Barbets [the Protestants] and captured some 400 French with many officers, and they raided until Pinerolo and until the place of Santa Brigida, with great fear by the place, which, by the cannon, managed to keep them far. After that, the governor of the aforesaid Place sent monsieur de Cattinat a courier to get relief, who was taken with the letter, and it was later known that the Lord General made a detachment of 10 men per company which he dispatched to Pinerolo.[5]

Between 10 and 17 June the Piedmontese protected the advance of the Spanish troops – 9,000 foot, 2,000 cavalry and 14 cannons – who arrived in Turin by the 16th, the day of the arrival from Milan of the General Field Master of the State of Milan: the Walloon Count de Louvigny.

The arrival of the first Spanish troops let Catinat withdraw. On 15 June he left 500 cavalry back to protect his rearguard, and marched to None, where his troops encamped and stayed.

On Thursday [23 June] all the infantry and the cavalry came to the camp between the Valentino and the Citadel in order to have the whole army gathered and ready to march, having order to be ready for every warning, as well as the troops who are in this city … My Lord Duke has prepared his magnificent equipment, but nobody knows exactly when they should march against the enemy, against whose parties skirmishes occur, and the worst is always on the French side, being many French prisoners in this City, where even some deserters come, and they would come in greater numbers if they did not fear to meet the peasants, who give the French no quarter. Here is assumed for sure that after the publication of the edict for the prohibition of introducing food in Pinerolo, their arrival there is so diminished, that in that Place they are short with all the comestibles; that there can not be got, but by the help of the subjects of this State.[6]

According to the nuncio, on the 27th the Duke was informed that the French had looted and burnt the towns of Rivalta and Orbassano and later that of Grugliasco too. A war council was held. It lasted until midnight, examined and compared all the available information and realised that

---

4   'They' are the French.
5   The nuncio of Savoy Mosti to Cardinal Rubini Secretary of State, Turin, 7 June 1690, in ASV, Nunziatura di Savoia, anno 1690.
6   *Idem*, Turin, 28 June 1690, in ASV, Nunziatura di Savoia, anno 1690.

probably Catinat wanted to build a bridge on the Po near Polonghera, to seize the local salt stores and send the salt to Pinerolo. Thus the Allied army moved to Moncalieri between the Po and the Sangone river and troops were dispatched to Polonghera. When more than 100 French cavalry arrived and tried to ford, the Allies waited until they were in the middle of the river, then started firing and killed them all.

On 28 June Prince Eugene arrived, as we know from the Papal nuncio, who wrote to Rome: '*Mylord Prince Eugene … left the marching troops, whose number is about 3,500, being all cavalry, except for a Regiment of 150 infantry…. The first that will come will be his Regiment of 1,000 dragoons, which is probably expected here on 12th of the incoming month.*'[7]

Meanwhile a Spanish cavalry regiment and a Piedmontese dragoon regiment advanced towards Verrua – halfway between Turin and Casale, on the right of the Po – to prevent any French march to Casale along that bank of the river, and the Spaniards planned a 10,000-man-strong blockading of Casale, which was achieved by the first week of July. Its immediate result was to prevent French raids from that city. Progressively, since July, the newly raised Milanese militia started relieving professional troopers in garrisons, and the professionals were gathered and redirected to Piedmont.

Actually, Victor Amadeus was more than lucky in having so close and huge a Spanish support, because the war in Italy started so suddenly that no Imperial or British-paid force was ready yet.

Spanish and Milanese officers were gathering 2,000 volunteers in Switzerland, to serve on Milanese pay. There were 800 French Protestants who passed through Genoa bound to Piedmont, whilst 300 more landed nearby, they too bound to Piedmont. An agent of William III's was gathering at least 400 Swiss soldiers on British pay, and by mid July 1,200 Religioners arrived in Turin, divided into three regiments.[8] But all those efforts originated only a relatively small flux of forces, coming drop by drop to the war theatre. In fact the Imperial troops arrived slowly and remained reduced to a few regiments, although quite good. Only since spring 1691 the Allied army in Italy could be considered on its full force, thus, had to rely only on his own small army Victor Amadeus would have been overwhelmed in a while by Catinat.

By the end of June the Spanish army, composed of Spanish, Italian and Swiss regiments, relied on more than 8,000 men in Piedmont and a force in the Duchy of Milan progressively increasing to 30,000 men, whilst further recruits arrived from Switzerland and Germany and other regiments were shipped from Southern Italy.

On 1 July the Piedmontese army moved to Lingotto, at that time three miles far from the city, and encamped there, leaving the Mondovì Infantry Regiment garrisoning the citadel, whilst the Turinese militia watched the walls and the gates of the city.

---

7   *Idem*, Turin, 28 June 1690, 2nd message, in ASV, Nunziatura di Savoia, anno 1690.
8   According to the *Avvisi di Foligno* issued on 15 July 1690, they were 400 Waldensians, 200 from Geneva, and 600 Swiss, Brandenburger, and French Protestants. They were shared under three flags 'which are those of England, Brandenburg, and the third they say of the Princes who joined the League; they are commanded by colonel Loche, from Dauphiny.'

Catinat tried once more to find a ford, or to build a bridge, but Victor Amadeus moved his army, committed 3,000 dragoons, and after a skirmish on 7 July prevented him succeeding. Thus Catinat on the next day, 8 July, tried to enter the town of Carignano, to seize the local bridge. The militia stopped him and held him off for many hours, until the arrival of the Allies. The French had to withdraw and 100 dead remained on the ground, along with many more wounded.

French logistical troubles increased. Pinerolo lacked salt and iron, thus nails for horseshoes could not be made, and cavalry and transports lost effectiveness. Moreover, the French camps were in a swampy area, diseases spread, and Pinerolo hospital became overcrowded. The French requisitioned a nuns' monastery in the city to lodge the sick and wounded, but that was not enough. The result was simple: French soldiers started deserting, initially one by one, and then team by team. Victor Amadeus let the French soldiers know that he would give every deserter a passport, and kept his word: he left them free to leave, but kept their horses, which he re-used to organise new mounted companies.

Catinat tried to get supplies from the surrounding country. Since mid July the French army had begun burning and looting the countryside up to the gates of Turin. As said, it was ferociously and stubbornly repaid by the Piedmontese peasants, thanks also to their militia training. Then Catinat decided the area was exhausted and it was time to concentrate his units, and moved to Pinerolo. During the night of 2–3 August, his men:

> … left their camp and crossed the small river Gelles and arrived between Pancalieri and Villafranca on the road to Pinarolo. Mylord Prince Eugene pursued them in the morning along with all the Milanese as well as the militia cavalry, but he succeeded only to lightly attack the rearguard on the banks of the aforementioned river, forded by the French, who left in their camp some part of their small baggage and some quantity of hay … The avant-garde of Mylord Duke's army, left Pancalè (Pancalieri) and advanced towards that enemy, between Vigone and Villafranca, nor does nobody have doubts about a general clash.[9]

On 3 August the French arrived near the village of Cavour. On the 5th they besieged its castle. The small garrison surrendered on 7th, but no matter: all the survivors were killed by the French.

The Marquess di Parella did not arrive on time, but, aware that Féuquières was not far, in Luserna, organised an ambush out of the town of Bricherasio. The result was different, for the Piedmontese trapped a convoy instead of Féuquières and killed 46 out of the 50 dragoons escorting it. Then they entered Bricherasio, and stormed the church, were 50 more French from Pinerolo garrison remained trapped with their captain. When kept, they all were killed without mercy in retaliation for the garrison of Cavour.

---

9   The nuncio of Savoy to Cardinal Secretary of State, Turin, 5 August 1690, in ASV, Nunziatura di Savoia, anno 1690.

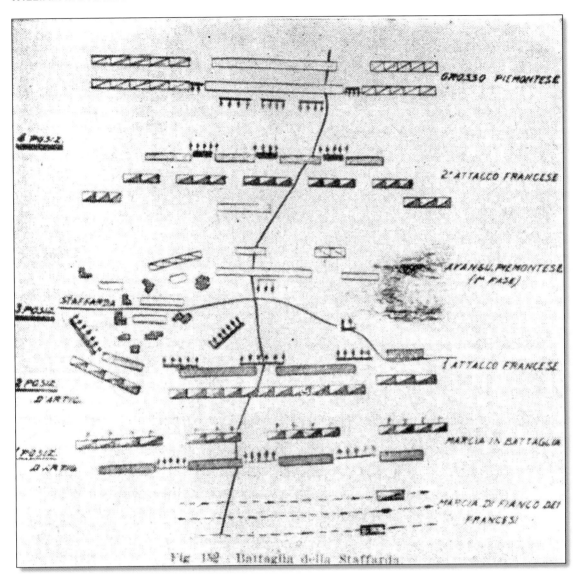

57. The Battle of Staffarda according to early maps

IV. Staffarda

On 15 August, Victor Amadeus was still waiting for the arrival of Imperial reinforcements. On that day he was informed that Catinat was moving to Pinerolo the supply train and the heavy artillery, had received materials and field cannons, distributed eight days of bread to the cavalry, four to the infantry and was requisitioning carts and draft animals.

Catinat's likely immediate target seemed to be Saluzzo, guarded only by militia. Thus the Duke ordered the concentration of the Allied army in Villafranca to approach the French from their left.

On the 17th Catinat left Cavour with 12,000 foot, 5,000 cavalry and 16 field cannons. He needed to go back towards Pinerolo, because his army was short of clothes and ordnance, and also if Pinerolo too had practically nothing left, it was not a good idea to have enemies between him and that city.

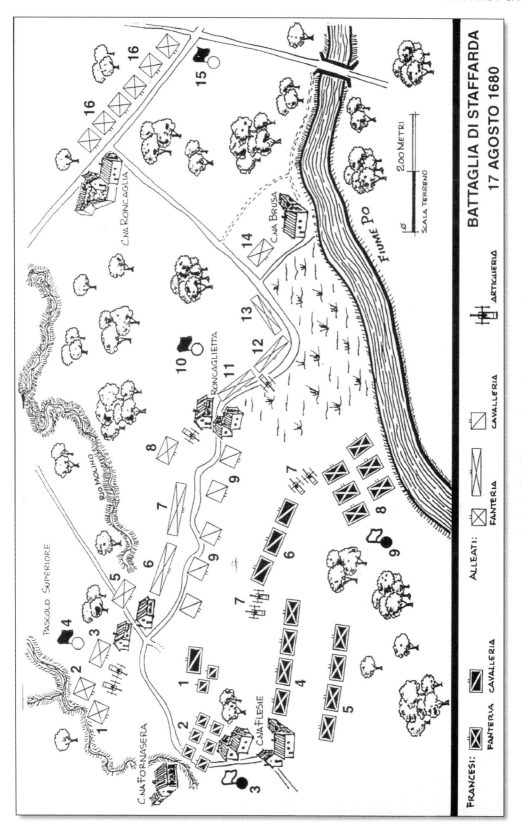

58. The Battle of Staffarda according to the most recent studies

123

Catinat shared his forces in two mixed columns of infantry and cavalry. These columns marched parallel, for in the case of an Allied attack, the soldiers had simply to turn left to have the battle line ready. All the wagons and the artillery were concentrated in a third column marching on the right of the other two, to be on the rearguard in case the first two columns were attacked and turned on their left. Then Catinat placed 400 cavalry under Montgomery in security on the left of his left column, to protect his flank on the enemy's side.

At 3:00 p.m. the first two French infantry brigades, Grancey and Artois, forded the Po near the Abbey of Santa Maria di Staffarda, not far from Saluzzo. They were followed by four infantry regiments – Cambresis, Chateaurenaud, Bourbon, and Hainaut – tasked with seizing the heights commanding the city, in spite of the Piedmontese militia targeting them from the walls of the city itself.

As we know, the Staffarda area was fundamental. Catinat destroyed the Carignano bridge on 10th June to protect his back whilst concentrating his troops in Pinerolo. Thus, the Po could only be forded at Staffarda or crossed in Turin, because there were no other fords or bridges downstream of Turin to Pavia.

Around 8:00 a.m., Victor Amadeus received the first news of the enemy movements and held a war council. The council decided to approach and attack the French with all the 15,000 infantry, 4,500 cavalry and 12 field cannons of the Allied army. The Duke rode at the head of the cavalry and preceded the bulk of the army, asking Louvigny to follow him along the Po with all the infantry and artillery.

The first infantry units reached Staffarda, where the Duke was waiting for them. They immediately joined the five cavalry squadrons commanded by the Marquess di Pianezza who had been sent ahead to try to engage the French rearguard. Around 5:00 p.m. they found it. But, as each side did not know the size of the opposing forces, both the Piedmontese and the French retreated, and informed their respective headquarters.

Victor Amadeus summoned another war council to attack the French. 'Don't do it,' said Prince Eugene according to his apocryphal *Memoirs*, written by Prince de Ligne, 'Catinat is an excellent general who has under him many old regiments, the best of the French infantry. Yours are new and mine have not yet arrived.' 'What does it matter,' answered the cousin, 'I know my country better than Catinat. Tomorrow I shall march to the Abbey of Staffarda.'[10]

So, the same memoirs conclude: 'Instead of delivering the battle, we were those who were attacked.'[11] According to some ancient historians, Catinat purposely marched that way,[12] just to attract the Allied army into the open

---

10 Rep. in Assum, Clemente, *Eugenio di Savoia* (Turin 1935), p. 29.

11 *Idem*, ivi.

12 Both Carutti, explicitly, and the Duke de Broglie in his biography of Catinat, wrote it, but I would not be so sure. Catinat had already written to Louvois that the French presence in Piedmont depended on luck and opportunities. My impression is that he was well aware of the bad situation due to the lack of supplies, and tried to keep his forces as much as possible.

Castello dei Principi D'Acaja a Fossano

59. Fossano – the castle

field and gain a battle. That may be, but what is sure is that his officers were really alarmed. As soon as he received their first worried report, Catinat dryly replied to the officer who informed him about the enemies: 'I do not ask you how many are they, but where are they',[13] then gave the order to come back from the area of Saluzzo, concentrated all the units on the left of the Po and committed the cavalry to reconnaissance.

Informed about an incoming column of enemy cavalry in reconnaissance, Victor Amadeus concentrated the available troops in a place narrow enough to be easily defended. That place bordered a river embankment, beyond which – and until the Po – the land was swampy and covered with shrubs. It looked like an impassable swamp and the Duke placed there his left wing, but did not care about the swamp, simply because it looked impassable, and that proved soon-to-be a decisive mistake. Then he deployed the Allied troops from there. The left was supported by three field cannons. The centre was on the only ground suitable for cavalry charges, and the Duke put there the cavalry, forward, on five

---

13   Reported in Broglie, op. cit., p. 66.

columns[14] and, on its back, from left to right, behind a hedge from a farmhouse to the next, he deployed the regiments Croce Bianca and Fusileers.[15] On their back he placed the artillery train and baggage.

The right wing was held by the Guards, Piedmont and Savoy regiments, and by the Marco Antonio Colonna's 'tercio' regiment of Neapolitan infantry, reinforced by the remaining nine cannons. The second line was held by German infantry units in Milanese service.

The rest of the Spanish infantry remained in column on the road along the embankment, because Louvigny did not expect the whole French army to arrive and wanted to be ready to ford the river quickly, covering his troops with part of his cavalry.

The French attacked, engaged the Allied centre and widened to the Allied right. Victor supported the centre moving the Saluzzo regiment from the left and then calling the Spaniards from the rearguard to strengthen both the centre and right. After a morning of fighting, some French units crossed the 'impassable' swamps and attacked the Allied left. The newly raised Mondovì Infantry Regiment was now alone. It was unexpectedly taken on the flank, collapsed and withdrawn. Thus the French had free movement and caused the collapse of the entire formation. Covered by the Guards, supported and relieved by the cavalry charges led by Prince Eugene and by the Count di Verrua, the Allied army eventually turned back to Turin.

The French casualties totalled 1,000, but:

> …the advantage that the Sieur de Catinat earned on this occasion was so considerable that most of the enemies remained on the ground. He took all their artillery [11 guns out of 12] and their baggage. More than a thousand prisoners were made, not counting 800 wounded, who after the battle were led to the French camp.[16]

The French then sacked Saluzzo and the villages nearby, causing serious damage and massacring the population. They then occupied Savigliano, Fossano, and Villafranca, to cover Pinerolo whilst waiting to open another way of communication through the Alps.

At that time it was estimated that the Allies had lost about 4,000 dead, 1,500 wounded and 1,200 prisoners out of the 19,500 men they had; but actually casualties were much less. The dead had been calculated the day after the battle, considering all the missing as dead. But many of them, however, were alive and simply dispersed, scattered here and there. In the following weeks they returned to the ranks. So, it was not surprising if in mid September the forces available to Victor Amadeus, including the finally arrived Imperial reinforcements, exceeded 20,000 men.

---

14 The first line included the State of Milan Dragoon Regiment – *Reggimento di dragoni dello Stato di Milano* – the second line was composed by the His Royal Highness' own dragoons – the Red Dragoons – and by the Dragoons of Genevois – the Green Dragoons. The third line included the four companies of His Royal Highness' Household and the Piedmontese Gendarmery; the fourth and the fifth lines were composed by the remaining cavalry of the State of Milan, including a regiment of Bavarian cuirassiers recently contracted in Milanese service.

15 Recently established just to protect the artillery in battle.

16 De Riencourt, op. cit., Tome II, p. 214.

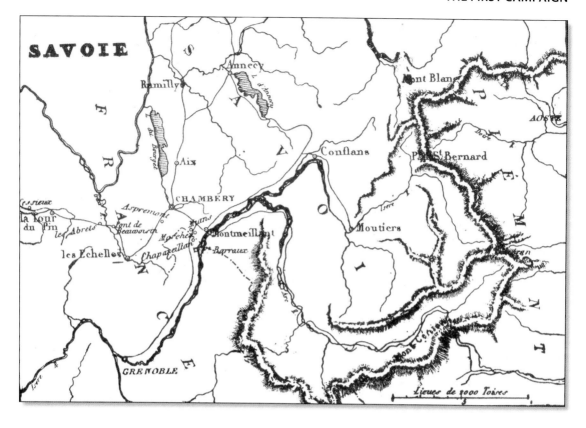

V. The French Invasion of Savoy

60. Savoy

Savoy was attacked a few days before Staffarda. The Sieur de Saint Ruth commanded a free corps on the border of Dauphiny. He entered Savoy only on 10 August and marched towards Chambéry, the capital of the Duchy. Count di Bernezzo could not try to hold in open field.[17] He had a relatively small militia detachment, because, as we know, in May Victor Amadeus called back to Piedmont the cavalry he had across the Alps, to have it at hand whilst concentrating his forces against the major threat by Catinat. Thus the Savoyard forces could not stop the French.

On 15 August, whilst in Piedmont Catinat reached Cavour, the French entered Chambéry. Once Chambéry was seized, Saint Ruth moved forward to Rumilly and then Annecy. His next objective was La Roche, not far from Geneva, where he placed his camp. Then, from La Roche, he sent troops to the remaining parts of the Duchy – Faucigny and Chiablese – whilst committing a strong column to Tarantasia, against the Count di Bernezzo, who had to withdraw across the mountains to Aosta Valley.

---

17 Italy geologically is a part of Africa crashing into Europe. The Alps are the result of this collision. On the Italian side, the side of the crash, they are very steep, but on the French side they are not, and the ground climbs more or less smoothly towards the heights. Savoy is on the French side of Alps, thus its small garrison could not rely on the ground to stop a French offensive.

On 9 September Saint Ruth's corps, now a little less than 7,000 strong, blockaded the castle of Miolans. Miolans was one of the two most important and strong fortresses in Savoy. It commanded the confluence of the Arc and Isère rivers, the Moriana valley and, most important, the Moncenisio and Fréjus alpine passes to Italy.

Miolans' walls were 200 metres long. It had four moats, two drawbridges, and five gates, including the strongly fortified main one. Its garrison was strong according to the contemporary standard for such a fortress, for the Marquess Graneri della Roccia, the local lord and thus the governor of the castle, had 50 militiamen and 50 soldiers commanded by captain Challandier, detached from the other major Savoyard castle, Montmélian. He rejected Saint Ruth's intimation for surrendering, and his troopers repulsed the French assaults, hence Saint Ruth abandoned the siege and moved to Tarantasia and Moriana. He seemed to have gone to his winter quarters, but it was a feint, because he was quickly back. On 1 October the French unexpectedly blockaded Miolans once more. The garrison was now weaker, no more than 30 men, and could not properly hold the long extension of the walls, thus, after 28 hours of shelling, had to capitulate.

VI. Operations in Piedmont Until the End of the Campaign

Catinat had troubles. After Staffarda his forces collapsed from roughly 17,000 to no more than 11,000 men. As we know, he was credited with 1,000 casualties in Staffarda, but what about the remaining 5,000? A good part of them were killed by the peasants – that is to say by the militia – when, after the battle, Catinat gave his soldiers free rein to loot, and sack. Disease killed the others. Dysentery spread all across the army, and probably malaria played an additional major role.[18] As Guy Rowlands underlines: 'Sickness was so widespread that the civilian administrator within the army and at Pinerolo also began to fall ill and die, threatening a complete collapse of the pay, supply and muster systems.'[19]

Why was this? Once more the answer is in the complete collapse of French logistics. Not only was Pinerolo short in clothes and ordnance, it lacked food too. The military administration tried to get meat, but two successive

---

18 It can be useful to underline that in the whole Mediterranean area people are often affected by the so-called Beta thalassemia, called Mediterranean anaemia. This kind of hereditary disease has, or may have, many bad consequences, although in spite of what one may think, normally – as I know by personal experience – it is not fatal and often does not cause any inconvenience. It has also a positive effect: whoever has Mediterranean anaemia cannot have malaria, because the red cells are too small to let the plasmodium, the unicellular protozoan parasite causing malaria, develop within the blood. Thus, whilst the French troopers, whose majority was not from the Mediterranean area, could be affected by malaria, a certain number of Piedmontese peasants, that is to say both militiamen and soldiers, probably were not because they came from malaria-infected areas and were probably affected by the Mediterranean anaemia. Thus, one may also wonder of how much Mediterranean anaemia may have preserved the Piedmontese army's combat readiness, whilst malaria put the French army out of order.

19 Guy Rowlands, 'Louis XIV, Vittorio Amedeo II and French military failure in Italy 1689–96', *The English Historical Review*, June 2000, p. 543.

61. Valley and citadel of Susa
in 1629

contracts failed within the end of July. There were frauds in the supply of wheat and flour, thus their prices arose, and the private contractor in charge of bread and flour supplies so widely extended his debt that was close to default and liquidation, because the government payment was late. Thus, apart for Louvois' orders to burn Piedmont just as the Palatinate, pillaging and looting were the only solution Catinat had to feed his men. He had no other choice, because the supply transport from across the Alps simply did not work due to the non-cooperation by the inhabitants of Dauphiny.

Catinat knew quite well how bad the French situation was. Louvois answered his request for reinforcements and to his analysis of the situation in Italy writing:

> The King knows well that to effectively manage the war in Piedmont it is necessary to seize Turin; but, for such an enterprise, one would need at least 20,000 foot and sixty or eighty squadrons, a considerable artillery equipment and to make expenses that in present times are hard to afford. It is impossible to know whether His Majesty will be able to do it in the forthcoming year. We must go day by day and catch the opportunities.[20]

At the end of the first week of September the two armies stood, opposing each other. The French were across the Po, between Polonghera and Carmagnola; the Allies were between Pancalieri and Villafranca.

---

20   Louvois to Catinat, quoted in Broglie, op. cit., p. 73

62. Gelassa Fort in the Susa Valley

Catinat was ordered to come back to winter quarters in Dauphiny, but he decided to take things 'day by day' and created and caught an opportunity. He moved to Saluzzo. The Allied army stationed on distance and engaged the French in small fights and skirmishes. On 26 September the French evacuated Savigliano and, at the beginning of October, Saluzzo too, and slowly moved to Pinerolo, Their target was the town of Susa, the key to the homonymous valley and the terminal of the roads crossing the Monginevro and Mont Cenis passes.

Victor Amadeus realised it and tried to prevent the manoeuvre, forming two 'flying camps' – that is to say, two speedy tactic combat groups:

> … the first commanded by Mylord Prince Eugene composed of his Germans, and the other of My Lord the Marquess di Parella, who, observing the movements of the French, have the order to attack them whilst on march, according to the opportunity they will have, to prevent the French to approach the Valley, and the city of Susa.[21]

On 11 November the news came that:

> … the army of the Allies went from Rivoli to Avigliano, a place on the road to Susa, with the aim of attacking the French and preventing the French from attacking that place. To this aim Mylord Prince Eugene went ahead with his regiment of

---

21 Mosti to Cardinal Rubini, on 7 November 1690, in ASV, Nunziatura di Savoia, anno 1690.

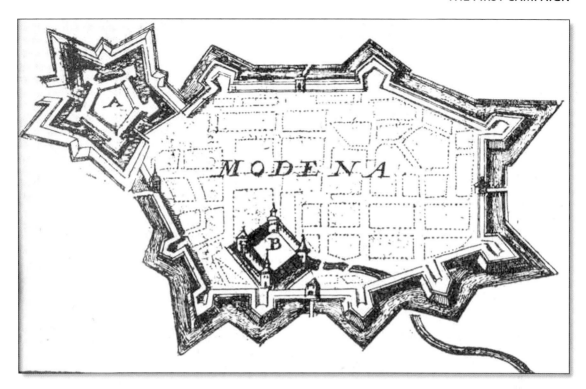

63. Modena

Germans, and visited the Place of Susa, ordered the defence, enhancing it with additional number of soldiers and left there the Mylord Duke's Regiment of the Guards. Meanwhile, every night a large number of wagons full of ordnance and food had been sent, and since yesterday it was published that a major fight had to occur today, the French having also gone with the Sieur de Cattinat towards Susa with the Cannon and Mortars along the road to Giaveno.[22]

But it was not enough. The Allied army was still far off when Catinat changed route, joined the other troops he dispatched and, with a marked numerical superiority, attacked Susa.

Bluntly, the Count di Lausa did not waste too much energy to defend the town, and the news of surrender arrived soon in Turin. It was then attempted to arrange a defence in Bussoleno, concentrating troops in the castle of San Giorio, but the French put their artillery in a commanding position and let it surrender after three days of shelling.

Susa was important because it was the head of the road to Savoy, the road to be used to relieve Montmélian. By seizing Susa, the French completely blockaded Montmélian for a siege to be undertaken during the next 1691 campaign. On the other hand, they opened an alternative route for their supplies, if they could get any, because the route crossing the Alps to Pinerolo passed through the Val Chisone, and supplies could be harassed or interrupted by the Waldensians.

---

22 *Idem*, 11 November 1690, in ASV, Nunziatura di Savoia, anno 1690.

Once this operation was achieved, Catinat went into winter quarters. Despite the resistance of Montmélian, the passages through the Alps were assured. In theory, reinforcements and supplies could now reach both Pinerolo and Susa and ensure the army's readiness for the incoming 1691 campaign. The French army was firmly anchored in Piedmont, and in theory it seemed ready to win the war. It had only to wait for the good-weather season and the supplies, if any.

The Allied army too went to the winter quarters. The Piedmontese took their quarters in Piedmont, the troops in Spanish service went back to Lombardy, the Imperial troops stayed in Piedmont as well as they relied on the Duchies of Parma and Modena; but, contrary to practice, fights continued. The Allied cavalry patrolled the roads and attacked columns and convoys wherever it found them. The foraging parties were turned into clashes of tenths, or hundreds, of men and, until March, everything could be said but that operations stopped.

On one hand this was the consequence of the organisation of the militia in Piedmont, on the other hand it could not be denied that the presence of Eugene of Savoy kept the combativeness high. We know it thanks to the letters by the Papal nuncio. According to him, in January Eugene focused on Casale, Victor Amadeus' other strategic problem, and tested its reactivity. The enemy reacted indirectly, and tried to raid Avigliana, but the raid was repulsed by the Imperial troops in Monferrato. Monferrato's population, as subject to the Duke of Mantua, was pretty pro-French and tried to react against Piedmontese and Imperialists. They assaulted the Austrian troops. Eugene reacted at first simply by jailing those responsible, but then he escalated, and when in January 1691 the inhabitants of Vignale supported by 100 French soldiers tried to rise up, Eugene ordered a severe retaliation. Many people were hanged, and this was enough to keep calm the whole Marquisate of Monferrato.

However, it was clear that the Allies needed more forces, and urged by Victor Amadeus, in March Eugene left to Vienna to ask for reinforcements.

12

The 1691 Campaign

I. Winter: Wishful Planning

In Vienna, Eugene found the Emperor and the most influential statesmen so well disposed towards his requests that it was decided to increase the Imperial corps in Piedmont to 20,000 men.

At the same time William III summoned the Alliance congress to decide the strategy of 1691. The members of the Grand Alliance sent their representatives to that great meeting, which was held in The Hague on 5 February, 1691, and known as the 'Assembly of the High Allies'. Victor Amadeus was represented by de la Tour, his personal envoy to William III.

The general situation was anything but good. The French seized Liège, defeated the Allies on land at Fleurus and Staffarda, at sea at Beachy Head. This happened mostly because the most of Allies' attention was focused on other issues. William III's major concern had been Ireland, and most of the British forces had been there. On the opposite side of the continent, Leopold too had troubles. The French actions in Germany attracted men and horses, for the members of the Empire, as was logical, had to worry and think of their own lands first, and then of Italy. Then another huge portion of his military assets had been destined for Hungary, because the Hungarian insurgence headed by Count Imre Tököly was supported by an Ottoman army 100,000 strong, and the Ottomans reconquered Bulgaria, Transylvania, and Serbia up to Belgrade.

However William won at the Boyne, Piedmont held, Spain was gathering money and men, and the Emperor was appointing Louis of Baden as his commander in Hungary, thus there was a possibility to look at a better future.

The Assembly of the High Allies decided that no member would negotiate with France unless Louis XIV undersigned three main promises: to give back the former owners all the conquests he made after the Peace of Westphalia; to give satisfaction and reparations to the Holy Siege for all the insults France made to Rome during Innocent XI's reign; to rehabilitate the Protestants in France, giving them back all the religious liberties they lost when he abolished the Edict of Nantes.

After a speech by William III, the Assembly held discussions. According to William, France could be weakened and perhaps won only acting from Italy. As it was later reported: 'he hailed as a special favour of Providence the

64. Louis, Margrave von Baden

faults of the ministers of Louis XIV, who forced the Duke of Savoy to throw himself into the arms of the allies.'[1]

The importance of Piedmont as a starting point for an attack on southern France was then reiterated, which had to match an Allied corps descending from the Rhine along the Alps, to join more or less in Savoy and then destroy Toulon and the French Mediterranean fleet. The tasked army had to be composed by Sabaudian, Imperial, Bavarian and Spanish troops. Its first task had to be an invasion of Dauphiny and/or of Provence.

Everybody agreed to increase the financial commitment of the Maritime Powers in order to enlist an additional 10,000 men, half of them Bavarians and half Imperial, to be employed in Italy, and the Assembly found a further agreement about the forces to be provided by each member. The United Provinces promised to field 35,000 men, the Emperor, Britain and Spain 25,000 men each; the Elector of Brandenburg 20,000; the Duke of Savoy and the Duchy of Milan a total of 20,000; the Elector of Bavaria 18,000, the princes of the House of Brunswick 16,000, the Elector of Saxony 12,000; the Landgrave of Hessen 8,000; the Circles of Swabia and Francony 10,000; the Duke of Württemberg 6,000; the Prince-Bishop of Liège 6,000; the Bishopric of Münster 7,000 and the Elector Palatine 4,000; totalling 237,000 men. All these men had to be found somewhere. This meant that each sovereign had to find his portion of the soldiers, but paying them was a different issue. Generally speaking the majority of the Allies were not rich, and needed funding.

II. Spring: Actual Funding and Organisation

Savoy fielded a little less than 14,000 men, that is to say 11,100 foot, and 2,776 cavalry and dragoons.[2] This figure seems to have included the militia too, at least for infantry. The Duke used militia for garrison duties and to fill the gaps of the standing regiments, but realised the military expenditure to be far more

---

1   Sirtema De Grovestijns (henceforth Sirtema), *Histoire des luttes et rivalités politiques entre les Puissances Maritimes et la France durant da seconde moitié du XVII Siècle* (Paris, 1853), vol. 6, p. 270.

2   Figures are from the '*Stato delle truppe d'Infanteria di S.M. Ces.ᵃ, Cattolica, Britannica e di S.A.R. – Stato della Cavalleria come contro*', p. 1, in AUSSME, L 3, busta 7, 4, handwritten copy of the original from AST, Imprese Militari, Mazzo 4°. The cavalry includes the Duke's Household, the Genti d'Armi – or Gendarmery – and the dragoons, that is to say His Royal Highness' own dragoons, Dragoons of Piedmont and Dragoons of Genevois, totalling exactly 176 officers and 2,600 men.

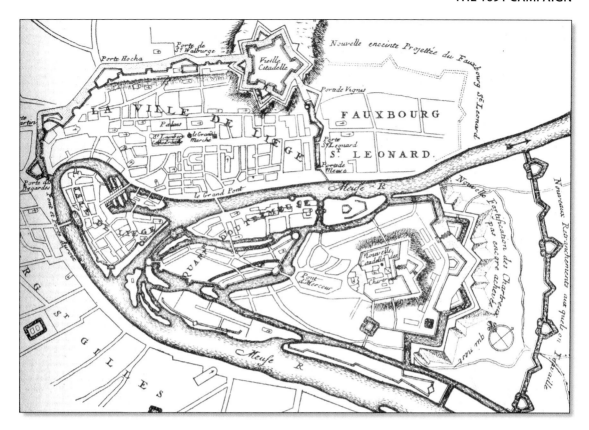

than the previous year. In fact the 10 months from January to October 1691 absorbed 4,045,440 *liras*, and this was still nothing when compared to the next budget. Moreover, the French conquest of Savoy and Nice deprived the Duke of their revenues, which meant, in general terms, a 25 percent less. What to do? In theory, had the yearly harvest been good, Victor could rely on high income from taxes and revenues, thus on a good amount of money, but it was not so. The war period added devastation to troubles caused by the weather, and harvest resulted not as good as needed, in the first years, and then decidedly bad. On the other hand, incomes had to raise, due to the increasing war needs. Thus Victor Amadeus had to impose more taxes, squeezing his states as much as possible. Incomes from taxes and revenues increased roughly 30 percent between 1689 and 1700, that is to say since the year before the war until the fourth after it, from seven and a half million to a little less than 11 million *liras*.[3] This proved to be not enough, and he sold offices – totalling 840,000 *liras* between 1690 and 1696 – and fiefs. Selling fiefs and related lordships allowed the State to gather 6,170,000 *liras* between the beginning and the end of the war. It was a compensation, but did not fill the gap.

---

3   Mario Abrate gives a 1689 figure of 7,543,841 *liras* in his 'Elementi per la storia delle finanza dello stato sabaudo nella seconda metà del XVII secolo' in 'Bollettino storico bibliografico subalpino', year LXVII, vol. I–II, January–June 1969, p. 397; whilst Luigi Einaudi in his *La Finanza Sabauda all'aprirsi del secolo XVIII e durante la guerra di successione spagnuola* (Turin, 1908), pp. 340–41 provides the 1700 figure of 10,917,442 *liras*.

There were some problems also with the British funding. On 3 March de la Tour was informed by the British Treasury about an assignation on a secure fund.[4] The whole amount – after fees – had to be paid cash in Genoa within 20 days. But when, after a little less than three weeks, de la Tour got the letters of change and discovered with his utmost surprise that they were neither payable in Genoa, nor within 20 days. When asked why, the banker answered that there were practically no letters of change available in England, and that the exchange costs increased. There was no loss, for the banker had already formally agreed the exchange rate, nonetheless it was a nuisance and a delay. Three months later, in June, it was the turn of Dutch funding: de la Tour sent letters of change for 16,000 *scudi* to be paid in Venice, but this was not that convenient, and he then received from Turin a couple of memoirs about the different rates one could find in Leghorn, Genoa and Venice.

Thus, the funding was late. it had been in arrears until then and continued to be in arrears until October that year. Late funding made things more problematic. Victor Amadeus resented a lack of trained soldiers and officers, due to the three regiments vanished in France. Actually, a part of that personnel could be recovered – for instance during the first week of December 40 Piedmontese and Savoyard officers passed through Bruxelles bound to Piedmont, and were followed during the next week by the brigadier of the Piemonte and Savoy regiments, who he too was going back to Turin along with many officers – but the lack of military manpower could be solved only contracting foreign professionals. Here the problems originated by the delayed funding came. The single unit on British pay existing in July 1690, now, by early 1691, increased to a relevant corps. In September 6,000 foot and cavalry from Brandenburg on King William's pay arrived in Italy. In January Sir Charles, 2nd Duke of Schomberg, the son of the first Duke, who had fought at the Boyne, arrived in Italy. William III had appointed him 'General of the Troops of His British Majesty in Piedmont', and he had to oversee the organisation of up to four religioners' regiments. In January 1691 the first two were established. One was commanded by the Marquis de Miremont, the other by the Sieur de Villefranche-Montbrun. A third and a fourth regiment, that of Montauban and Deloche, were to be organised soon, along with a small dragoon unit, called Balthazar's Dragoon Regiment, totalling only 160 dragoons and 20 officers. It was a matter of 2,400 men – some 2,200 foot and 120 dragoons[5] and this was what a half of the British

---

4   The sum was in pieces of eight. The weight of a Spanish piece of eight was 550.209 Spanish grains, that is to say 27.468 grammes, and its purity was 930,55 percent which meant it contained 25,560 grammes of silver. This was just a bit more than the Piedmontese white *scudo*, whose weight was, as we know, 27,321 grammes, and whose purity was 916.67, hence contained 25.04 grammes of silver, that is to say the 91.16 percent of the silver contained in a piece of eight. At that time, and during the entire following century, the money change was made simply putting the coins on a scale, looking at their weight and giving or receiving the same weight in the desired currency, according to the related silver titles. Thus one needed (or received) 109 and half *scudi bianchi di Piemonte* for 100 pieces of eight. As already said, a Piedmontese *scudo* equalled 86 *soldi*, or four *liras* and six *soldi*. Ordinary exchange fee rates at that time were around five percent.

5   Figures come from the above mentioned 'Stato delle truppe d'Infanteria di S.M. Ces.ª, Cattolica, Britannica e di S.A.R. – Stato della Cavalleria come contro', p. 1, in AUSSME, L 3, manuscript copy of the original from AST, Imprese Militari, Mazzo 4°.

and Dutch subsidy to Piedmont was paid for. But the soldiers came, and the money did not, thus Victor Amadeus had to anticipate sums for wages and equipment on his own, relying on the money he had at the moment – regardless of incoming from taxes, borrowings, or from Spain – subtracting it to other vital but still less urgent purposes.

The Imperial contingent included six infantry[6] and seven mounted regiments,[7] totalling on paper 16,995 foot and cavalry, with 6,550 horses; but actually, including sick, they were 16,500, and their mounted troops lacked more than 250 horses. They all had to be paid by the Maritime Powers, who, by the way, expected them to be 18,000, that is to say 2,000 more, thus the Emperor would get 300,000 *scudi*, and the Elector 100,000. But, in spite of Anglo-Dutch funding, the Imperial engagement in Italy could not be bigger than so, due to strategic priorities the Emperor had.

The Spaniards deployed in Piedmont 15 tercios – regiments – of foot, including Swiss and German-levied ones, and six horse regiments: four cavalry and two dragoons; but Milan too had some problems. On 20 July 1690, Fuensalida had to pay 175,000 *liras* to the colonels contractor of the newly raised Swiss regiments in Milanese service, who, by the way, in June had urged him to contract them. Thus, short of money, he urged the viceroy of Naples to send troops and money, above all money. He needed it to pay the soldiers, their supplies and ordnance and also to pay the uniforms they lost in battle. On the other hand, on 6 September, the viceroy of Naples asked the bankers for a loan, granted by the military treasury with six percent interest. It was a matter of 100,000 Neapolitan ducats, but was not enough, and the viceroy decided to tax the nobles too. This too proved to be not enough. In January 1691 Fuensalida asked the Milanese government for a further 300,000 *scudi* to pay the war. Provisions were gathered quickly, and the Arsenal in Pavia prepared a great quantity of bombs, shells, grenades and military tools for the coming campaign.

III. The French Conquest of Nice and the Shelling of Oneglia

Lack of money did not let things in Italy go as planned, because financial complications affected and someway dictated Allied operations.

Victor Amadeus was not happy with his allies. The Germans did not come, and the Spaniards were not committing as many troops as needed. In April he

---

6   Infantry Regiments: Stadl, Württemberg, Coburg, Lothringen, Merseburg (Bavarian) Guards and Steinau, the latter was Bavarian also. They totalled 9,921 men, 230 less than they were supposed to have, see 'Stato delle truppe d'Infanteria di S.M. Ces.ᵃ, Cattolica, Britannica e di S.A.R. – Stato della Cavalleria come contro', p. 1, in AUSSME, L 3, handwritten copy of the original from AST, Imprese Militari, Mazzo 4°.

7   Cavalry regiments Caraffa, Palffy, Taaffe, Montecuccoli and Commercy, dragoon regiments Barheit and Prince Eugene. They totalled 6,591 men (including 1,933 dragoons), instead of the 6,804 they were supposed to have, and lacked 254 horses; see 'Stato delle truppe d'Infanteria di S.M. Ces.ᵃ, Cattolica, Britannica e di S.A.R. – Stato della Cavalleria come contro', p. 2, in AUSSME, L 3, cit.

wrote to de la Tour that he could field only 6,000 or 7,000 men, that is to say a half of his army, due to delay of the promised funds.[8] A first consequence was the French conquest of the County of Nice between March and April. Catinat gathered 12,000 men in Briançon, and, on 12 March 1691, crossed the Varo, the river marking the border between France and the County of Nice. The military harbour of Villafranca was besieged, capitulated on 21 March and was occupied on the following day. Then the French besieged Nice. The garrison was not big. It was composed of 500 militia, and five regular companies, but could hold. Unfortunately the enemy shelling made a first gunpowder magazine explode, and, on 1 April, a second. The garrison was now very short of gunpowder, the explosion caused relevant damage, and the governor accepted to capitulate on 2 April 1691, and received free withdrawal. Thus, also the second transalpine base of departure the Alliance could exploit to attack Provence and southern France had been lost to the French. Moreover, if, in the domain of the wishful thinking, one could speak of a maritime Anglo-Dutch intervention in spite of the French naval forces in Toulon, no support could now be provided by the Anglo-Dutch fleets for a possible operation against southern France, because no Mediterranean landing point remained in Allied hands. The next French attempt was against Oneglia. The French fleet arrived there in June and bombed the small town, but the garrison had been enhanced by that who capitulated in Nice, so it was strong enough to hold.

Victor Amadeus did not know what to do. De la Tour tried to cheer up his master, writing: 'King William talked to me about Y.R.H. with such a tenderness and esteem, that I would not be able to repeat, assuring me that he cared his own interests no less than yours, and that he was in extreme anxiety due to the dangers surrounding Y.R.H.'[9] But Victor Amadeus did not need words, he needed men and money.

Catinat continued marching north, bound to Savoy and Montmélian, whilst the Duke was alone and nobody knew where the Allied troops were.

The Spaniards were slow. In March they moved from winter quarters to the Ticino, and the bulk of their forces started marching to Piedmont only in the second half of April. But the Spaniards acted that way for they had a broader extension of lands and many more problems than others. For instance, in January they knew that the French commander of Casale, Crenan, was organising two regiments of local people, 1,500 strong each. In March they moved against pro-French Mantua, and seized and raided many towns not far from Mantua, for that Duke started organising a new regiment. Thus Fuensalida ordered 3,000 militiamen to be called to arms and relieve the professionals to be committed from garrisons to Piedmont. The men were never enough. Reinforcements could come from Naples, of course, but Naples too had some engagements: 700 foot and 13 bombers to be shipped to the *Presidii* in the last week of May, for instance, not considering other

---

8   Victor Amadeus to President de la Tour, Turin, 3 April 1691, in AST, Lettere ministri, Olanda, m. 1.
9   De la Tour to Victor Amadeus, 27 April 1691, in AST, Lettere Ministri, Olanda, cit.

shipping here and there.[10] And shipping were not always possible. The navy was in charge of them, but on that July the Neapolitan navy was urged to join the Spanish, Sicilian, Tursi's and Sardinian galley squadrons to chase and pursue North African pirates trying to raid southern Italian coasts. This meant no ship was available for shipping troops north. In theory, troops could march along the Adriatic coast, but the pirates' presence meant increasing the land-based watch and reaction system. On the other hand, when the piratical threat seemed over, the French fleet in August shelled Barcelona, and Alicante in September; nonetheless, in spite of all these troubles, Spanish troops were approaching Piedmont.

The Imperialists too were approaching, or at least so they say, but were very slow, much more than the Spaniards, and had a longer trip to make. The first two German companies bound to Piedmont arrived in Como during the first week of March, but the next four arrived only two months later, and the bulk of the Imperial troops appeared in Lombardy only by mid June.

William III was upset. In May he wrote to Heinsius:

66. Antonie Heinsius, Grand Pensionary of the United Provinces

> The slowness of the march of the Imperialists and Bavarians towards Piedmont is distressing, and I fear they will arrive too late. The difficulties which the Elector of Bavaria arouses are incomprehensible, and his refusal to let his troops march, unless those of Brandenburg and Hesse proceed towards the Upper Rhine, is without motives, since, as the enemy is, in this respect, the presence of Saxon troops suffices. I hope, then, that the Elector of Bavaria will no longer make objections to the march of his troops, and that they will be already on their way.[11]

This time Imperial troops were commanded by Count Antonio Caraffa, or Carafa, an Italian general in Imperial service, with a good experience in Hungarian campaigns against the Ottomans. But Caraffa was not Eugene, he was higher ranked, older and slower than Eugene, and William was impatient. A week later he added to Heinsius:

---

10 Nobody was surprised when, to fill the gaps caused by all these commitments, in May the viceroy of Naples proposed to the Neapolitan nobility to raise a foot regiment 6,000 strong. It had to be commanded by the governor in person and composed of companies – 200 strong each – to be provided by each noble from the people of his fiefs.

11 William III to Heinsius, 22 May /1 June 1691, reported in Sirtema, op. cit., vol. 6, p. 271.

The slow march of the troops destined for Piedmont is a very distressing thing. I've noticed that almost surely they will get there too late, and therefore our money is lost.

I assess, however, that if we can find letters of credit, they must be sent to Caraffa; but it must be well explained that we shall not agree to any payment, before the troops will be arrived in Piedmont.[12]

De la Tour in the same period commented : 'H. British M. and the States General are lively and ardent in providing fast helps to Y.R.H. in order that nothing better can be desired, and I must give good witness that they do for You what they did not do towards whoever person in the world.'[13]

IV. The Siege and Relief of Cuneo

In June Catinat seized Rivoli, Carignano, and Carmagnola and proceeded to besiege Cuneo. By the way, a siege on Cuneo was less dangerous to Victor Amadeus than on Turin, who so much expected his capital to be besieged, that he made Duchess Anne and the family move, and appointed Eugene to command the Turin defence. It would have been a problematic major engagement. As he wrote to de la Tour, no less than 12,000 foot – that is to say almost all his infantry – were needed to defend Turin.[14]

But Cuneo too was important a fortress. Lying at the mouth of many valleys, Cuneo was a hub, the terminal of the roads coming from no less than nine mountain passes, linking Piedmont to France, Nice, and Liguria. Its conquest would allow Catinat to firmly settle on the right of the Po, to open an additional supply route to France and at the same time to cut Piedmontese and Allied communications to Nice, Liguria, and the Mediterranean. The Cuneo garrison was relatively small, but the fortifications were good and the city held.

Catinat committed a large corps commanded by general Bullonde, whose men opened the trench in the night from 18–19 June. The first attack occurred on the 19th in the morning, and was repulsed. The small garrison consisted of 1,200 men including local countryside militia, Mondovì militia, Waldensians, city militia, and some Religioners, in that case French Protestant, commanded by Count Roero di Revello. They repulsed the second attack on the 21st and made some sallies, which eased the entrance of the Regiment of Saluzzo, part of a 3,000 strong relief column headed by the Marquess di Voghera.

In a week the French lost about 2,000 men and got no result; then Prince Eugene came. On 26 June at dawn, he left the Allied army along with 2,500 cavalry and a convoy of ammunition wagons. On his way, he gathered units of militia informed in advance about the operation, and advanced very speedily.

Catinat warned Bullonde and wrote that he had already sent him a detachment of 2,000 cavalry and 300 grenadiers, who would join him on

---

12   William III to Heinsius, 28 May/7 June 1691, reported in Sirtema, ivi.
13   De la Tour to Victor Amadeus, 7 May 1691, in AST, Lettere Ministri, Olanda.
14   Victor Amadeus to President de la Tour, Turin, 17 June 1691, in AST, Lettere ministri, Olanda.

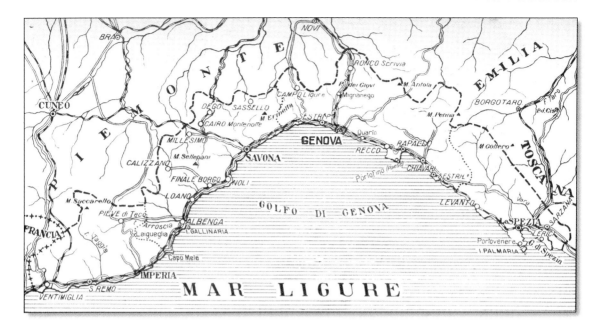

the 28th. Bullonde, he concluded, had to hold the position at any cost and continue the siege.

67. Liguria in the 19th Century

Eugene knew it, sped up the march advancing only with cavalry and fell on the enemy before the French reinforcements: it was a triumph:

> From Cuneo it is known thanks to an express sent by Lord Prince Eugene that, as soon as they got the news of his march towards them, the French in front of that place decided to leave the siege, and that, meanwhile, they were surprised by the aforesaid Lord Prince, hence he succeeded in defeating 1,500, including eight grenadier companies, the wounded and the prisoners, and in taking one hundred ammunition wagons, fifty supply ones, a big cannon and a mortar, and then succeeded in making safe the passes the French could come back through to restart the siege.[15]

Catinat bitterly commented in his memoirs:

> The army then forded the Stura in the greatest disorder of the world; all the battalions forded in a crowd, each mixed with other, the rearguard like the avant-garde, hurrying everyone to save themselves. Nothing has ever made a route remembered better than the passage of that river.[16]

The minister of the Duke of Modena wrote to his master:

15　The nuncio of Savoy to Cardinal Secretary of State, Turin, 11 July 1691, in ASV, Nunziatura di Savoia, anno 1691.

16　Catinat, in Le Bouyer de Saint Gervas, Bernard (ed.), *Mémoires et correspondance du Maréchal de Catinat de la Fauconnerie* (Paris 1819), vol. 2, p. 35

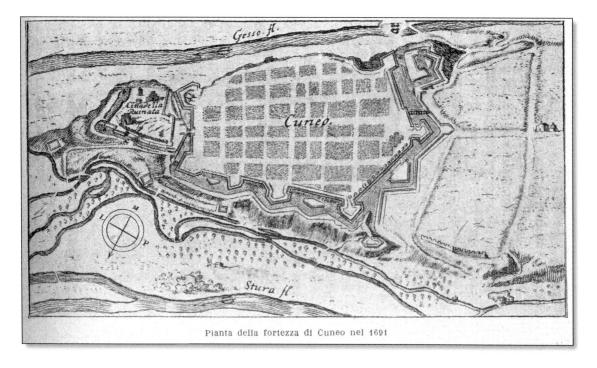

Pianta della fortezza di Cuneo nel 1691

68. Cuneo

The besieged lost 300 men, including six captains, the besiegers 4,000 not including deserters and wounded ... they left in the camp quantities of bombs, grenades, cannonballs and gunpowder. They also left in the camp all the wounded and sick and a great amount of luggage, and the terror of the enemy must have been great, because Mr. de Fichiere [Féquières] left his wounded nephew in the tent.[17]

Bullonde was jailed in Pinerolo for cowardice and incompetence, but the damage had been done. Relieving Cuneo, Eugene closed to the French the door towards the Allied rearguard. Nor did he stop there, because he pursued the retreating enemy, though not always successfully:

Lord Prince Eugene, with 500 of his Germans wanted to assail the rearguard of the French, while they were leaving Carignano, as he did earlier with success on a similar case in the Asti countryside, but he was caught in the middle by an ambush by 2,000 of them and had to defend himself, as he did with extreme gallantry, until the arrival of Mylord Duke, who in person went to rescue him. In the fact Lord Prince Eugene lost three good officers, and some one hundred of his soldiers; a similar number of French remained on the ground, with the loss of a flag.[18]

When he was informed of the Cuneo disaster, Louvois, who was not well, had a heart attack and died. Meanwhile, the Imperial troops commanded by Caraffa and the Elector of Bavaria arrived, raising the Allied army to some 40,000 men, including Piedmontese militia.

---

17 Abbot Leporini to the Duke of Modena, Turin, 30 June 1691.
18 The nuncio of Savoy to Cardinal Secretary of State, Turin, 28 July 1691, in ASV, Nunziatura di Savoia, anno 1691.

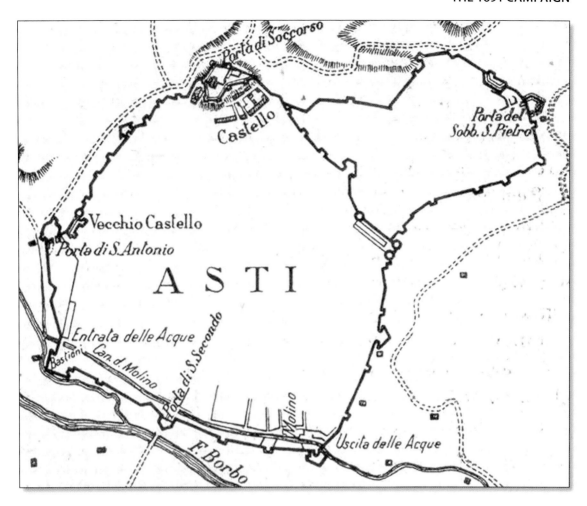

69. Asti

The Piedmontese plain was now firmly under Allied control. Also, despite the Imperial reinforcements arriving slowly, and immediately starting quarrels with the Spaniards, by the end of August Victor Amadeus felt strong enough and asked the Allies to relieve Montmélian, because that fortress was besieged since the previous year. Unfortunately he faced a marked obstruction. The Austrians had no interest in strengthening Piedmont, and the Spaniards were worried about the closer threat to Milan by Casale and by the French army in the Po valley. Thus the Austrians were happy with engaging the French in Italy, distracting them from the Rhine at the lowest cost, and the Spaniards preferred to stay close to Lombardy instead of going across the Alps.

Prince Eugene suggested crossing the Po, threatening the enemy communications and forcing Catinat to chose between a field battle and a retreat. In any case there would be still time to relieve Montmélian; but he was not the commander of the Imperial troops, and Caraffa had different ideas, thus the war council on 21 September decided nothing but the siege of Carmagnola.

Carmagnola fell on 9 October and 'fifteen cannons were found there, five more than those that were there four months ago when the French entered

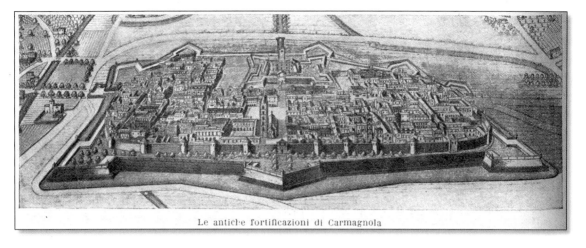

Le antiche fortificazioni di Carmagnola

70. Carmagnola

… [Catinat] made a big detachment to send it to Monmegliano and try to reinforce the place before the Allies can let the relief enter there.'[19]

The next step was against Susa, hoping to be able to retake it. So, on 13 October the nuncio could write that:

> The army of the Allies went to Carignano. From there they sent Lord Prince Eugene with a strong group of soldiers to recognise and take places around Susa to form that siege, which must follow if the French do not hold the mountain commanding the place, which is the only way to seize the town in a few days.'[20]

Meanwhile Catinat strengthened it, and for a month it had been known that 'All the French troops who were in Savoy have all come down into Susa.'[21] On 19 October it was reported that:

> The army of the Allies went until Rivoli where they stopped, and General Stenau with about 6,000 men and 1,500 horses was sent following the dragoons of Lord Prince Eugene marching towards Susa, to support him in the march and in the plan of seizing the heights around Susa … So far it is not yet known whether they met opposition, although it is publicly said that the strongest passes are already occupied by French infantry sent by Monsù di Cattinat.[22]

Actually, on 24 October, 'The news comes from Susa that the Allies have occupied all the major heights, but that of the Capuchins where the French are too well entrenched, and that tomorrow morning artillery fire had to start against the Place and the Capuchins' position.'[23] But the enemy positions were considered so strong that on the 25th the Allies were ordered to withdraw. The French exploited their retreat for a sally; and it was up to Eugene, commanding

---

19 The nuncio of Savoy to Cardinal Secretary of State, Turin, 10 October 1691, in ASV, Nunziatura di Savoia, anno 1691.
20 *Idem*, Turin, 15 September 1691, in ASV, Nunziatura di Savoia, anno 1691.
21 *Ibid*.
22 *Idem*, Turin, 19 October 1691, in ASV, Nunziatura di Savoia, anno 1691.
23 *Idem*, Turin, 24 October 1691, in ASV, Nunziatura di Savoia, anno 1691.

71. Ivrea

the cavalry in the rearguard, to cover the Allies' movement with the Regiment of Lorraine and His Royal Highness' Household.

The failure of the manoeuvre against Susa implied the abandonment of any coordinated and shared Allied project in favour of Montmélian. Caraffa decided to drive his troops to winter quarters. So, Victor Amadeus decided to act alone. Eight Piedmontese infantry and two dragoon regiments left Asti on 7 December. Via Ivrea, they arrived in Aosta on the 15th and immediately sped to the Piccolo San Bernardo pass. But as soon as they reached its top they knew that Montmélian, half-destroyed and mined under the *maschio* of the citadel, had surrendered after a very long and terrible siege.

V. The Siege and Fall of Montmélian

Montmélian – *Momigliano* in Italian – was a pillar of Sabaudian rule across the Alps since long ago. The last time the French besieged it, in 1630, its garrison, commanded by Goffredo Benso Count di Cavour, had successfully held out until their withdrawal.

The fortress was on a big, wide, relatively flat rock beside the River Isère, not far from Chambéry. The town was at the foot of the hill and along the river. The original castle had been built in the early Middle Ages, and its first landlord seems to have been a certain Aymon de Pierre-Forte, a nephew of Humbert by the White Hands, the first Count of Savoy. Counts Amadeus III and Amadeus IV of Savoy were born there in the 12th and 13th centuries, and thus the fortress was very important to the family. In fact it was important

72. Montmélian in 1690

also and especially as a major defensive asset, if not as the major strongpoint of the whole Savoy, and, for sure, the hardest to be seized.

The garrison, commanded by Carlo Gerolamo Del Carretto, Marquess di Bagnasco, spent the first three months of the spring 1690 in a feverish activity to allow the fortress to withstand the forthcoming clash. When the enemy vanguards arrived in June, the fortifications were in order, stocks had been made, cellars filled, gunpowder magazines too, and the garrison had risen to 12 infantry companies and 100 gunners.

Del Carretto was a tough commander and did all he could to stop or at least to slow the approaching French. After the capitulation of Miolans in early October 1690, he started ambushing night and day the enemy around Montmélian and continued until 9 January 1691, when 3,000 French approached the city further. Del Carretto reacted by a furious sally of 200 foot and dragoons, who killed 30 French, wounded several, and took no casualties.

Nothing happened until, on 4 February 1691, Catinat arrived from south, having planned the invasion of Nice. On 6 February, before leaving to Piedmont, Catinat placed the first two batteries, which, two days later, 'two hours after midday … began to salute the fortress, one by twenty cannon shots … and the other by seven bombs.'[24]

The bombing continued uninterrupted in the following days. Its intensity increased due to the arrival of further guns, caused fires in the fortress and damaged its walls. Then there was a relative calm until 14 July, when the French received nine more infantry battalions and a regiment of dragoons back from raiding the Aosta Valley.

Two weeks later the actual artillery duel between the fortress and the besiegers began, and there was a first general attack on the night from 31 July

---

24 Bagnasco, Carlo Gerolamo del Carretto, Marquess di, *L'assedio di Mommeliano 1690–91* (Rome, 1936), p. 48.

to 1 August. It failed. The following morning the French bombed and shelled, and damaged the walls. On 2 August they tried a further attack, which was repulsed. Then they succeeded in opening a couple of breaches, thus on 4 August Del Carretto allowed the city to capitulate, accepted a four-day truce and retreated with the garrison into the citadel, up on the top of the hill.

Meanwhile, the situation of the garrison was getting worse. By 1 September, one third of the soldiers were ill; every day up to half a dozen died, and the most of survivors were so weak that they were not fit for combat. In October, the situation further worsened. The average guard in arms on the walls did not exceed 70 men at a time and moreover they were short of shoes and clothes. Obviously there were deserters, whilst, on the other side, the French received reinforcements.

On 26 October there was general rejoicing when the garrison received a letter from the Duke. Victor Amadeus announced the seizing of Carmagnola, the start of the action against Susa and his intention to relieve Montmélian. But the joy did not last long, because in November 'On the night of the sixth, the enemy published the retreat of the army of H.R.H. and that of the Allies from in front of Susa.'[25]

That news depressed the soldiers. Desertions increased, as well as the enemy activity. On 15 November the French were inspected by Catinat, who, moving to the winter quarters in France with the bulk of the army, let the works of approach continue, increased the artillery and ordered to start the bombing again. 'On the first day of December, the two new batteries began at dawn. Pulling at the same time the other five, together with the eight Mortars, you could see the air all crowded with bombs, balls and smashed stones.'[26]

The garrison reacted using hand grenades, stones, and rockets, but it was clear that the peak of the siege was next. It was expected to be when the French fired the mine they had been preparing for long time. Del Carretto had prepared a countermine composed of 11 barrels of gunpowder, but he was unlucky. The French shelling made the countermine explode in advance. The explosion opened a further breach in the walls, and it was so wide that it looked impossible to prevent the enemy entering the fortress.

Del Carretto summoned a war council and asked his officers for their opinions. They all agreed: it was impossible to hold further, it was now time for a honourable capitulation. Nonetheless Del Carretto pushed ahead the defence 24 more hours but, when he spotted the French sappers starting digging also under the *maschio*, at noon on 21 December he let the drummers roll the call.

The French were tired. They admitted to have lost 1,500 dead, but were credited to have lost 2,000 and that was not all: including wounded and deserters,

> … it is believed that Momigliano costs the King of France six or seven thousand men … after nineteen months of blockading, without assistance and without provisioning, in the middle of a conquered country, after two days bombing, a

---

25 *Idem*, p. 102.
26 *Idem*, p. 117.

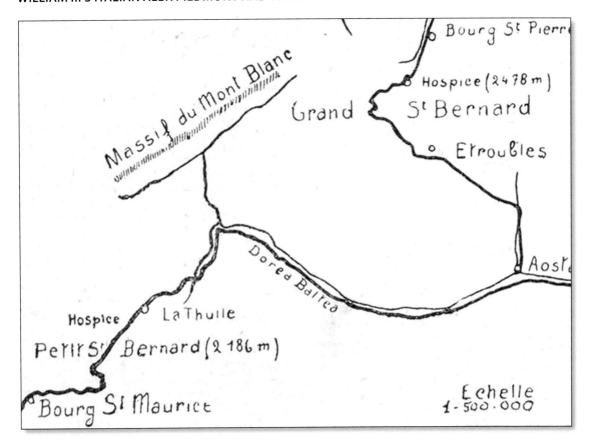

73. The Great and the Little
Saint Bernard Passes

formal siege of ten days to the Land[27] and thirty-five of open trench under the castle, with eighteen mortars and thirty-two cannons in batteries, which reduced it [the castle] to such a state that it could not be recognised by its friendly forces.[28]

It was a bloody result, and the French knew Victor Amadeus was coming. It was a matter of days before he reached Montmélian, for the Piccolo San Bernardo was only 115 kilometres away. Thus Catinat conceded to Del Carretto all the best possible surrender conditions. Then he went up to the castle to pay him a visit, followed by his highest ranked officers. He was amazed when realised how the fortress looked from inside, and was more amazed when realised the garrison was reduced to only 284 men, half of them absolutely unfit for any kind of service. Catinat praised the defenders. No governor of an enemy fortress – he said – ever held so long against the King's troops.

On 23 December 1691 the garrison left along with Del Carretto, holding three cannons[29] and their rifles ready to fire, rolling their drums, and waving

---

27 That is to say the town of Montmélian.
28 *Idem*, ivi.
29 Actually transporting three light cannons across the Alps in that period was so difficult, that a further agreement was made: all the guns remained there, but the French would give the Duke in Turin three similar cannons from Pinerolo.

their flags, with all their baggage and personal properties on wagons provided by the French, bound for Avigliana, in Piedmont. But as soon as the leaving parade ended, only 84 proceeded to Piedmont, because Del Carretto on the previous day gathered the garrison, and told them that the Savoyards were not allowed to follow him to Piedmont. They had simply to promise not to join the French, for they had to keep their oath to the Duke.

VI. Consequences, and a First Lesson Which Was Never Learned

Victor Amadeus was furious. He wrote to Vienna, highly complaining about Caraffa. Prince Eugene supported his cousin's complaints, providing his own report. The Emperor tried to put water on the fire, thus relieved Caraffa, and appointed Caprara, who had proved himself quite well, as usual, against the Ottomans. Then Leopold released an Imperial patent, appointing Victor Amadeus as the supreme commander of the Empire's forces in Italy, and started negotiations

74. Imperial Marshal Enea Caprara

to let Victor Amadeus' eldest daughter, Maria Adelaide, marry Archduke Joseph of Habsburg, his eldest son, who had just been elected the King of the Romans, thus his successor to the Holy Imperial crown. Unfortunately for Leopold, Victor Amadeus did not rely on simple promises, he looked for facts, and until that moment practically no fact existed, including the fiefs of the Langhe he paid in advance and the Emperor had not yet given him. No, Victor Amadeus was very upset with Leopold, and was not alone. In fact Leopold had another ally who was upset with him, quite upset, and unfortunately he was a man nobody could neglect: William of Orange.

As soon as he was informed of what was going on in Italy, William III wrote to Heinsius, on 28 October:

> The recall of the Imperial troops back from Piedmont would be a great misfortune; we must try to prevent it, but I can do nothing to prevent it; for if I speak of it, I shall be immediately tormented for a new subsidy, which it is impossible for me to grant: this puts me in a great embarrassment, for it is a very important question, and Piedmont is the only point from which one can enforce France to reason.[30]

The House of Habsburg tried to act friendly and to somehow calm, if not bribe, William. Spain offered him the government of the Low Countries.

---

30   William III to Heinsius, 28 October/8 November 1691, reported in Sirtema, op. cit., vol. 6, p. 288.

75. Max Emanuel, Prince Elector of Bavaria

William rejected it for, as a Dutch Protestant, he perceived himself to be not well accepted by Flemish and Walloon Catholics, and this could weaken and endanger the alliance. He suggested that post to be given the Elector of Bavaria. Spain agreed, and Max Emanuel left Italy, but ordered his troops to follow him, which was not exactly what William expected him to do. On 13 November William wrote to Heinsius:

The state of affairs in Piedmont does not like to me; the divisions which reign there are deplorable; the withdrawal march of the Bavarian cavalry is a loss impossible to be repaired, and I expect the Elector will soon give his infantry the order to follow the cavalry. I do not see any possibility of remedying something so unfortunate.

I hope that President La Tour will soon arrive here, and that, in advance, all necessary measures will be taken to act vigorously on this side during the next campaign; because that is the vulnerable point of France.[31]

Then he, as the King of England, asked Leopold to appoint the Prince of Hannover as the ninth Elector of the Holy Empire. Leopold wanted neither to have a ninth Elector, although foreseen since the Treaty of Westphalia, nor got the new Elector to be a Protestant, but William insisted, and there was not that much to do other than say yes. Thus the crown of Britain, within less than a generation, would start being involved in every German quarrel occurring in the 18th century.

Leopold supposed himself to have made a favour to William, but William considered it as a pure act of policy and not certainly as a payback for the huge quantity of money Britain was pouring into the Austrian treasury. There was a lesson to be learned here, but whoever had to learn it at that time did not, and also refused to learn it during the next century. The lesson was simple: Piedmont had not to be left alone against France, otherwise soon or later it had to find an agreement with France, simply in order to survive, and, if that was the case, consequences would be the worst.

Now, Vienna left Turin without help, or was ready to withdraw her help as soon as possible, in 1690–95, and later too. The consequences were the military collapse of the Grand Alliance in 1696, then the French alliance forced on Piedmont in 1701, the French-Piedmontese alliance in 1733–36, and, above all, the armistice of Cherasco, which in spring 1796 opened the

---

31   William III to Heinsius, 3/23 November 1691, reported in Sirtema, op. cit., vol. 6, pp. 271–2.

gate to a further 20 years of death, disasters, defeats and humiliation by Napoleon on Austria and Europe until Waterloo.

If in 1691–93 this was still a lesson in progress, after 1696 who was broad minded – as Britain, and the Netherlands too – and knew how to manage world politics, already had clear ideas about it and learned it. William III realised it, no matter if he liked it or not, and acted accordingly. The British cabinets ruling during the 18th and 19th centuries shared William's vision, simply because that was the situation they had to deal with, hence that was the most rational thing to do.

Unfortunately, the House of Habsburg never learned this lesson. They were so selfish and narrow-minded that they looked only for their most immediate advantage and gain, and did not think nor care of consequences. They wanted the others to fight, and pay, supporting Austrian interests in exchange for nothing, including the necessary military support. The Austrians never learned that lesson, especially about Piedmont. Had their behaviour's consequence affected only them, it would have not been too a big problem, but unfortunately it was not so, ever. In 1692 the consequence was simple: Victor Amadeus started negotiations with France; and in 1696 the result exploded: the whole Alliance had to accept an armistice with France.

13

1691–1692 Political, Diplomatic, and Military Problems

I. Discussions

1692 started with a concentration of French troops in northern Europe for the greatest operation of the whole campaign and perhaps of the whole war: the siege of Namur, the most important and hard-to-seize fortress in all of Flanders.

In Spain the French simply continued to threaten Barcelona and widened the area they had occupied since the beginning of the war in Catalonia. Seeing the enemy focus on Flanders and Spain, William III urged his allies to invade southern France, as decided at The Hague in 1691.

In fact Eugene and Schomberg wanted to enter Dauphiny, but the Spaniards wanted to seize Casale, and Victor Amadeus, once Montmélian was lost, preferred to seize Pinerolo first. That would cut off the French from Italy, and secure the Allied rear line, and it was just what Louis XIV worried much about, for he ordered Catinat not to worry about any Dauphiny 'cabanas' the enemy could burn, but to take care of Pinerolo, which had to stay at the top of Catinat's mind.

But William had a different vision: an invasion of France would attract French troops from Flanders, thus it had to be made. There were further problems, as Heinsius reported to William III in early January:

> I conferred with the Earl of Winditsgrats,[1] about the offensive war in Piedmont; he replied that he shared my opinion, that he had written to that aim to his Court and would continue to do so. He approved the proposal to instruct Milord Paget, in the name of Your Majesty, and Mr. de Heemskerk on behalf of the States, to make further inquiries in this respect at Vienna. He showed me much zeal, but also some fears of the obstacles that might be encountered, first of all in the

---

1   Windischgraetz.

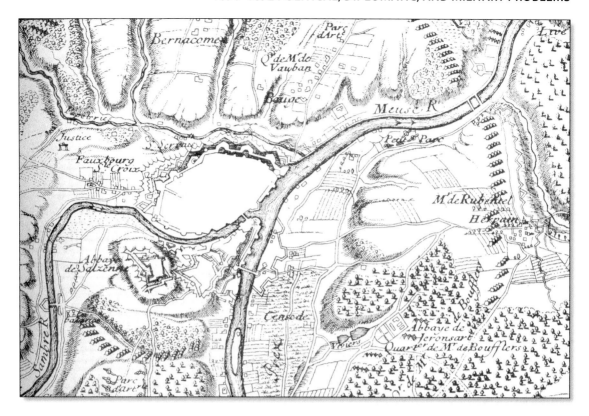

diversity of minds dominating in this Court, then in the person of Caraffa; Since the Elector of Bavaria has already withdrawn his cavalry from Piedmont, he also fears that the Elector may withdraw his infantry, because he is in charge of the general government of the Spanish Netherlands, and that it was rumoured that he had pledged to the Court of Spain to keep a large corps of troops in the Netherlands.

The current policy of the Court of Rome must be added to all this. They want not only to remove the theatre of war from Italy, but they declare themselves openly in favour of a peace with France. This is a point of the greatest importance not only in regard to Piedmont, but even more so in the interests of the Allies and of the general cause; for, in Vienna, they speak of acting only defensively in Piedmont, and thus [the Austrians] may rightly be regarded as the promoters of the peaceful views of the Court of Rome. We must act with all possible vigilance to counter this blow; the Earl of Winditsgrats has promised to do so, and I will charge M. Heemskerk to watch over it; for it is essential that this be done before the arrival of the nuncio carrying the pacific recommendations of the Pope. As for the person of Caraffa, it is a very delicate question; it would only be the Emperor himself who could remedy it.[2]

76. Namur besieged in 1692

---

2   Heinsius to Willam III, on 8 January 1692, in Sirtema, op. cit., vol. 6, pp. 292–293.

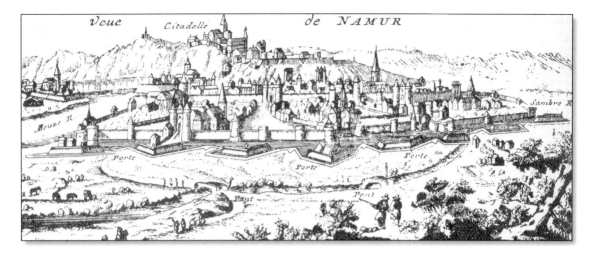

77. Namur in the 17th century

II. The Complicated Diplomatic Situation in Italy

Actually Caraffa had been a problem. Due to the rules of the Empire and to the lack of money perpetually affecting the Habsburg's treasury, Caraffa had been ordered from Vienna to demand support to the Imperial feudatories in Italy. According to the rules, whenever the Empire was involved in a war, all its members, that is to say all the feudatories, had to support it with men and money, or in men, or in money.

However Imperial authority over Italy had been dramatically weakened when the Italian cities defeated the Emperor in Legnano in 1176. They gained substantial autonomy and kept it during the next three and a half centuries. Charles V more or less re-established it, but it was more formal than a matter of substance. In a certain sense no Habsburg tried to enforce the Italian princes to act according to the rules from the beginning of the 16th to the end of the 17th century. Italian troopers or volunteers committed to Germany during the Thirty Years' War, or to Hungary against the Ottomans, could be considered enough as a support, especially if they were such skilled generals as the Duke of Parma, or Count Montecuccoli. But now, in the last decade of the 17th century, Leopold asked the Italian feudatories for money, and Caraffa was ordered to enforce them to pay. The Empire was involved in a war, actually it was involved in two, against the French and against the Ottomans, and money was needed. The Pope, and Venice were out of the Imperial body. Genoa was half and half, the Republic did not like to be in the Empire, but could hardly demonstrate that it did not belong. Milan and Piedmont were out of question, for the Duke of Savoy was fighting supported by Milanese troops, but what about the Grand Duke of Tuscany and the Duchies of Parma, Modena, Mantua and Guastalla, and the Republic of Lucca? They had to pay, a lot. Parma tried to avoid it. The Duchy had already committed an infantry unit – the Battalion of Parma – against the Ottomans in Levant, but no matter, that was another, better: that was 'the other' war; what about this one against the French? Thus Caraffa raised money, a lot of money, from Genoa, Lucca and Tuscany, and enforced Parma and Modena to accept the honour to provide the Imperial troops with money and winter quarters on their own soil.

Caraffa was not mild. The Italian princes were not happy, and this caused a problem. In the short term they all greeted the Papal proposal for neutralising Italy. Their mid-term reaction was their pro-French attitude during the subsequent War of the Spanish Succession. Their long-term reaction – triggered by Parma alone – was the storm caused by Alberoni in 1716–18. But, by now it was still January 1692, and the only actual problem William could see was in Rome.

There was a new pope in Rome. Louis had severe quarrels about the Electorate of Colony with pope Innocent XI, who died in August 1689, and it was against him that he ordered his troops to seize Avignon. The clash continued but ended too during Innocent's successor's reign: Alexander VIII. Alexander was a Venetian, whilst Innocent had been from the Duchy of Milan – thus originally a subject of the King of Spain. Louis XIV during 1690 had time to realise

78. Pope Innocent XII

how bad his situation was, thus he did his best to calm the waters in Rome, gave Avignon back to the Pope, renounced all the demands he made in the past and promised not to support the French clergy demands for autonomy. As a result, the pope appointed cardinals three French bishops, and Leopold was so upset that decided to withdraw his ambassador from Rome.

On the other hand Alexander VIII too was upset with the Austrians, because Leopold was not pushing as much as he could the war against the Ottomans in the Balkans, now mostly managed by Venice and the Italian contingents – the Papal one included – in Greece and in the Aegean Sea.

Alexander died in February 1691, but only in July 1691 the cardinals elected the new pope, and once again it was a subject of the King of Spain. Innocent XII was from the Kingdom of Naples, and his late mother belonged to the Caraffa family. He was quite friendly to Leopold of Habsburg, but succeeded also in having good relationship with France. Basically his idea was to neutralise Italy. This sounded fine both to French and Imperial ears: one front less meant much less trouble and expenditure and all the Italian princes liked this idea too. There were some people who were not happy with such a proposal. One was Victor Amadeus, unless the neutralisation gave him both the lands he lost to France and those he sought to get. There was another who was not happy and it was William III.

William was not happy because he wanted to go on with his strategic plan. At the beginning of January 1692 he answered to Heinsius confirming his opinion:

Although the loss of Montmélian is fatal, I still maintain that it is in Piedmont, more than anywhere else, that we can hope to get the major success by acting offensively. We must work tirelessly to let the Imperial Court coming into these views, and to have the Spaniards be constantly urged to give the proper assistance to the governor of Milan, as well as to the Spanish Low Countries.[3]

Heinsius answered William, saying:

I urged the Bavarian Minister to urge the Elector not to withdraw the troops he still has in Piedmont, because of the necessity of acting vigorously on this side. He told me that he had no doubt that His Electoral Highness was ready to comply with what might be considered necessary by your Majesty.[4]

And a week later added:

I received a letter from the Duke of Schomberg; he hopes the loss of Montmélian not to be perceived fatal in Geneva and in the Swiss cantons; He considers as indispensable that we support them, and thinks that we should assist them with money, as well as increase the number of troops under his command, in order to protect Switzerland if necessary.[5]

And, after having remarked that the winter quarters the Spaniards provided to Allied troops in Lombardy were bad, Heinsius added a further bad news: 'Business does not go well in Switzerland for I am told daily that the cantons, both Reformed and Catholic, are pronouncing themselves more and more for France.'[6]

The uncertain diplomatic situation also let the Republic of Genoa enhance her military organisation, to protect her neutrality, and it was decided to muster 3,000 men on the Riviera, to increase the number of cannons in the fortress of Gavi and to recall as many troops as possible from Corsican garrisons.

III. Men, Money, and Planning

As far as he was concerned, Victor Amadeus in theory had 17,242 men, that is to say 14,467 foot and 2,775 cavalry and dragoons, but only a little less than 14,000 were really available to be used on the ground. It was a lot of men, at least when compared to previous figures. The Duke achieved that result in two steps. In February 1692 each town and village in Piedmont was required to provide a certain number of men and to have replacements ready in case of casualties. Then, two months later, in April, when preparing the incoming campaign, one third of the Battalion of Piedmont was inserted into the regular regiments, enjoying the same wage and benefits as the

---

3   William III to Heinsius, on 1/11 January 1692, in Sirtema, op. cit. vol. 6, pp. 292–293.
4   Heinsius to William III, on 11 January 1692, in Sirtema, op. cit. vol. 6, p. 294.
5   Heinsius to William III, on 18 January 1692, in Sirtema, op. cit. vol. 6, p. 295.
6   Ivi.

professional soldiers. Anyway the Duke did not like that much this system: it was dangerous, because it took too much manpower away from agriculture. The solution could be to rely on foreign professionals, but this meant a long chain of long and fatiguing negotiations to be undertaken with foreign princes, especially German ones.

As Heinsius underlined in February, 'The Duke of Savoy is very zealous for the cause of the Allies, but is very much in pain about where to find money.[7] by that time, the British funding was still five months late, which meant 100,00 *scudi* according to the old ratio.

The financial problem was partially solved when Charles II of Spain assigned Victor Amadeus a monthly subsidy of 30,000 *scudi* on the revenues of the Kingdoms of Naples and of Sicily. This increased the Spanish funding which, at the end of the war, totalled 5,777,184 *liras*, that is to say more than one third of the 15.7 million Piedmont globally received from abroad. In spring 1692 Victor Amadeus received letters of change from Naples and Sicily for 100,000 *scudi*, covering the costs of the just ending 1690–91 winter quarters, but in fact the 100,000 *scudi* was less than that.

There was some good news from the Maritime Powers who had to increase their support from 30,000 to 36,000 *scudi* a month, but sending money was still problematic. In April de la Tour sent letters of exchange for 144,000 *scudi*, which put the British subsidy up to date, but it was just an illusion. Once more de la Tour had problems in finding in Amsterdam letters of change drawable at least on Geneva, thus the 20,000 *scudi* given by the States General in July 1692 was late and diminished. Moreover during summer the British subsidy was late again, and de la Tour could send 72,000 *scudi* in September, but this covered three months and a lot of the promised money was still missing and would be missing until next March 1693.

On their side, the Spaniards too had troubles. It was more a matter of lack of men than of money. Actually, money seemed to be more than enough, but Spanish commitments in Flanders, Italy, Levant, and Catalonia rendered sustainability problematic. In January 1692 the French credited the Spanish army in Catalonia to be 21,000 strong, that of Flanders to be composed of more than 51,000 men, including also three Italian infantry tercios, each 800 strong, and one Italian cavalry tercio 400 strong. If the Flemish front was demanding, the Catalan one was more demanding, for it was in metropolitan Spain, thus in March all the troops levied in Lombardy were ordered to go to Catalonia, whilst in April the viceroy of Naples was urged for 2,000 soldiers destined for Catalonia and for money to Milan. He ordered to muster all the vagabonds, idles and beggars the police could find in Naples[8] and in May told the aristocracy it was necessary to use the 100,000 *ducati* existing in the Neapolitan banks. Meanwhile, a new regiment 3,000-foot strong was organised in Gaeta to protect the littoral and all the Neapolitan barons were

---

7   Heinsius to William III, on 22 February 1692, in Sirtema, op. cit., vol. 6, p. 302.
8   It may be interesting to know that the tercio was composed of 1,000 men and left to Catalonia on 22 April, but it included only 200 vagabonds, for the majority fled as soon as they knew the authorities were looking to muster them.

urged by the viceroy to organise their people in military units to watch and protect the coast.

The King of Spain's forces in Italy could not decrease, due to both the commitment in Piedmont and the risk of a French naval raid on Neapolitan coasts. Thus the Spanish troops serving with the Venetians against the Ottomans in Levant were recalled, destined for Lombardy, but with scanty results: in April only 300 out of 3,000 came back, the missing having been killed in Levant by enemies or by diseases. This was not enough, for the governor of Milan wanted to have no less than 15,000 men in Piedmont in the next campaign.

The Spanish navy – Spanish, Neapolitan, and Sicilian galley squadrons – shuttled between southern and northern Italy and Barcelona, shipping soldiers and money, and then gathered in Port Mahon, joining Tursi's squadron and the Spanish vessels to repel any French naval attempt.

IV. Strategy

Eugene came back to Turin from Vienna on 6 July. On the 7th he reached the camp and planned with Victor Amadeus the first invasion of France in the last 50 years.

Victor Amadeus was all but happy. Apart for Pinerolo, he underlined once more what a problem such an invasion was in terms of power projection and sustainability. It was logistically very hard. Piedmont knew it, for such an invasion failed twice in the previous century. In 1536 Emperor Charles V, backed by the Spanish and Genoese fleets and with no opposition from the French navy, had nonetheless been compelled to fall back into Liguria with heavy casualties. Victor Amadeus' and Eugene's great-grandfather, Duke Charles Emmanuel I, at the end of the 16th century had tried to conquer the same region, but without success, even though he had the support of part of the local population. When attacked, both times, the French had always had time to put strong garrisons into the threatened places, before retreating north with the main body of their army, burning and laying waste everything behind them. They halted their retreat near Lyon, where they could be supplied with ease from the Rivers Rhône and Loire and wait for the enemy to be worn down, a process possibly speeded up by raids and attacks on his flanks. On every occasion, the invading army had been forced to leave, pursued by the French who, descending from Lyon, were well supplied from the River Rhône as they proceeded down to Marseille and the sea.

The other Allied corps were strong too. Including 11,200 foot and 2,600 cavalry comprising the Piedmontese field army, the Allies had 37,310 foot and 12,480 horses.

According to contemporary sources, the Allied army in northern Italy was a little more than 50,000 strong, all included.

14

Marching Through Dauphiny

I. The Failed French Landing in Oneglia

The first action of 1692 campaign in Italy occurred in May, when on the 19th a French fleet composed of 35 galleys commanded by the Duke de Noailles appeared in front of Oneglia and shelled the town. As soon as the shelling started, the garrison entered the castle and the people immediately abandoned the town and fled to the mountains. The French landed 1,500 men, that is to say three battalions, and started looting and burning the town. The landing force was far less than expected,[1] so the local militia, which retired protecting the fleeing inhabitants, came back and joined the Piedmontese garrison, composed of companies of the Chiablese Infantry Regiment and of a few Mondovì militiamen. The Piedmontese surrounded the French and destroyed the landing force, killing more than a half of them and retaking the booty.

II. Planning in Piedmont

Catinat was in Perosa Argentina, halfway between Susa and Pinerolo, to relieve whichever of the two could be attacked by the Allies. His situation was bleak. According to French sources, the Allied army in Piedmont was now more than 51,000 strong, far more than he had.

The Allies considered many offensive plans, not all against French metropolitan territory. At last the Piedmontese general the Marquess di Pianezza was tasked to blocke Casale with 6,000 men, and the Hungarian General Pálffy with 5,000 men[2] had to act in the Chisone Valley, threatening both Catinat and Pinerolo at the same time.

---

1   A galley could have on board up to 100 infantrymen to be landed, thus a squadron of 35 galleys could – and was expected to – ship up to 3,500 men, especially on such a short distance as that between Toulon and Oneglia.

2   According to the list existing originally in the Turin State Archive and now in AUSSME L 3, busta 7, number 3, in July Pálffy had formally under his orders 14,647 men. This figure should include also Schomberg's corps, although, according to the lists we have, neither his regiments –

The expeditionary force bound for France had to move east to west, from Piedmont to Dauphiny and had Catinat on its right flank, thus north. So, Pálffy's corps was vital. It was between Catinat and the expeditionary force, faced Catinat and protected the right flank of the expeditionary force itself whilst it moved to France. Catinat was not strong enough to engage Pálffy successfully. Had Catinat turned around, Pálffy could choose between attacking Pinerolo, or engaging Catinat's rearguard. Moreover, Catinat received clear orders from Versailles: no matter how many cabanas and villages could be burnt by the Allies in France, he had absolutely to keep Pinerolo in French hands. Thus Catinat did not move, and, anyway, it being that his logistics were as much affected by disorders and disorganisation as in the previous year, how could he act?

The Allied expeditionary force was 29,000 strong and marched to Dauphiny divided in two columns. The first and stronger one was a bit more than 21,200 strong. It was commanded by Victor Amadeus, along with Eugene, Caprara, Parella, and Leganes. Parella was in avant-garde with 1,860 dragoons and 3,583 foot.[3] Victor Amadeus, Caprara and Eugene followed him with the bulk, including 8,348 foot, 450 dragoons and six field guns. The new governor of Milan, Count de Leganes, commanded the rearguard, including 6,062 foot and 968 dragoons. The second column was roughly 8,000 men strong, and was commanded by the Duke of Schomberg.

Victor Amadeus had to leave the area of Cuneo, move towards Argentera, cross the Maddalena Pass and enter France bound for Vars and then to Guillestre. Schomberg had to march up the Luserna Valley, cross the Alps at the Colle della Croce pass, and then join Victor Amadeus in Guillestre on 1 August.

III. Logistics Across the Mountains

On 23 July the army left Saluzzo bound to Cuneo. One week later the nuncio could write:

> The news came that the troops of Mylord the Duke arrived at the barricades across Cuneo and that the Marquess di Parella, who, with a corps of soldiers, moves more or less a half day ahead, depending on the opportunities, is already in Barcellona [Barcellonette] only five Piedmontese miles[4] far from Ambrun [Embrun] … Mylord Duke is in Demont [Demonte] across Cuneo, with Lord

except for one infantry regiment and the Balthazar's dragoons – nor his name appear. However, considering that neither his name nor his regiments are listed among the troops marching with Victor Amadeus, all the sources agree on 6,000 men staying with Pálffy and 8,000 following Schomberg across the Alps, and considering that Schomberg had to march along a road between Pálffy and Victor Amadeus, it is reasonable to think that a portion of the 14,647 Pálffy's men were Schomberg's.

3   From Saluzzo to Cuneo they were organised in a different way, because Parella was with Commercy and had 6,044 men, including 3,883 foot and 2,661 dragoons, and Victor Amadeus had 7,578 foot and only 200 cavalry.

4   The original says 'only five of this country's miles', that is to say only five Piedmontese miles.

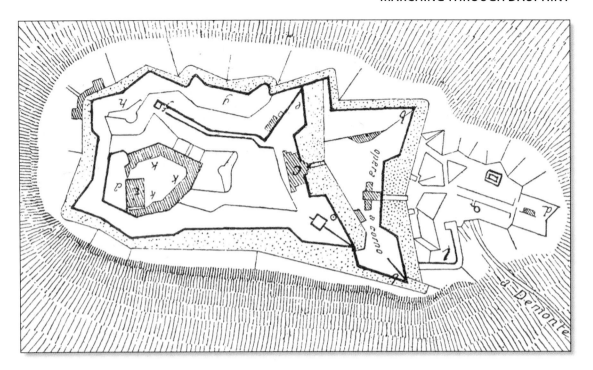

79. Demonte

Governor of Milan, with G.nal Caprara and with Mar.ss di Parella, whilst the troops of the latter passed ahead along the route going to Ambrun in the Dauphiny, and it is said as a sure thing that Mons. di Cattinat passed with a great part of troops in that Province.[5]

The last time the Piedmontese army had to sustain a power projection across the mountains was during the war against Genoa in 1674. That experience was not completely lost in anyone's minds, but the situation was completely different, and besides, there were plenty of experts.

How did they manage logistics? Quite well, it seems. 'The baggage will follow the artillery' was the standard rule in all the March Orders[6] when the army was on the Italian side of the Alps. And artillery had to move along a different route, due to the need for better and wider roads and the necessity of not making the other troops' march slow.

The regimental and General Staff's baggage had to follow the artillery and were forbidden to move along with the quartermasters, who were normally at the head of the columns and were in charge of choosing the camp locations.[7] The March Orders do not speak that much of the baggage and transports and clearly suppose them to move along with the artillery.

5　The nuncio of Savoy to the Cardinal Secretary of State, Turin, 30 July 1692, in ASV, Nunziatura di Savoia, anno 1692.

6　*Ordini di marcia pel 22, 23, 24, 26, 27, 28, 29, 30 luglio 1692*, handwritten copies in AUSSME; L 3, 7–3, Stati Preunitari – Piemonte, *Notizie sulla Campagna del 1692 nel Delfinato*.

7　*Ordini di marcia del 27 luglio 1692*, handwritten copy in AUSSME; L 3, 7–3, Stati Preunitari – Piemonte, *Notizie sulla Campagna del 1692 nel Delfinato*.

After entering France, artillery moves along the same route of all the other troops, in rearguard. On 3 August, marching from Guillestre to Embrun, '20 dragoons placed at the head of the Camp under the orders of the General Provost will prevent the passage of any baggage before or between the troops.'[8] This could be evidence of a regiment's likely desire to keep their own baggage close, as well as evidence of the transport staff feeling safer among the troops instead of in the rearguard. On the other hand, the commanders clearly preferred to have at the head of the column all the troops fit for a fight – in this case five infantry regiments and the dragoons – keeping a sixth infantry regiment ending the column.

Further information can be found in the orders issued on 26 August about the march the next day from Embrun to Savine saying:

> Tomorrow if God likes we shall leave the camp in good order to march until Savine, where the camp will be formed…

> 7°

> The small artillery will march to the old camp of the Dragoons of Savoy across the bridge on the Durence and will remain there together with all the baggage and will not cross until a new order.

> 8°

> The General Provost will remain where the army passes and will not leave any baggage march ahead, nor in between, nor after the Regiments.[9]

What is interesting is how long they marched every day. From Saluzzo to Busca, in Piedmont, on 23 July, the march was 16 kilometres long. On the next day, 24 July, from Busca to Vignola, it was 20. Then the troops rested one day, and on the 26th they marched up the mountains, until Demonte, 20 kilometres away. On 27 July they reached Sambuco, 21 kilometres from Demonte. On the 28th they marched along the road from Sambuco to Argentera: 16 more kilometres. On the 29th they arrived in Saint Paul sur Ubaye, in France, 30 kilometres away and across the mountains. On the 30th they proceeded to Guillestre, 25 kilometres away. Then they stopped until 3 August, because they had to seize the city, and once Guillestre taken they moved to Embrun.

As we see, the schedule of three days marching and one resting, according to the general rules described by Perjés, which so many authors think to be the absolute standard, in fact in this case was not followed, and this case is not an exception in Italian campaigns[10] between 1690 and 1748. We have here a two-day march, followed by a one-day stop, and then by a five-day

---

8   *Ordini di marcia del 3 agosto 1692,* handwritten copy in in AUSSME; L 3, 7–3, Stati Preunitari – Piemonte, *Notizie sulla Campagna del 1692 nel Delfinato.*

9   *Ordini di marcia del 26 agosto 1692,* handwritten copy in AUSSME; L 3, busta 7, number 3, Stati Preunitari – Piemonte, *Notizie sulla Campagna del 1692 nel Delfinato.*

10 Exemples to be given can be: Eugene of Savoy's march to Turin in 1706, Eugene's and Victor Amadeus' march to Toulon in 1707, Piedmontese march from Palermo to Siracusa in 1716, Charles Emmanuel III's march from the Adriatic coast to the Western Alps in 1742.

uninterrupted march, followed by a three-day stop, which is a fake one, because they stopped to seize a city, thus to fight, not to rest.

We have 148 kilometres covered in only seven days, thus a daily 21 kilometres average, that is to say at least five kilometres per day – if not nine – more than the 'rules', and, moreover, climbing the mountains. This should be enough at least to start questioning all the authors blindly supporting Perjés as an absolute rule.

IV. Raiding Dauphiny

Going back to operations, all was achieved according to the plans. On 29 July the Piedmontese captured 600 French soldiers from two Irish companies[11] and of the Dauphiny militia.[12] On the 30th Victor Amadeus entered Guillestre. He ordered his troopers to be disciplined, and formally forbade any robbery, but the city had already been robbed by its Irish garrison before they retreated into the castle. The Allied troops stayed in Guillestre on the next day to rest and to build a bridge, which was achieved on 1 August.

Eugene was tasked for investing Embrun. On 3 August he crossed the Durance in front of Saint-Clément and marched along its left bank. Then he took position on the heights and started the siege, no matter if Catinat was said to be with some troops on the other side of Saint-Clément. On 5 August the bulk of the army arrived and blockaded the city. On the following day the Allies opened the trench and the siege began. The siege of Embrun went not as easily as one may think. On the 10th Catinat was said to have reached Briançon, to have advanced towards Saint-Crispin and to be gathering troops in Gap to relieve Embrun. Victor Amadeus committed Schomberg and the Religioners towards Saint-Crispin to stop any attempt by Catinat.

Six cannons arrived on 12 August in the evening. Two were immediately placed, but two others fell down in the moat, due to the continuous fire from the walls which wounded both the oxen of the train and their drivers. The next day and the following were spent in trying to retrieve the fallen cannons from the moat, and firing them against the place with the others.

On the 15th the place asked to capitulate and on the 16th surrendered after a fight hard enough to have cost several casualties:

> Immediately after the surrender of Ambrun, Lord Prince Eugene was sent with a large detachment of cavalry to Gap, a big and mercantile city, on the road that leads to Grenoble, akin to imposing the contributions, and demanding them from neighbouring country.[13]

---

11 They should have been inserted in the Chiablese Regiment, because we know that only in 1692 it received a second battalion, mainly composed of Irish from the French army.

12 The *Mercure Historique* of that month admitted the Piedmontese had captured four regiments of Dauphiny militia, whose men were sent to Turin.

13 The nuncio of Savoy to the Cardinal secretary of State, Turin, 20 August, 1692, in ASV, Nunziatura di Savoia, anno 1692.

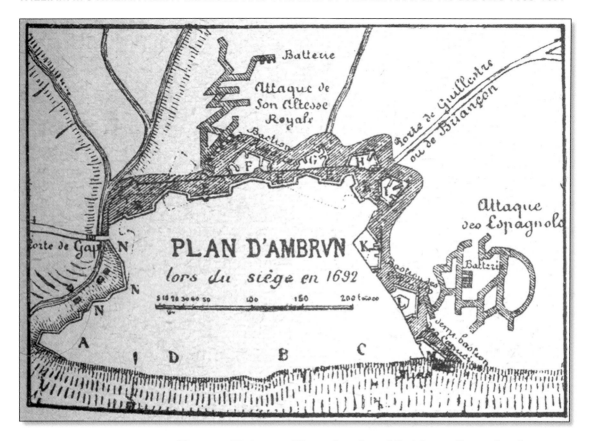

80. The siege of Embrun, 1692

Then, on 27 August, Victor Amadeus fell sick: smallpox, the physicians said. Duchess Anne left Turin to take care of him and arrived to the camp on 5 September. But, contrary to expectations:

> Such an accident could not so far delay on that side the military operations in the army of the Allies, which has finally crossed the Durance, and has extended until Gap without finding any opposition, and the French cavalry who came in that neighbourhood immediately withdrew at the appearance of Lord Prince Eugene with his Germans.[14]

In fact operations went ahead under Caprara's and Leganes' operational command, also if Victor Amadeus formally kept the command and moved along with the army.

The Allies remained in Gap no less than 15 days, 'with abundance, better, with superfluity of all the necessary.'[15] Raiding parties were spread 15 leagues – 45 miles – far around Dauphiny, and down to Provence to get contributions from everywhere. The result was quite good, both in terms of looting and of

---

14   *Idem*, Turin, 3 September 1692, in ASV, Nunziatura di Savoia, anno 1692.

15   'Relazione della ritirata dell'Armata da Gap e dei danni in tale occasione causati al nemico con incendio, contribuzione ed altri', handwritten copy of an original from Turin State Archive, in AUSSME, L 3, 7/3, p. 48.

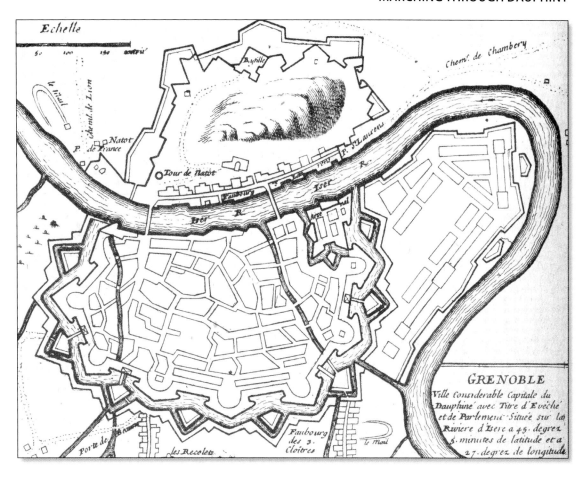

81. Grenoble in the early 18th century

propaganda: it was the first time since the Thirty Years' War that France was invaded and raided.

Gap had been abandoned by its inhabitants and was sacked and burned. Imperial and Sabaudian troops had too many pending bills due to what the French did in the Palatinate and in Piedmont, not to miss the opportunity of revenge.

Eugene commented: 'Nothing prevents us from advancing to Grenoble', and he was right, because Catinat, weakened by the detachments to the army of Flanders and stopped by the royal order to protect Pinerolo, had not enough forces: 2,000 out of his 16,000 men were needed to protect Pinerolo. The remaining 14,000 were at that time around Palons, but they were too few to protect Briançon, and Grenoble, and to threaten the enemy retreat and its lines of communication.

In spite of how easy could be to seize Grenoble, on 12 September Gap was abandoned and the Allied army began retreating, to be back in Saluzzo by the end of the month. The Allies left behind them 4,000 buildings burnt in towns, villages, castles and farms, they took away 200,000 bags of cereals, 10,000 cattle and sheep, a huge number of horses, mules and donkeys and an incalculable amount of values in goods and money:

> We … have forced the enemy to fight in his territories, and to devour his own entrails and by the grace of God we bring back the army in very good conditions, and there is no Officer, nor soldier who does not enjoy the convenience of some booty.[16]

William III was anything but happy:

> The orders sent by the Emperor and the efforts that could be made to let the Allied troops spend the winter in Dauphiny, will certainly arrive too late, because I have seen letters from the Marquess de Leganes and from Louvignies to the Elector of Bavaria, in which they say that this is impossible, and that, had the illness of the Duke of Savoy not prevented it, the retreat would have been faster. Thus there is no doubt that, as things are, it must have been so. Hence this expedition will have done more harm than good to the common cause; it will have served only to indicate to France its vulnerable side, and certainly they will take precautions that will impede that next year we can go in again.[17]

On 9 October back in Piedmont, Caprara summoned a war council to state what to do about Pinerolo. The generals agreed: nothing could be made due to the lack of siege mortars. By now, only reconnaissance could be performed to get information about what to do, and to prepare a siege to be undertaken in the next year's campaign. Then everybody went to winter quarters.

V. A Case of Smallpox and its Consequences

Victor Amadeus' smallpox had several consequences on military, diplomatic and political levels. The most immediate and apparent result was said to be the interruption of operations. As we have see, in this case his illness let the Allies stay longer in France. But we must underline that September on the Alps was the last month before the snow. The longer the Allied army waited, the harder its return across the mountains, and it was not a good idea to spend winter in France, with Catinat in Italy, still holding Pinerolo and Casale.

The Spaniards and the Imperialists, or at least Leganes and Caprara, intended not to do too much and the former wanted simply to defend Lombardy in the Alps, whilst the latter had no interest in wasting too many men and resources in a late autumn campaign.

Once more Victor Amadeus was upset. The strategic result was far less and the military expenditure far more than expected. If the former was not that great, the latter increased to more than 6,100,000 *liras* from November 1691 to the end of October 1692.

But the scanty military result of that campaign was compensated by some interesting new perspective opened up by his recent smallpox. Smallpox was over in a relatively few days, but Victor Amadeus' health remained poor at least

---

16 Author unknown, reported in Sterrantino, 'La malattia del Duca di Savoia', in *La guerra della Lega d'Augusta fino alla battaglia di Orbassano* (Turin, 1993), p. 43.

17 William III to Heinsius, on 22 September 1692, in Sirtema, op. cit., vol. 6, pp. 347–348.

until April 1693. This long illness caused a deep change in the French and Sabaudian relationship, for Victor Amadeus had no son yet, only two daughters. Had he died, who could inherit the crown? According to the laws of that time, the heir was the oldest male of the closest branch. The closest branch was that of Savoy-Carignano, started at the eve of the century by Prince Maurice of Savoy, the younger brother of Victor Amadeus I, Victor Amadeus II's grandfather. The Savoy-Carignano family, who gained the throne in 1848 and unified Italy in 1861, in the first half of the 17th century moved to France, but, just before the Nine Years' War, the family was very badly treated by Louis XIV in person. Prince Eugene of Savoy belonged to that branch, and it is well known that he left France due to having no prospect of a career left to him by Louis XIV. But Eugene was not the chief of that branch, for the chief was his uncle, his father's eldest brother, Emmanuel Philibert of Savoy, Prince of Carignano, who was on the worst terms with the Sun King. Emmanuel Philibert was deaf-mute, thus originally nobody cared of him. Being exceptionally clever, thanks to a special teacher the young prince learned to speak and to communicate. Later he served in the French army, became a colonel, commanded the Carignan-Salières Infantry Regiment, was appointed the governor of the city of Asti in Piedmont and then, in November 1684, when he was 62, he suddenly decided to marry Maria Angela Caterina d'Este, a 28-year-old member of the ducal family of Modena, which Mary, the next-to-be queen of England, belonged to.

82. Emanuel Philbert of Savoy, Prince of Carignano

Louis XIV was upset and did not consent. One may wonder why the King of France's consent had to be considered relevant about the marriage of two foreign princes, but this was not Louis' opinion. There was a slight possibility to obtain Savoy through some rights of succession, hence that marriage had not to be made, unless the bride was French. But how could she be French if the engagement and the marriage had been negotiated by Abbot Grimani, the Imperial diplomat?

Louis' fury fell on Emmanuel Philibert, who refused to leave his wife. Louis hence ordered – please, note the verb 'order' – Victor Amadeus to turn Emmanuel Philibert out of Turin's court and out of Piedmont. In early 1685 Victor Amadeus could only obey, and Emmanuel Philibert had to leave his country. This was a major scandal and went down very badly among the Italian princes. But it had two other bad consequences for France: after this insult to his family, Prince Eugene became angrier than ever with France, and above all Emmanuel Philibert became an enemy of Louis. Now, in 1692, in case of Victor Amadeus' death, Emmanuel Philibert – that is to say an enemy of France and a supporter of the Empire – would be the duke, and, since

167

83. René Froulay Count de Tessé

he had a male heir born in 1690, no possibility remained to France for a further attempt to seize the Duchy, or at least to keep it somehow under her influence.

All the possible hypotheses were made about every possible case. Gossip and rumours spread everywhere and were reported to Versailles by the Count de Tessé, the French governor of Pinerolo. It is absolutely useless to report these rumours, for they had no consequence and no importance on further facts, but for one: Louis decided it was time for a negotiation with Victor Amadeus in order not to lose everything.

It is very difficult to discover who started the negotiations. Both the courts had their own unofficial agents and spies one into the other. Contacts were kept more or less secretly. A word told on one day by a person to another could mean all by noon, and nothing by midnight. Letters reported a version, which could and could not be true, both for the writer had interest in shaping some aspects and to put others in the shadows, or simply because he was in good faith, but had purposely been misinformed. What we know for sure is that, after many unofficial contacts in the previous years, a negotiation started in early 1693, a negotiation that ultimately had to led to peace in Piedmont within three years, and in Europe within four.

15

The Four Seasons of 1693

I. Winter Plans

The 1693 general Allied strategy was to make a new raid in France from Piedmont, a raid to be supported by the British fleet in the Gulf of Lyon.

A war council was held in Turin in the first week of February, whilst the Piedmontese cavalry patrolled the country to prevent French raids. Victor Amadeus, Leganes and Caprara agreed: the first step had to be, as in the previous year, the blockading of Pinerolo and Casale, to prevent sallies by their garrisons. Leganes was in charge of both the fortresses. The other generals had to pass in France. They were also informed that they had to act with a strong naval support. The Spanish navy had to gather in Naples, take on board at least an infantry regiment, which was already in Naples, and then join the Anglo-Dutch fleet, which was expected to reach the Mediterranean.

But things did not go as sought. On 19 March 1693, suddenly the French fleet appeared on the Neapolitan coast, offshore from Pozzuoli and Baia. It was 27 vessels strong, and the Spanish ships were still in the Baia dry docks with their works in progress. Nothing happened, and the French left without consequence, but the surprise had been bad. Nonetheless, soon after their departure, the traditional military shuttle between Naples and Finale restarted, preparing the incoming 1693 campaign. The Allies were expected by the French to field 48,000 men in Piedmont, but in fact they fielded more. Instead of the 12,000 men the French credited him, Victor Amadeus had a little more than 17,000, but as usual he needed money, and it was not that easy to get it from abroad.

William III was in a bad political and financial condition, for everybody was seeking money from him and the Dutch. German princes above all asked him to fund their armies on the Rhine. Hence he wrote to Heinsius:

> As for me, I am unable to contribute because the funds I shall get from Parliament will not even be enough to cover essential expenses. I can not, therefore, do anything extraordinary, especially since I must give my share to the money intended to attract the Elector of Saxony, and that I must contribute to the

expenses of the campaign in Piedmont, or, without that, we shall do nothing important. You can assess, from all this, of my helplessness.[1]

He was also worried due to the Imperial troops:

I am informed with the most sensible pain about the deplorable state of the Imperial troops in Italy, and that they will not be able to start the campaign until June or July. There will be nothing to expect from the operations in Piedmont, which is an impossible thing, because that is the only place from which one can hope to be able to attack the enemy with some hope of success. Count de Winditsgrats must necessarily be talked about this subject, in the hope of finding some remedy for it.[2]

So, once more Victor Amadeus had to rely basically only on his own forces. The ducal army was more or less the same size as the previous year, that is to say 17,200 men, divided into 14,500 foot, and 2,700 horses, and this time too it was due to the militiamen called to arms.

Someone in the last quarter of the 20th century underlined this Piedmontese army increase to be 'part of a much longer-term growth in armies in early modern Europe.'[3] Written as it is, this is a clueless comment, for one should realise – and say – that, between 1688 and 1713, Europe had one of the bloodiest, longest and most serious periods of uninterrupted widespread war it had ever seen, and that normally, during a war, during every war, every involved state does its best to raise as many soldiers as needed to survive and, possibly, to win.

As usual, more men meant more money, and more money was not that easy to obtain, especially when considering how hard it was to get on time that already promised.

Foreign funding was further complicated by the risks affecting European economy and finance during a war. By the way, the funding was late until March 1693, when de la Tour received and forwarded the subsidy covering the last four months of 1692, and the months of January and February 1693, but, when operations started, March was not covered yet, nor was April.

II. Spring Offers: Perracchino, Chamlay, Tessé, and Gropello

The secret contacts between France and Savoy were going on practically since the beginning of the war and neither Louis nor Victor Amadeus had ever considered them really decisive, but they both knew that one day they might reach a result. As it was reported to Versailles, at the beginning, in December 1691 a certain Perracchino, an attorney-at-law in the city of

---

1   William III to Heinsius, on 10/22 January, 1693, in Sirtema, op. cit., vol. 6, p. 385.

2   William III to Heinsius, on 7/17 March 1693, in Sirtema, op. cit., vol. 6, p. 388.

3   Christopher Storrs, *War, Diplomacy and the Rise of Savoy, 1690–1720* (Cambridge: Cambridge University Press, 2000), p. 25.

Pinerolo, told the Marquis d'Harleville, at that time the governor of Pinerolo, that the Abbot di Cumiana had reported to him that the Duke could leave the Grand Alliance and come back to the French alliance if the King would encourage him at least a little, for instance by a three- or four-month long armistice.

Louis XIV was not naive and realised that Victor Amadeus wanted only to gain time, hence his answer was a substantial confirmation of the 1690 ultimatum presented by Catinat.

Anyway things were not going that well for France, so, pushed also by the Pope, Louis sent to Pinerolo the Count de Chamlay with a letter to the Duke.[4] When informed by di San Tommaso, Victor Amadeus let him answer on his behalf that, during the war, it was unfair to receive letters from the King of France, but if the Count de Chamlay wanted to talk with the Marquess di San Tommaso about the business and interests of their respective masters, they could meet in Pinerolo.

84. Giovanni Battista Gropello, later Count di Borgone

San Tommaso did not go in person to Pinerolo, but sent one of the men he trusted more, a finance official named John-Baptist Gropello. Disguised as a peasant – clothing to which, according to Tessé, his rough features gave a very truthful appearance – Gropello went to Pinerolo. The King's proposals revealed by Chamlay sounded not so appealing to Victor Amadeus, thus nothing was concluded, and by the end of February 1692 Chamlay returned to France, whilst two months later Gropello was appointed at the intendancy of Susa. When there, Gropello proved once more what a skilful man he was. After the French occupation, he organised the local intelligence network covering the area from Susa to Briançon across the Alps, and provided the Duke with all the information one could need about the French military and logistical situations. On the other hand, he was the soul and the head of the resistance against the invaders. He coordinated the militia, harassed the French logistics, attacked their convoys, cut their communication lines and provided the Allied army with the needed food and provisions. Victor Amadeus deeply appreciated and trusted him, which is why, once the operation stalled, he chose him for further negotiations with France.

As soon as he came back to the town in the autumn of 1692, the governor of Pinerolo René de Froulay, Count de Tessé, told San Tommaso he had

---

4   It must be underlined that nothing of that is reported in Tessé's memoirs. According to Tessé negotiations started when Gropello came by the first at Tessé in Pinerolo on 30 December 1691. Tessé informed Versailles and then Louis XIV sent Chamlay. See, *Mémoires et lettres du Maréchal de Tessé*, 2 vols. (Paris, 1806), vol. I, p. 20.

85. Mary Adelaide of Savoy, Dauphine of France in 1696

some important things to tell him.[5] Tessé had no formal diplomatic patent by Louis XIV, hence Victor Amadeus sent him Perracchino, then Mrs Perracchino was committed, and then a Jesuit father, and through them the Duke promised only, as Tessé later reported: 'some nice and well written nothings'.[6] This game went on until Tessé showed documents crediting him as a plenipotentiary. Then the Duke called back Gropello, who later, in 1699, was ennobled and known as the Count di Borgone, and committed him to visit Tessé in Pinerolo twice a week and negotiate.

Disguised as a peasant this time too, Gropello sneaked across the lines during the night, met Tessé and proposed, listened, negotiated, talked, promised to report to his master, disappeared and went back to Turin, to reappear a few nights later, perhaps in different clothes, as when he was recognised in Frossasco dressed as a tinker.

The contacts continued during the next part of the war, and gained a growing importance in the eyes of Victor Amadeus as much as Allied support diminished. In modern history, Victor Amadeus is an example of political skill. His had a great ability to measure and mix military and diplomatic action, subduing the former to the latter. He really rendered war the continuation of politics by other means, instead of the aim or the end of politics itself.

As early as February 1693, Louis seemed to agree to what Victor Amadeus wanted. Had the Duke signed a treaty with France, the King would give him back the Duchy of Savoy, and Susa, whilst the County of Nice would be given back after the general peace. The Duke had to receive 800,000 *scudi* in four yearly instalments, and Casale would be put in neutral hands until the general peace. Louis would no more threaten nor harass Savoy about the Waldensians, and would never more compel the Duke to provide him military support. Lastly: Maria Adelaide di Savoia, the Duke's eldest daughter, had to be engaged and then married to the Dauphin, the Duke of Burgundy, Louis XIV eldest grandson and future heir.

This was not exactly all Victor Amadeus wanted, although it was quite close, hence this time negotiation started seriously, but this was not a good reason to stop operations. In case, operations were a good way to push France

---

5 Tessé had been the governor of Pinerolo since the beginning of 1691. In Spring 1692 was promoted to lieutenant-general and moved to France. D'Harleville became the governor of Pinerolo, but left that post to Tessé again, when he came back by the end of that same year. Tessé was said to be a witty and clever man, his memoires are nicely written, but they are not that objective.

6 Rep. in *La guerra della Lega d'Augusta fino alla battaglia di Orbassano*, cit., p. 31.

and get better conditions. The Duke knew how weak Catinat was, and had no doubt that during 1693 campaign Pinerolo would be seized. Could it be obtained before the campaigning and without fighting? On 30 May 1693, a real comedy occurred in Pinerolo, played by Tessé and Gropello. The latter told the former that his master renounced all the money promised if the King gave him Pinerolo. Tessé immediately stood and dramatically replied that, according to him, that was only an excuse to break any further discussion or to consider the suggested treaty broken.

Gropello, according to his own instructions, knew he had only to try to get Pinerolo, but had to avoid any halt in negotiations, thus explained that the Duke was actually suggesting an alternative between Pinerolo and the money, leaving the King's mind to choose. Tessé proposed a different exchange: Luserna Valley to France and Casale and the whole Monferrato to Piedmont.

Gropello left and reported to San Tommaso. San Tommaso sent him back to tell Tessé that it was a negotiation about the skin of a bear which had not yet been captured, and by the way it would be a long and very complicated thing, and in case such an exchange would not be confirmed by a further general peace, it would be the seed for a new war. Then, whilst waiting for Tessé's answers after the reaction from Versailles, Victor Amadeus informed the Allies about his contacts with Tessé, and prepared the next operations.

III. Summer Operations

For the English fleet did not appear in the Mediterranean as concerted, and therefore the hope of being able to operate against France with its support on that side was lost, once Casale blockaded and the Spaniards arrived in Piedmont, H.R.H, in order not to lose the whole campaign unsuccessfully, held a council with Marquess Leganez, Marshal Caprara, Prince Eugene, Co. Pálffy and P.nce Commercy. And it was decided to engage the back of Pinarolo and reject the enemy from the heights where they stood and tighten Pinarolo. On July 19th H.R.H. along with Marshal Caprara went to the Spanish camp in San Secondo di Pinarolo, to enhance the movement on both the sides and take the enemy's back. And it was established that M/s Leganez had to march behind the Chisone in the Perosa valley. And on 21th H.R.H. with M/l Caprara and a detachment of 3,000 foot took the road to Rivoli and Avigliana, bound to Col de Bas and Prà della Bas and Cà del Coch, all hills where the enemy stood. And on 24th P.nce Eugene with another similar detachment marched to Cumiana, and another unit with 600 horses went to Val di Susa, and Pálffy to threaten S. Brigida and Pinarolo had to remain with the cavalry in the same place.[7]

By a carefully planned sequence of movements the Allies let Catinat move towards Susa, leaving Pinerolo unprotected:

---

7   The nuncio of Savoy to the Cardinal Secretary of State, Turin, 18 July 1693, in ASV, Nunziatura di Savoia, anno 1693.

The news from the camp … is that Milord Duke advanced with his troops far beyond the mountain, seizing on one side all the places along the road to Susa, whilst from the other side, Lord Marquess de Leganez, Lord Pnce Eugene and Lord di Schomberg did the same, in different ways, each of them with a large detachment, thus the French withdrew from their places.[8]

Then:

… once they got the result of deplacing the enemy without bloodshed, H.R.H., M/l Caprara, Lord P.nce Eugene and P.nce Commercy went to visit the Perosa to assess the place and determine whether to keep it or ruin it, and it was decided for the latter option.[9]

Pinerolo in itself was quite strong, but in 1692 the French had further strengthened it, building a new fort on an old bastion. This new fort of Santa Brigida, a four bastion star-pointed one, commanded the citadel of Pinerolo and was linked to it by a covered road one mile long.

Due to the strategic importance of Pinerolo, at the eve of the war, as we know, Catinat had been ordered by Louvois to hold it at any cost. That is why, when going to the winter quarters in December 1692, he left there seven infantry battalions, commanded by Tessé.

At the end of winter, whilst he was still in Exilles, waiting for reinforcements from France, Catinat sent Tessé five more battalions out of his 47 and three squadrons. This enhanced the garrison to some 6,000 men. It was enough to withstand the impact of the 25,000 men with whom Victor Amadeus was approaching.

The Allies arrived in front of Pinerolo in July. They left a portion of their troops on their rear, to counter any French relieving army. All the others were committed against Santa Brigida. The idea was simple: Santa Brigida commanded Pinerolo's citadel, once Santa Brigida was seized, Pinerolo had to surrender.

The siege was uneasy. The Allied logistical effort was impressive, and the fights were hard. Once the batteries were achieved, on 5 August the Allied artillery opened fire. In less than two weeks an avalanche of more than 6,500 different shells[10] fell on Santa Brigida, devastating its fortifications. Tessé defended the place tenaciously, and his adversaries fought as tenaciously as him. In spite of high casualties, the Allied troops managed to settle fast, and on the night of 7–8 August attempted an attack to Santa Brigida: they lost 800 dead and got no result. They pretended to have won and on the following morning, 8 August, Prince Eugene:

---

8   *Idem*, Turin, 23 July 1693, in ASV, Nunziatura di Savoia, anno 1693.

9   *Idem*, Turin, 29 July in ASV, Nunziatura di Savoia, anno 1693.

10   That is to say 781 mortar bombs 10 calibre, whose weight was between 46 and 49 kilogrammes (about five *rubbi*), 567 mortar bombs 8 calibre (35–37 pounds, or four *rubbi*), about 1,200 12-pound cannon balls (about 4.5 kilogrammes each) and about 4,000 30-pound cannon balls, each weighing about 11 kilogrammes.

… [talked] with the governor of the fort, who, being sick, had to be brought up the walls and said that [the fortress] was not yet in state of surrendering. H.H. replied that he could now have more advantageous conditions than he could later. The other replied that the breach was not made yet and that at that time he would think about it, for he knew that he had to deal with Generous Princes and that they knew what his duty and the rules of war did foresee.[11]

Given the bad result of the negotiation, Victor Amadeus ordered shelling to restart, and they opened two wide breaches by 13 August. Then the defenders retreated in the citadel on the 16th, after having blown up all remaining Santa Brigida fortifications.

The retreat cost the French no casualties; and this made suspicions arise among the Allies – though unaware of the activity of Gropello – about a possible French-Savoyard collusion.

Meanwhile, 5,000 soldiers and good artillery came from the Duchy of Milan, but it took a long time to put the pieces in battery, for only on 20 September could they start firing against the citadel of Pinerolo. On 25 August the Allied began general shelling, using 80 cannons and 15 mortars. The fire damaged houses and walls, but not the garrison, which suffered light casualties.

It seemed the siege would have to continue indefinitely, considering that, by the end of August, compared to the 35 dead of the garrison, the Allies had lost about 3,000 men; to be increased to 6,000 when adding the deserters, the sick and wounded. This was the discouraging Allied situation in front of Pinerolo when Victor Amadeus was informed that Catinat had reinforcements from the Rhine and Catalonia and was coming from Susa.

Not to get locked by the enemies, credited to be 40,000 strong, the Duke summoned two war councils, and on 1 October ordered the siege to be lifted. The Allies let the few standing walls of Santa Brigida be blown up, sent the heavy artillery to Turin along with the mass of the carriages and marched against the enemy.

IV. Autumn Battle: Orbassano or the Battle at Marsaglia Plateau

On 4 October 1693, on the Marsaglia Plateau, or rather on the left of the Chisola creek, near Orbassano, thus very close to Turin, the French army clashed with the Allied army from Pinerolo.

Just before nine o'clock in the morning, 40,000 French attacked along the whole line of the entire 25,000 Austro-Hispano-Piedmontese front, pressing against both the opposing wings. The Allied right wing – composed of Piedmontese, Imperialists and Religioners – held quite well and repulsed all the enemy attempts. The French Gendarmerie smashed the Guards and the

---

11   *Relazione dell'assedio di Santa Brigida*, 14 August 1693, in AST, Sez I, Lettere Ministri, Spagna – Mazzo 39, H.R.H. the Duke of Savoy to Knight Commander Operti.

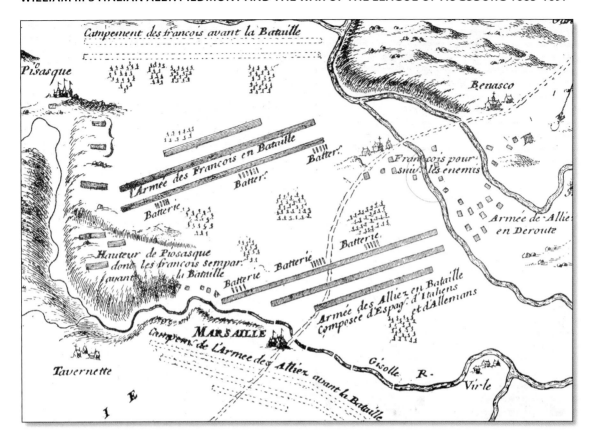

86. Plan of the Battle of Marsaglia, 1693

Religioner regiments and opened a breach, but was stopped by the cavalry units just behind, who counter-charged:

> … and five infantry battalions were entirely cut to pieces by our cavalry and most of them by H.R.H. Red Dragoons. … Never had a victory been more certain for us than this one, whilst it was hoped that the left had at least held if not charged the enemy, but when some squadrons of the Cavalry of the State[12] made a withdrawal and some battalions from the first line of the left wing retreated, no General Officers were found to repair such a disorder …[13]

wrote the author of the Piedmontese official report. And added:

> The truth is that the troops of the left wing retired immediately, the first line did not make, one can say, any resistance and that the second line, far from rushing to support, made a hurried withdrawal from which the loss of the battle derived, because had the left wing held up somehow, the right could charge and let us have a victory which we already hoped.[14]

---

12 'State' means the Spanish-ruled Duchy of Milan.
13 *Relazione ufficiale piemontese*, rep. in *La guerra della Lega di Augusta…* cit., p. 114.
14 *Relazione della battaglia di Orbassano*, Ufficiale – riservata, in AST, Sezione 1ª, Imprese Militari, Mazzo 4, n. 26.

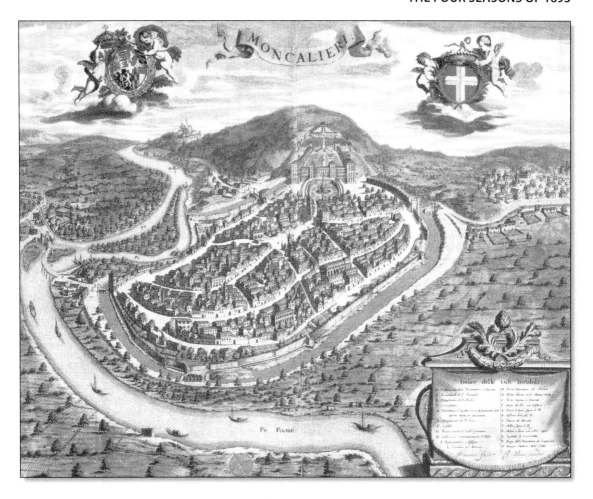

87. Moncalieri

As a matter of fact, the indecision of the Allied command generated a one and a half hour inaction, and due to that lack of orders the collapse of the left wing, mainly composed of troops of the crowns of Spain. Thus by 11:00 a.m. the French pierced the line. The White Cross Regiment tried to hold:

> … seeing the Tercio di Bonesana collapsing on them, and the enemy cavalry charging it, they made those actions in the time allowed. They threw away their muskets and, with sword in hand, sold at a high price the lives of their Officers and Soldiers, and actually only 200 of the latter remained alive, and half of the Officers with the Commander; only one captain was saved unharmed and two lieutenants.[15]

Enemies flooded everywhere and started encircling the Allies: 'And not be enveloped' on the right wing also, it was necessary to:

> … charge on every side. Which was made by the outmost strength, for, having taken back from the enemies many colours they had seized on the left wing, and

---

15 *Relazione ufficiale piemontese*, rep. in *La guerra della Lega di Augusta...* cit., p. 115.

without counting them, our right wing counts more than 25 enemy [colours], and many pairs of kettledrums; with all this we had to withdraw.[16]

Prince Eugene, and Marshal Co: Caprara, were warned about the bad condition of their left; and, however, since they always fought with remarkable advantage, they exploited it to withdraw their right, step by step, in good order. They rescued eight cannons to safety, and they would have taken away some others had the train horses not perished in advance.[17]

Some 6,000 Allies remained on the ground, French casualties were probably as many.[18] The Piedmontese lost very few.[19]

Due to this victory, Catinat seized back Santa Brigida, or its ruins, re-opened his way to Casale and enforced the Allies to remove that blockade. But, once more, Victor Amadeus proved to be a skilful military organiser because:

… after a short time, having gathered those missing in action, and joined them to the others withdrawn from the blockade of Casale, the Most Serene of Savoy gathered twenty four thousand fighters; with whom he advanced to Moncalieri on a favourable place, no more than five miles far from the French camp at Prolonghera. Nor did other things follow by now; the winners being happy of having obtained a large quantity of food, and other profits from Piedmont. Then they passed across the Alps.[20]

---

16 *Idem*, p. 114.

17 Ivi.

18 'Casualties on our side, after the calculation of the tables, are reduced, between cavalry and infantry and dragoons from all the nations to 5,500 men out of action including injured, dead and prisoners: Imperial = 1,500, Spanish = 2,500, Piedmontese and Religioners = 1,500. That of the enemies is calculated by themselves, according to what was reported by many deserters and prisoner officers sent back to some 6–7,000 out of combat and that particularly the Gendarmerie, consisting of 1,600 horses, has suffered greatly, and it's assumed to be reduced to a half.'; Report of the battle of Orbassano. Official – classified, cit., conclusion. Besides, it must be underlined that the French casualties were calculated in different ways, and were assumed to be between a minimum of 1,000 up to a maximum of around 8,000 dead, wounded, deserters, those missing in action, and prisoners.

19 The Duke of Schomberg died after that battle. He was succeeded as Duke of Schomberg by his brother, Meinhardt, 3rd Duke of Schomberg. His regiment was given to a French Huguenot in British service, Henri de Massue, 1st Viscount (later 1st Earl) of Galway, thus it was later known as the Galway Regiment.

20 Ferrari, G., *Vita e campeggiamenti del Serenissimo Principe Francesco Eugenio di Savoja, supremo comandante degli eserciti Cesarei, e dell'Impero*, Napoli, appresso Domenico Lanciano, 1754, pp. 31–32.

16

1694: A Year of Negotiation

I. Problems

By the end of 1693 Louis XIV's armies had won at Fleurus, Staffarda, Marsaglia, Steenkirk, and Neerwinden, occupied Catalonia, Savoy, Nice, a part of Piedmont, a wide portion of Flanders and mastered Mons, Namur, Charleroi, Dixmude and many other Flemish cities. The war was not going as well as the Allies may have hoped, but Louis too was not that happy with its results.

In his corner, Victor Amadeus too was quite unhappy. His objectives were known. He wanted to expel the foreign powers from Piedmont, to regain the full control of the Alpine passes, and to increase his territory. But none of these results were in sight, better: there was no result in sight at all. Austria did not support the Italian front. Britain and the Seven Provinces were late in payments. The British fleet appeared only once in the Mediterranean. Montmélian had been lost. Pinerolo had not fallen, and Casale was barely blockaded. As things were, it was not realistic to think of a victorious conclusion to the war. Meanwhile, it was unclear when such a conclusion, any conclusion, may come, and, moreover it was all but sure that, during the final peace negotiations, Savoy would be able to get what it wanted, above all Casale and Pinerolo.

There were further problems affecting military and political activities. The harvest in Piedmont was becoming worse and worse, thus incomes and revenues did not provide as much as needed. In January 1694 the Duke forbade any export of wheat and grains, for the last harvest had been poor, and it was unclear how good the next would be. To avoid speculation, he ordered to keep the grain market closed until the harvest in July. In late spring it was clear the 1694 harvest would be worse than that of 1693, also if nobody yet knew that the worst of all would occur the next year, 1695. In spite of these great problems the army increased to a little less than 18,500, including 15,745 foot, and 2,682 cavalry and dragoons, still exploiting the militia, and getting professional recruits from Switzerland to fill the gaps in Swiss units in Savoy service.

The defeat suffered at Marsaglia and the poor harvest let Victor Amadeus represent to the Maritime Powers how hard it was to manage the war. Thus, after Marsaglia, Britain and the Dutch increased their support by another

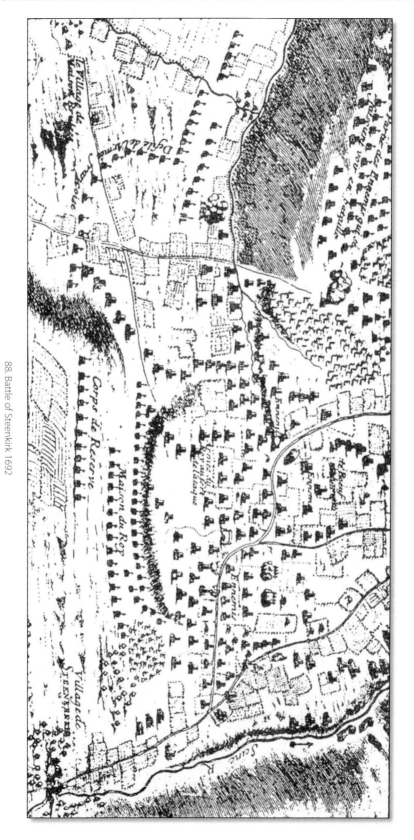

88. Battle of Steenkirk 1692

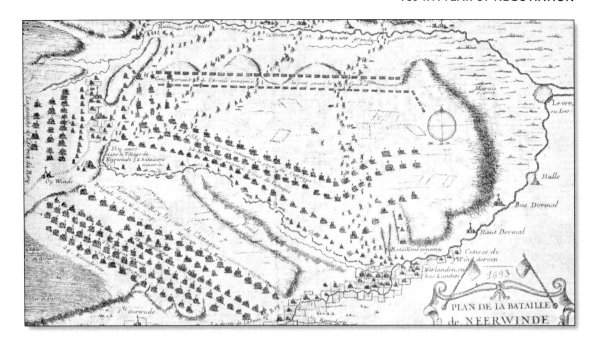

12,000 *scudi* a month. In theory Victor Amadeus now got 48,000 *scudi* a month, one third – 16,000 – paid by The Hague, and two third – 32,000 – by London. It was the largest subsidy paid by Britain during that war, and considering the whole war, the British treasury gave a little less than 6.7 million *scudi*, that is to say roughly 5,350,000 English pounds.[1]

It was the largest funding, of course, but it was always late, and charged by fees. Actually, by the end of 1693 campaign, Britain still owed Victor Amadeus 100,000 *scudi*. They were paid in December, but covered only the period including September 1693, thus they did not include the recently agreed increase. The same happened with the 50,000 *scudi* special grant William III and the States General promised to fill the losses consequent to Marsaglia. Moreover in 1694 in Amsterdam, de la Tour had to face an unexpected eight percent raise in the exchange costs in one year, thus the amount of the subsidy by the Maritime Powers seemed in fact further reduced due to financial fees and costs, but King William intervened and decided to pay also those exchange costs, to let Turin integrally receive the expected sum.

In 1694 British funding to Victor Amadeus became a bit more problematic. The British Treasury founded an agreement with two prominent London bankers, Herne and Evans.[2] They had to remit the October 1693–October 1694 subsidy to be paid in Genoa or Leghorn in six parts. The first – 128,000 pieces of eight – had to be paid in April 1694. Then there had to be four more

---

1   In 1670 a British Guinea's weight was 8.387 grammes of gold 11/12, title 916/000, whilst a French Louis' weight was 6.724 grammes title 910/000.

2   Herne and Evans were considered very reliable for in 1692 they advanced, together with John Childs, 50,000 pounds to the crown to meet the expenses of the government of Ireland, and in 1692–94 they also remitted money to the British army in Flanders.

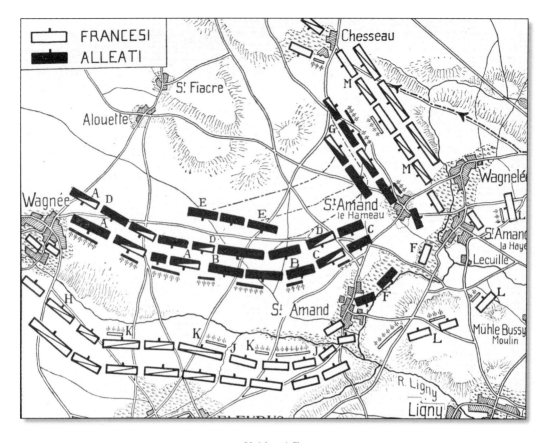

90. (above): Fleurus
91. (below): Mons besieged in 1691

92. (above): Leghorn – the fortress
93. (below): Map of Leghorn

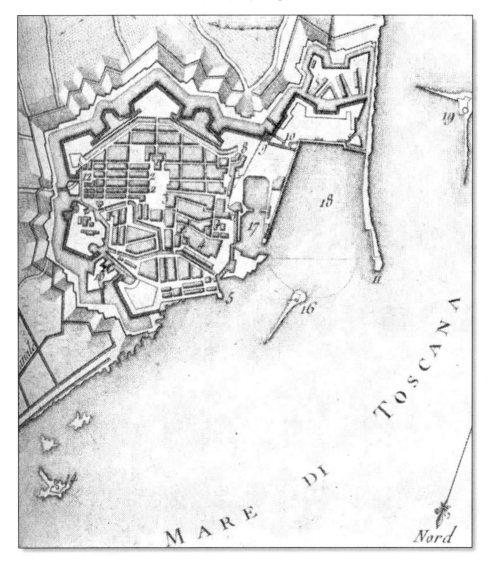

payments until September, and the sixth and last had to be made in October. But this operation was not free of charge. This time the system more or less worked, because in November 1694 the global British arrears were only 10,000 *scudi*. But de la Tour had greater troubles than the previous year in finding letters of change in Amsterdam and in London, and some of those he found were rejected, due to the lack of funding covering their guarantee.

Now, in 1694, France suffered a heavy famine. The wheat harvest was much less than necessary and Versailles ordered the generals to slow down operations on less important fronts, to save forces. Catinat was on the defensive and limited his movements as much as possible. Such French inactivity had an immediate impact. The Imperialists acted accordingly, for they could not fight against the Ottomans and Hungarians in the east while consuming resources on two other European fronts in the west. If one of the two could be left in peace, the best for all.

Spain had problems in holding both in Flanders and – more seriously – in Catalonia. Since Milan was defended in Piedmont, Spain did not see the need for greater efforts in Italy: on the contrary, the less her army provoked the French in Piedmont, the less the risks of seeing a French invasion in Lombardy. As a result, the Spanish commitment in Piedmont was reduced to 13,000 men – 10,000 foot and 3,000 cavalry – who in fact were fewer, for only 8,000 foot were actually at arms. Spain needed to focus on Catalonia, and after the defeat suffered in June at Palamos, with the loss of 8,000 men and of the whole artillery and supply train, the situation appeared to be dramatic there.

The French too were exhausted. Sustainability on three different fronts was not easy, especially when thinking of the logistical problems due to two of those fronts being across the mountains – the Pyrenees and the Alps – and further enhanced by the systemic disorganisation of the French supplies.

Louis XIV was seriously looking at a possibility, any possibility, for ending the war. According to him, the Allies were like the bricks of a wall. Had one of them left the Alliance by a separated peace, the wall would collapse. Thus, contacts were established in Rome, among the German Princes, in Flanders, and in Italy.

II. Negotiations Before the Campaign

William III too wished the end of the war, but he could not accept an enforced peace. In fact, negotiations with the Maritime Powers began only in the last months of 1693 and Louis played on two different tables at the same time. In Brussels one of his agents, the Abbot Morel de Saint-Arnoul, met Dijkveld in 1693, whilst a healthy merchant acting as the Polish resident in Amsterdam, Francisco Mollo, started meeting the burgomasters of Amsterdam after 1694. On the other hand, both Denmark and Sweden acted, the latter seeking to play the role of mediator.

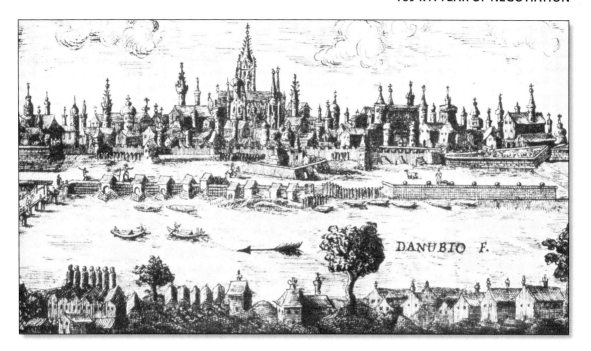

94. Vienna

On 29 November 1693, Louis sent Catinat a letter melting threats and promises to the Duke of Savoy[3] and speaking about possible negotiations. It is not clear why did he chose Catinat instead of Tessé, and what exactly happened later, but also if this letter is reported by Sirtema, it was not mentioned by the instructions later released to Tessé. According to them, the King:

> … in the month of December 1693 gave the aforesaid Sieur Count de Tessé two projects of a treaty to be concluded with the Duke of Savoy … His Majesty also added to those two projects the draft of a marriage contract between Monseigneur the Duke of Burgundy and Madam Luisa of Savoy … and he gave the said Lord Count de Tessé a plenipotence to agree with the aforesaid Lord Duke of Savoy or with his ministers about all the articles of the said projects.[4]

The Marquess di San Tommaso, after the Duke's order, invited Tessé to Turin. Tessé came on 30 December 1693, dressed as a coachman, and as reported in his memoirs was received by Victor Amadeus. The Duke, after some courteous words, declared that first of all he would make as much as he could to get in Vienna a pacification of Italy. Had he not succeeded, he would inform the concerned parties.

Victor Amadeus' next step was to send Abbot Grimani to Vienna to reveal to Leopold I the intentions of France. Grimani had to underline the damage suffered by Piedmont in the last four years, and assure the Emperor of Victor's sincere devotion to the League. But, on the other hand, Grimani

---

3   Sirtema, op. cit., pp. 400–401.

4   *Recueil des instructions données aux ambassadeurs et ministres de France: Savoie-Sardigne et Mantoue*, tome I (14th of the collection); Instructions to Tessé, on 18 March 1696, pp. 174–178, rep. in Moscati, op. cit., p. 42.

had also to ask Leopold for the actual release of the Imperial fiefs of the Langhe mentioned in 1690. More: Grimani had to push Leopold, for the proposed engagement of the Princess of Savoy to the Duke of Burgundy made the conclusion of her marriage to Leopold's eldest son, Joseph, the King of the Romans, urgent.

At the same time in Turin Victor Amadeus kept his unfriendly attitude to France so well that, as William III told Heinsius in April: 'After the letters I got from milord Galway, we can completely rely on the Duke of Savoy's perseverance.'[5]

These optimistic words to Heinsius were written in April, when the campaign had not yet begun, negotiations were still at their starting point and, above all, when no answer yet came from Vienna. Then Leopold's answer came and was not good. In fact Grimani spent several months in Vienna and got only delays and postponements, with no conclusive answer, neither about the feuds, nor about the marriage. The only answer Grimani received was about the neutralisation of Italy: Leopold rejected it, at all; but he did not look willing to enhance the Imperial commitment. As usual, the House of Habsburg wanted all at other people's expense, an attitude they would keep also in the next wars.

Once the Emperor's answers were received, Tessé suggested Victor Amadeus ally to France. The sincere declarations the Duke made in Vienna, he said, fulfilled any need of honesty, sincerity, and loyalty to the Allied cause, thus Victor Amadeus could now feel free to get the peace everybody was invoking in Italy.

The Duke did not think it was time for such an engagement, and simply offered to arrange a dull military campaign. He could act in order to avoid any major success, thus not altering things as they were. Tessé asked him for at least a written document; but Victor Amadeus refused, for it would give Louis XIV a diplomatic weapon against him.

III. 1694 Campaign and Further Negotiations

Victor Amadeus II acted according to his promises to the French, also he obtained from Leopold I Prince Eugene's appointment as the Imperial commander in Italy.

The main military event of 1694 Italian campaign was the Allied reconquest of Santa Brigida. The French had taken and repaired it after Marsaglia. Now Eugene directed and achieved the operation within three days, by 28 August. However the seizing of Santa Brigida was anything but decisive. In the best case it could be a good preliminary local success, certainly it did not damage the enemy that much.

The Allied council of war then discussed besieging Casale. Victor Amadeus opposed such a plan, and William III too, for he feared that if such a siege failed, the Allied cause could be heavily affected during the negotiations.

---

5   William to Heinsius, 3/13 April 1694, rip, in Sirtema, op. cit., p. 423.

95. (above): Charleroi shelled in 1692
96. (below): Huy

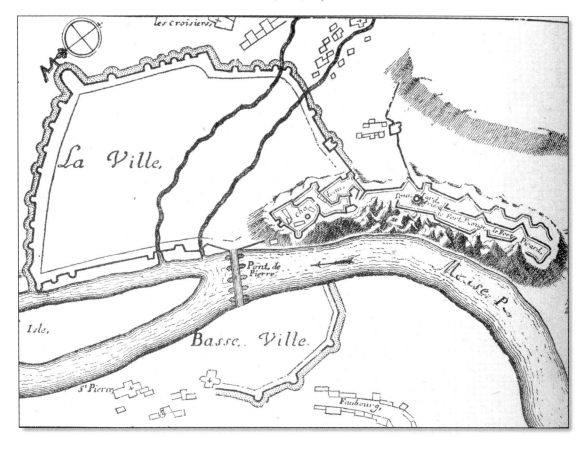

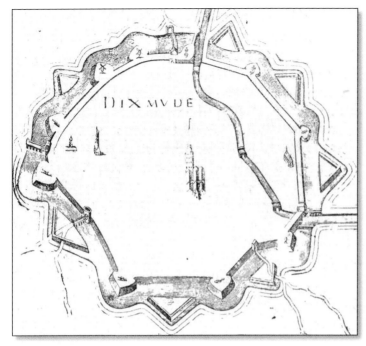

97. Dixmude

Thus Casale was blockaded, but operations started too late in the autumn, and when the snow came the siege was postponed to the following year.

William was not that wrong. During 1693 alone, the French won major battles at Heidelberg, Rosas, Huy, Landen, and Charleroi, besides Marsaglia. If it was right that in 1694 the French had been short of men and money, this did not mean that the Allies could risk a further defeat or simply a failure. Negotiation depended on military results, and military results were as a pair of scales: they could fall either way.

The French repulsed an Allied landing in France in June, and in Spain that same month won at the River Ter, then seized Palamos, Gerona and Hostalrich and marched to Barcelona; and the city could be held only due to the Spanish-Anglo-Dutch fleet activity in the Mediterranean.

In Flanders the Allies reinforced Dixmude and, on 27 September 1694, recaptured Huy. These were good results, but, on a global level it was clear that a failure in front of Casale could be a diplomatic risk.

Victor Amadeus tried once more to push Leopold about both the fiefs, and his daughter's marriage. He complained about the relatively small Imperial and Spanish support, and underlined how exhausted Piedmont was. San Tommaso wrote to Vienna that, seen the proposals by France, nobody could reject such a peace, so why should the Duke? Leopold practically did not answer.

In autumn 1694 the French–Allied talks in the Netherlands ended with a draft, and in November William III informed the Allies about the French propositions and asked for comments, and remarks. The ground was to have the Treaties of Westphalia and Nijmegen as a starting point for a general pacification. Then France had to recognise William as the King of Great Britain, and make restitution for all the conquests made since the beginning of the war, as much on Spain as on the Duke of Savoy. More: France had to give back the lands seized during the so-called *réunions* period, give Strasbourg or an equivalent for Strasbourg, to the Empire, and the same for Luxembourg to Spain. Lastly: the Duke of Lorraine had to be restored to his Duchy.

As far as he was concerned, Victor Amadeus was completely unhappy. The drafts did not speak of Casale and Pinerolo, whilst the restitution of Pinerolo to him had been explicitly foreseen in Article IV of the alliance signed in 1690. The Allies were not keeping their word. Had the peace been made that way, he would be back to 1690 situation: a client state of France, again, moreover with the Duchy devastated and weakened by a terrible five-year war.

17

Casale

I. Contacts and Attempts

Once he had seen the peace draft, Victor Amadeus urged in Vienna for the Emperor to keep his word about the Langhe and the marriage. He underlined that during the 1693–94 winter he refused the French offers and in 1694 continued the war. His envoy, the Marquess di Priero, better known in the Piedmontese dialectal way as the Marquess di Prié, asked the Emperor for a new, personal and written commitment not to sign the general peace. Leopold promised, but in his letter to Victor Amadeus dated on 18 March 1695, he insinuated that first of all the Duke had to act upon King William and the General States.

This was a problem. Mary Stuart suddenly died on 7 January 1695, and William, who was not a merry man on his own, was much more depressed and sad than usual. As de la Tour reported, during their talk William:

> Came back to the danger Y.R.H. has of being overwhelmed. He told me that this did not look so a big danger to the eyes of everybody … That Y.R.H. has been reduced to situations worst than the present one … That you have acquired by such a conduct an immortal glory. That, according to his statement, one must neither retreat nor stop when he has gone so far. That Y.H., delaying his peace until the one made by all the Allies, will bring his reputation to the highest point it may ascend. That you have in your hands the liberty and servitude of Europe. If Lord the Duke of Savoy is, due to the necessity of his own business, forced to make his own peace, beg him on my part to do it for us all; we will be extremely obliged.[1]

This was a sort of free way signal. Could it change or be confirmed? De la Tour had to talk once more with William III in London about the Savoyard situation, and later, on 25 February, reported: 'I then spoke in person to the King, and although he did not speak this so openly, he admitted enough that the Allies will not be able to support neither the war, nor your demands.'[2]

---

1   De la Tour to Victor Amadeus II, on 29 January 1695, rep in Carutti, *Diplomacy*, p. 220, note 1.
2   De la Tour to Victor Amadeus II, on 25 February 1695, rep. in Carutti, *Diplomacy*, p. 224, note 1.

98. Ercole Turinetti, Marquess di Prié / di Priero

The Duke already knew it, but wanted a further confirmation: had a general peace been arranged, could he rely on getting Pinerolo? When asked whether would he support the Duke's interests or not, William was honest, and de la Tour reported from The Hague: 'The King replied that he had that same intention, but that, frankly speaking, he did not see that we could force France to the cession of Pignerol, if we made peace in the situation we are now.'[3]

All was now clear. Victor Amadeus realised that the Allies were focusing on getting the Barrier in the Low Countries, and back from France, Strasbourg to the Empire and Luxembourg to Spain, and nothing to him. If everybody was looking only for his own interest why should he not?

Getting back Pinerolo was of basic importance, whilst Casale could not be a problem if he got something in exchange: Lombardy, for instance; and he decided to ask Madrid for it.

The 1695 campaign was next to start. No further delay could be arranged, and Victor Amadeus had to warn Tessé that he could no longer postpone the siege of Casale once the Allies arrived. Worse: this time he could no longer exploit the reasons he used the previous year not to undertake the siege.

In winter Louis XIV doubted Victor Amadeus' negotiating position to be weak, and had ordered Tessé to stop the talks. He wanted to focus on negotiation with William III, but here a surprise came. As William had feared, the draft of peace conditions distributed among the Allies caused a sole reaction: everybody wanted all, and possibly more than all, with no compromise. The obvious result was to stop the talks, because the Allies could not find an agreement among themselves. Thus, Louis realised how endangered Casale was and ordered Tessé to restart the talks with Victor Amadeus.

The Duke was aware of how complicated the Allied internal diplomatic situation was, and lost no time in playing his game: gathered his cards and started.

II. The Actual Negotiation and the Fake Siege

On the eve of 1695, funding to Piedmont was a problem as never before. In 1695 the Bank of England took direct responsibility for the payment of the

---

3   De la Tour to Victor Amadeus II, on 25 March 1695, rep. in Carutti, *Diplomacy*, p. 224, note 2.

British funding. For there were no letters of change available, and due to the firmly established and uncontested Anglo-Dutch naval power, this time the subsidy was shipped in cash and offloaded in Genoa and Leghorn, to be paid to Victor Amadeus in six monthly instalments.

The Duke, in trouble, simply reorganised his military administration and enhanced his army to the unexpected and never seen before figure of more than 23,000 men.[4] On the other hand he exploited these men as a concrete threat against France to gain advantages during the negotiation.

As the commander of the Allied army, in spring 1695 he arrived in front of Casale to besiege it. He fielded 54 cannons, 70 mortars and 25,000 men, including 6,000 Spanish and 6,000 Imperial soldiers. The French garrison was only 160 officers and 2,700 men. The weather suddenly froze on 8 April. The Duke exploited that delay and intensified his diplomatic pressure on his Most Christian uncle. He started from the already existing negotiations, and on 11 April, in spite of the low temperature and of the recent snow, he sped up the siege works and increased the artillery. On 21 April he sent Gropello to Tessé with a letter, and on the 26th he let embark on barges in Turin the cannons bound for the siege. They were shipped downstream to Casale, and he let the French know it.

The siege park had been enhanced by 20 more cannons, when Victor Amadeus met Prince Eugene and the Marquess de Leganes to discuss the incoming campaign, but at the same time he gave Tessé extensive assurances of his good faith to achieve a separate peace.

The first proposal he made to Tessé was simple. The Marquis de Crenan, governor of Casale, had to capitulate as soon as the breach was opened, and capitulation conditions would foresee the destruction of the fortifications. This was fine to both Piedmont and France. France promised to William III to give back Casale, and, once it was dismantled, it would no longer be a military tool in foreign and probably enemy hands. On the other hand, Savoy prevented the Duke of Mantua, or Spain, or France, or the Empire from obtaining such an important commanding place.

Thus the condition was accepted and Victor Amadeus agreed to destroy Casale and not to act against Pinerolo, Susa and the French metropolitan territory across the Alps until 1 November 1695, that is to say during the whole campaign. On their side, the French promised not to undertake actions against the Duke and the Allies in Italy. Both the sides promised each other not to increase their armies, and had the other Allies opposed the demolition of Casale, the Duke would leave the League and join France, according to what had been laid out in 1694.

In May the countervallation and circumvallation works were achieved. Early that same month Victor Amadeus dispatched the Count di Vernone to Madrid. Officially Vernone had to talk about the Spanish financial support; in fact, according to his instructions, he had to ask Charles II to appoint Victor Amadeus and his heirs as the perpetual governors of Milan.[5] Victor

---

4   That is to say 20,752 foot, and 2,537 cavalry and dragoons.
5   In *Diplomacy*, cit., p. 227, Carutti reports a resume of the instructions issued to Vernone on 2 May, and on 18 May, 1695.

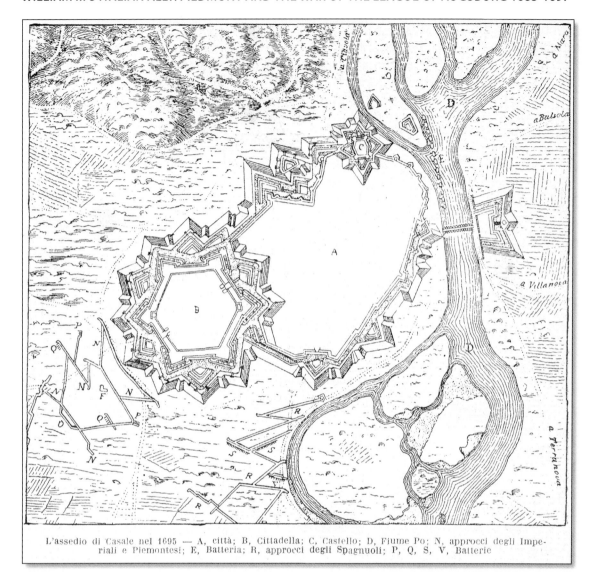

L'assedio di Casale nel 1695 — A, città; B, Cittadella; C, Castello; D, Fiume Po; N, approcci degli Imperiali e Piemontesi; E, Batteria; R, approcci degli Spagnuoli; P, Q, S, V, Batterie

99. Casale besieged by the Allies in 1695

Amadeus informed William III of what was he trying to get from Spain, and William agreed to support him in Madrid.

On 25 June 74 Allied cannons and 70 mortars started shelling Casale. The garrison answered with 210 pieces – 120 in the citadel, 30 in the castle and 60 on the city walls – but Crenan received positive orders and knew what to do: only to seem to hold.

On 26 June the trench was opened and, on 9 July the garrison was demanded for surrender. In spite of what they expected and to their outmost surprise, the Allied generals spotted the white surrender flag rise, and were informed that the Marquis de Crenan had agreed to surrender, if the citadel and all the other fortifications of Casale would be razed.

Pleased with such an opportunity to end the matter quickly, Leganes immediately accepted. Lord Galway was suspicious: why did such a fortress surrender if its magazines had still plenty of gunpowder and food, as it was confirmed by the inspections after the surrendering? Prince Eugene protested and said no: the suggested capitulation meant the enemy to be weak; by insisting, the Allies could get the fortress intact. But this was precisely what Victor Amadeus did not want, and consequently he joined Leganes to accept the French proposal, which actually was his original one. Moreover he was the supreme Allied commander, and the final decision was up to him, and he accepted, of course.

The capitulation, containing 26 articles, was signed on that same day by Leganes and the Duke. Eugene refused, for he did not consider it convenient to the Empire. That changed nothing. Crenan came out with all his men and went safely to Pinerolo. The Allied and the French sappers and miners started to work and gave the dismantled city back to the Duke of Mantua on 25 September.

By that time Victor Amadeus had been informed that Vernone had obtained no result in Spain. Had he succeeded, the Duke would be the master of Milan once Charles of Spain died, and Charles had no heirs and a real storm was expected to rise after his death, hence, having Milan in hand could be a major result. But, as said, in Madrid they refused. Once more the situation looked without a solution. The only improvement was the destruction of Casale, but it was not enough.

Victor Amadeus was sure it was time to finish the game. His military budgets in the last four campaigns increased year by year, from the 7,284,629 *liras* of November 1692–October 1693 period, through the 9,050,134 of 1693–94, and 9,919,623 of 1694–95, and were expected to reach the horrendous amount of 10,597,074 *liras* in the last budgeted year 1695–96, rocketing the total war expenditure to 50,231,823 *liras*, that is to say three times the total long-term debt the State had before the war in 1689. Of course, he received subsidies, but they did not exceed 15.7 million during the seven years of war Piedmont faced. What about the missing 35 million? Moreover, the country had been severely devastated by the French, but also by the Allied armies, and the harvest had been not that good in 1693, bad in 1694 and terrible in 1695, that is to say during the last three years. It was definitely time for a definitive agreement.

18

The Pilgrim Who Made Peace with France, and War on the Former Allies

I. The Pilgrim Who Went to Loreto and What He Did

The Grand Alliance was renewed in The Hague on 18 August 1695, and negotiations between England and France restarted the following winter. Strasbourg, Luxembourg and the Barrier were still obstacles, whilst nobody cared about Pinerolo.

This helped Victor Amadeus, for if Pinerolo was neglected, nobody actually cared about it in The Hague, Vienna, and London. So, when in spring 1696 the campaigning began, and the Allied army marched to Pinerolo, Victor Amadeus could inform Tessé, and promise to prevent the city being seized on that year. This meant that Louis XIV had to negotiate seriously, for the release of the town to Piedmont was the main condition for a separated peace.

Since long before, both Pope Innocent XII and the Republic of Venice acted in order to gain the neutrality of Italy. The Pope did not like to have an Imperial military presence in Italy and disliked the idea of a weakened France facing the Protestants. On the other hand Venice too preferred Italy to be neutral, for she had so many commitments in the Levant that needed none on her backyard. The joint Papal-Venetian initiative was more or less openly supported or at least favoured by all the Italian princes, to whom the reestablishment of the Imperial authority sounded like a threat.

Louis XIV too wanted to get at least a truce in Italy, as a first step towards a general peace, possibly according to his conditions. Piedmont seemed the only possibility he had, thus he agreed to give Pinerolo back to the House of Savoy. Pinerolo's walls and forts had to be razed, but this was the only real condition he made.

Once this obstacle was removed, there were only some details left, to be directly discussed. Meeting in Turin was impossible; meeting in Pinerolo too, for there were too many Allies around. The Dutch agent in Turin, Fagel,

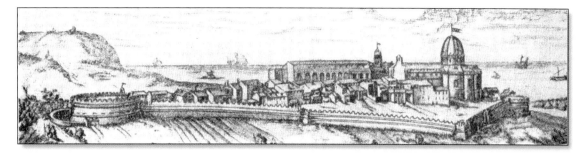

100. Loreto

was one of them, and Lord Galway was another one. Moreover the latter was quite suspicious after what occurred at the siege of Casale.

What to do? Or could somehow Victor Amadeus wait a bit more, until – let us say – the general peace? The answer was no, and it was not only a matter of politics; it was also a matter of money. As said, the military expenditure budgeted for 1695–1696 exceeded 10,500,000 *liras*. Attrition due to war had been severe in Piedmont, and the ducal treasury afforded it how it could. Taxes increased and some interventions on the coins occurred. They affected the copper coins, and the silver-coppered ones, for they both were the most used, especially for soldiers' daily wages, and also because the Treasury could gain more on their preparation than on other coins. During the war the ducal mint produced 1 million *liras* in copper and silver-copper alloy coins,[1] and introduced a new coin as an exchange for the German florins carried by the Imperial troops. Further 20,000 *liras* were minted using copper in 1695, and 98,521 and half in 1696. The result was seen in 1700, when the bad currency in copper coins was retired, and the Treasury took back more than 1 million *liras*.

The financial gap in theory had to be filled by the Anglo-Dutch funding, but we know how normally late and affected by fees it was, and in 1696 the situation was worst than ever. On that year British financial condition was so difficult that the Treasury found only a way to pay the subsidy to Savoy: de la Tour was offered with tallies.[2]

This happened because no banker in England accepted Treasury's promises for future payments, so, the Treasury decided to give de la Tour the tallies corresponding to funding. Then he was told that he had to take the tallies, sell them – which meant to lose some 12 percent – and look for exchange letters, losing an additional 10 percent. Moreover, when de la Tour looked for exchange letters, the only bankers who accepted the transaction asked for a 20 percent fee on the whole 1695–96 financial exercise.

So, the long-sought agreement with France had to be reached by Victor Amadeus, not only because it was a good political idea, but also because day by day it appeared to be the only financial solution left. But how to turn around the Allied diplomatic sentries?

---

1   The *soldi* were minted using a silver-copper alloy, whilst the denari were made of copper alone. If one recalls a *lira* to be equal to 20 *soldi*, or to 240 denari, he may easily realise how many of those coins could compose a million *liras*.

2   To know what a tally looked like, see William Hogarth's painting *The Distrest'd Poet*: the milkmaid shows her bill carved on a tally to the poet's wife.

101. Louis of Bourbon Duke of Burgundy, the grandson of Louis XIV and Victor Amadeus' son-in-law after 1696

Long, very long before, Victor Amadeus had started scattering the news that he promised to pay a pilgrimage to the Holy House in Loreto, in the Papal States as an acknowledgement for having being rescued from the smallpox by the Holy Virgin in Embrun during the 1692 expedition. Now he desired to dissolve the vow, thus announced he wanted to go to Loreto.

Before leaving, he entrusted Lord Galway with the preparation of the forthcoming campaign, and recommended that he had to be obeyed as he was the Duke in person. Lord Galway felt sure of the ducal commitment in the war, and wrote praising letters to Vienna and to London, saying that there was no doubt the Duke was seriously preparing the next operations.

Then in March Victor Amadeus left, bound for Loreto. He had a few people with him, and Annibale Maffei, a diplomat he trusted very much, was among them. Also a French diplomat dressed as a clergyman was waiting for him in Loreto, or at least it was said later.[3]

What they discussed and agreed is not directly known. Baron Carutti too, the most accurate historian of the Sabaudian diplomacy and the author of the most important biography of Victor Amadeus II, admitted that he could find nothing in the archives, for most of what the Duke and Tessé said was never written down. Indirect evidence about what they decided may come from the treaty later agreed on 19 June, and then signed by Gropello and Tessé in Pinerolo on 29 June 1696. It said that:

> There will be forever from now on a stable and sincere peace between the King and his Kingdom, and His Royal Highness the Duke of Savoy and his States, as if it had never been troubled.[4]

Then Victor Amadeus promised to leave the Grand Alliance and to do everything possible to obtain from his soon-to-be former Allies the neutrality

---

3   See Ottieri, Francesco Maria, *Istoria delle guerre avvenute in Europa e particolarmente in Italia per la successione della monarchiu delle Spagne dall'anno 1696 all'anno 1725* (Rome, 1753), book I, p. 54; and Muratori, Ludovico Antonio, *Annali d'Italia*, 13 vols. (Napoli, 1870), vol. 12th, year 1696: 'The mischievous people, who did not believe such a prince to bother himself as much as to go so far to implore the protection of the Virgin, rather thought that under the cloak of piety it was concealed a secret meeting with some unknown person about his business, and this was, no matter how much the fame said, a French minister disguised as a clergy.'

4   *Traité de paix entre Victor Amé II Duc de Savoie et Louis XIV Roi de France*, done in Turin on 29 August 1696, premise, rep. in Solaro della Margarita, op. cit., vol. II, p. 155

102. Nice – fortifications in
the 17th century

of Italy, under the guarantee by the Pope and Venice. He promised also to
join Louis XIV in a defensive and offensive league until the general peace,
acting, as good ally, with the French troops against the State of Milan and all
those who wanted to oppose the treaty. In addition – *au surplus* – 'as a clear
evidence of the actual return of the King's friendship to His Royal Highness,
His Majesty' wanted 'to really consent' and promised that the fortifications
of the 'City and Citadel of Pinerolo, forts of Santa Brigida, Perosa, and other
forts depending on them' will be razed and demolished at his own expense:

> … [giving all] in the hands of Victor Amadeus, as well as the lands and domains
> included under the name of Governorate of Pinerolo, and which had belonged
> to the House of Savoy before the transfer that Victor Amadeus the first Duke of
> this name had made to King Louis XIII, and the demolished City, Citadel and
> forts, and territory, will as well be remitted to His Royal Highness to keep them
> in sovereignty and to rejoice fully and in perpetuity by Him and His Successors in
> the future, as of something belonging to them on their own.[5]

Just pro forma, for probably nobody actually believed it, Victor Amadeus
committed himself and his successors not to rebuild the destroyed fortifications,
and not to build new ones; but everybody knows that one says so many things…
Furthermore, His Majesty would:

> … [return] to His said Royal Highness the conquered countries, places, castle
> of Montmeillan, of Nice, Villafranca, of Susa, and others with no exception,

---

5   *Traité de paix…*cit., article I, rep. in Solaro, cit., vol. II, pp. 156–7.

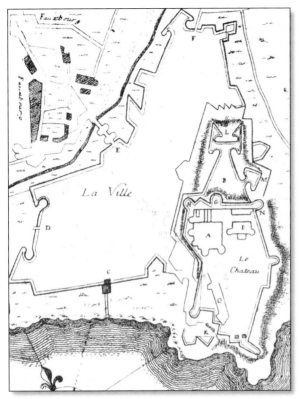

103. Nice – map of the city in 1692

without demolition, and in their entirety, with the quantity of war and mouth ammunitions, cannons and artillery, and all which they were provided and equipped of when they fell into the hands of His Majesty.[6]

Moreover, according to Article IV, the court of Versailles would assure the marriage of the Duke of Burgundy to Maria Adelaide of Savoy, Victor Amadeus' daughter.

The following Article V granted to Victor Amadeus the Royal Treatment he already enjoyed by the courts of Madrid, Vienna, and London.

So, after six years of war, the Duke achieved his goals and could be considered politically satisfied. Only, now, once the Treaty signed, the foreign troops had to leave Italy and actually re-enter Germany[7] – the Imperialists – and Milan, the Spaniards. How to let them do it?

II. The Comedy of Horrors

Louis XIV ratified the Treaty on 6 July 1696. On that same day by two separate letters, one addressed to the Pope, the other to the Venetians, he promised to give back the Duke the city of Pinerolo, his dependencies and Perosa, as well as the conquests made during the war.

According to Carutti,[8] the pacts were inserted into two separate documents. The former, divided into 14 articles, concerned the territorial matters and delegated the Duke to negotiate the neutrality of Italy with the Emperor. The latter document consisted of 22 articles, and the most important stated that, in case no neutrality was obtained, Victor Amadeus would join his army to the French.

And here started the comedy Louis and Victor agreed on, which, due to the casualties, resulted a real comedy of horrors.

Catinat advanced from Pinerolo to Rivoli. Then, by a threatening letter, he announced the siege of Turin, and the sack and fire of the surrounding country, unless the Duke accepted a generous offer by the King. The offer was, of course, the already signed and ratified pacts, which among the Allies nobody but Victor Amadeus knew to have been made.

---

6   *Idem*, p. 157.
7   Thanks to the Venetian mediation and guarantee, the Treaty said: 'and if there are some of the said troops who, in fact, enter the States of the Republic of Venice, they will be considered to be returned to Germany since the moment they will be on the Venetian State, and returned to the said Republic of Venice.' This meant that the Treaty could work as soon as the last Imperial soldier arrived in Bergamo or Brescia, thus in Eastern Lombardy, at that time part of the Republic of Venice.
8   Carutti, *Diplomacy*, cit., p. 232.

The Duke properly played his character. He published a brave manifesto calling the people to the war without mercy. The French answered the same way and massacres started by both sides. Victor summoned a council of war and put the question flat on the table: it was an extreme situation, thus an extreme action was due; a decisive battle, win or die once forever; what did they think? Their reaction was just as he expected. The Allied generals had heard rumours about the impressive strength of the French. Catinat was a gallant and skilled general who won both the times they engaged him, the Imperial contingent was not yet arrived, the Spaniards were relatively few and were now focusing mostly on sea warfare, thus the only solution was to harass the French as much as possible with guerrillas, until the arrival of the Imperial troops. After such a generally shared opinion, Victor Amadeus proposed to let Catinat know that he would accept the peace and the neutrality only if all the Allies agreed and that, by the way, he would never raise in arms against the Alliance, and ended asking for a one-month truce. The Allied generals agreed. And obviously Catinat accepted it too.

Couriers were immediately dispatched to the Allied capitals, and provoked appalled reactions. Leopold I rejected any neutrality and sent Count Mansfeld to Turin. Mansfeld had to underline to the Duke all the dangers of this new French friendship. On one side the Duke would get back his lands, but actually he would be back under Louis XIV's rule. Moreover, after such a desertion he would be rejected from any future alliance and would never more find support.

Leganes supported Mansfeld, but he felt much more unsafe, for if Piedmont became neutral Catinat's next step would be Milan. The Duke protested he was only trying to do the best for his country, acting according the Pope's and Venice's wishes, not forgiving that the general peace, that is to say the neutralisation of Italy, was deeply desired by all the Italian princes.

William III was informed by Victor Amadeus by a letter written on 17 June,[9] which he received on the 24th. The news made him quite upset, but what could he do? He opposed the arrangement, for he realised quite well what a disaster such a separated peace would be, but he was far away and Louis was close. He had always honestly admitted to de la Tour that he could do nothing more than he was doing, and here the result was. Moreover, he realised very soon what was in the wind in capitals other than Turin. On 26 June he wrote to Heinsius:

> I realise, from what they write from Vienna, that we should not expect a positive answer from that Court; the language used by Kinsky is gallant; but if business go badly in Piedmont, we shall have to speak in a different tone, and if peace is concluded separately, I'm afraid we must blindly accept the conditions that France will see fit to offer.[10]

On the other hand the Imperial attitude too was a concern:

---

9   See in in Sirtema, op. cit., p. 556, note 2.
10   William to Heinsius, 24 June 1696, rip, in Sirtema, op. cit., p. 556.

The answer written by Count Kinsky is, with no doubt, the most bizarre olla-podrida I have read in my life. It tends principally not to consent directly to the secret negotiation, whilst it tolerate that they can be undertaken; that is the form, to express myself in the same terms than Count Kinsky's. As for the material part, it is positive: the restitution of Strasbourg and Lorraine; the whole question rolls on these two points. When suddenly communicating this to Callière, I'm afraid I'd give him an opportunity to break all the negotiation.[11]

William made what he could to let the war in Italy go on. He ordered to no longer pay funding to de la Tour – whom he correctly assessed to have been unaware of the negotiations – and stated he would address the money directly to Lord Galway. But in the same letter, dated on 14 July, he admitted that in Amsterdam there was no will for a further resistance, and in Vienna they seemed ready to accept the neutralisation of Italy:

If … the Imperials recognise the neutrality of Italy, I do not see how we can continue the war without expose us to a sure ruin, and in this case, we shall be forced to receive such a peace as France will see fit to give it to us.[12]

So, neither the promised money nor the expected soldiers came from the Allies, only a lot of words, more or less harsh; and Victor Amadeus went ahead.

On 29 August 1696, a few days before the end of the truce, San Tommaso and Tessé signed a treaty substituting and basically confirming in every detail the agreements signed in June. The treaty made Savoy completely free from any French intrusion or influence, and engaged the Duke to reduce his army to no more than 7,500 men – 6,000 in Piedmont and 1,500 across the Alps – until the general peace.

Then Victor Amadeus demanded the Allies accept the treaty and the neutralisation of Italy before 16 September. They refused. He joined Catinat's army and a new war started.

III. The Turn of the Screw

On 28 June 1696 the Emperor had ordered Prince Eugene to assess with Leganes and Galloway if, in the case of a Piedmontese defection, the Allied troops could continue the campaign without, or even against, the troops of the Duke of Savoy. Had they received all the expected soldiers, in theory they could, but, actually, the most of the Imperial soldiers were still missing when, on 18 September 1696, two days after the stated term, operations restarted.

Victor Amadeus' 24,000 men joined Catinat's forces, composed a manoeuvring mass 50,000 strong, and marched along the Po to besiege Valenza. Local peasants fled immediately, and panic spread. By 9 September the Allied troops were all out of Piedmont. Leganes had asked for a further

---

11   William to Heinsius, 2 July 1696, rep., in Sirtema, op. cit., p. 557.
12   William to Heinsius, 19 July 1696, rep. in Sirtema, op. cit., p. 562.

50,000 *scudi* in August, then on 22 August had called to arms the Lombard militia, which was now garrisoning many places along the border, but this did not prevent the French and Piedmontese reaching Valenza, opening the trench and starting the siege.

The Spaniards were worried, for the place reacted less and less to the enemy. They had no more men or resources, unless the Imperial reinforcements came, but they did not come. So, the Allies looked for an agreement. Leganes and Mansfeld met San Tommaso in Pavia and on 7 October 1696, in Vigevano they concluded the peace. They signed two copies. The first said that His Royal Highness would undertake the negotiation about the neutrality of Italy. The second said that His Royal Highness would be the mediator of the general peace, offering and accepting the proposals by the Most Christian King universally to everybody, and individually to each of the Allies. Thus it would be up to the Duke to assign the terms for the answers and to intervene in the final treaty with all the guarantees that the other Allies would take.

This was the true treaty, according to the declaration made by Leganes to San Tommaso. The other copy was made only to be shown to the Emperor. Mansfeld insisted on writing this second version, 'to let, with a plausible reason, the Emperor withdraw his troops from Italy, which he disliked very much.'[13] But Leopold refused to ratify it, for he supposed it to be strongly opposed by Britain and the Netherlands too.

He was wrong. William was upset with Austria. As soon as the last week of July he had already written to Heinsius:

> It is clear that the Emperor's ministers have no scruple in taking the most important resolutions, and in implementing them without our participation; thus it will exempt us, on our side, from being as much scrupulous as we are, and we shall act in the future according to our particular convenience.[14]

The Dutch acted accordingly, and Leopold, left alone, in the end had to accept the Treaty. The only thing he could do was not to ratify that part of the article concerning the negotiation of peace in Italy to be made through the Duke of Savoy.

Back to September, according to the Treaty, hostilities had to stop from the day it was signed and the French had to leave the siege of Valenza. Then the Imperial, French and Spanish troops had to leave, and the Duke of Savoy had to occupy Pinerolo.

The Austrians trickily tried not to leave Milan, for, they said, their soldiers had not yet received their wages. Thus, they said, the Italian princes, as the feudal lords of the Empire, as well as the Republics of Genoa and Luques, had to pay wages and travel to the Imperial troops, that is to say 300,000 doubles, whilst the governor of Milan had to provide food to the French, who, otherwise, would loot Lombardy. There was not that much that could be done. Those were the Imperial rules and the Imperial army could enforce them. The

---

13   Carutti *Diplomacy*, op. cit., p. 239.
14   William to Heinsius on 23 July 1696, in Sirtema, op. cit., p. 568.

104. Cosimo III de' Medici, Grand-Duke of Tuscany

Grand Duke of Tuscany paid 75,000; the Duke of Modena 40,000. Ferdinando Gonzaga paid 40,000 as the Duke of Mantua, and 25,000 as the Marquess of Monferrato. The Duke of Parma gave 36,000; the Republic of Genoa 40,000; the small Republic of Lucca 30,000; and the Pope voluntarily contributed with 40,000.

This greed by the Austrians caused bad consequences in a few years, and worst consequences within less than a generation. In the short term, when the War of the Spanish Succession began in 1701, all the Italian princes supported the House of Bourbon, and this was a major obstacle to the Imperial army during five long years. But longer-termed consequences were worse and basically originated the War of the Quadruple Alliance in 1715.

Going back to 1696, William III was absolutely upset with Victor Amadeus, and with the Austrians too, but he was a good politician and knew when it was necessary to accept a situation he did not like. Incidentally, both the Seven Provinces and Britain were short of money, and their financial situation was not good. Both the Emperor and Spain were gallantly declaring their will to go on with the war, but in fact were looking for further money and support by London and The Hague. Asking the Parliament in London for further money and men in these conditions would be useless and perhaps dangerous. It was clear that there was no possibility left but the general peace, and William acted accordingly. In December he wrote to Heinsius:

> I realise more and more that the Imperialists seek to avoid negotiation; it is an incomprehensible thing when I consider their situation; but I think they are trying to let our negotiations begun in Holland fail, which would not be good for us.
>
> Personally, I am reluctant to admit the Duke of Savoy in the general guarantee of peace; for I can not forgive so easily the infamous trick he has just played us. I do not see how the mediation of Venice can be very useful to us, although I expect nothing but troubles from Sweden; but, if we need a second mediator, Denmark or Portugal seem to me more suitable.[15]

The game, the wargame, was over now; it was time for diplomats to sit and discuss.

---

15   William III to Heinsius, on 27 November / 7 December 1696, rep. in Sirtema, op. cit., vol. 6, p. 593.

19

The Peace of Rijswijk

Peace talks made things ripe enough to negotiate the peace. The peace conference was held in Holland. The Allied ambassadors had to lodge in The Hague, the French in Delft, five miles away. The meetings had to be held in the manor of Rijswijk, halfway between the two cities. The Swedish Baron of Lilienroth and Count Bonde mediated in the name of the King of Sweden.

Victor Amadeus II committed de la Tour and the Count of Frichignono as his representatives to the peace conference. They had not to demand to be recognised as ambassadors, but simply to care of the interests of Piedmont and to implement them.

As the Duke underlined, their main task was to insert into the final treaty:

> … what was stipulated here on the 29th of the past August, between the Most Christian King and us … about the particular peace of Italy, the restitution of the occupied places, the cession of Pinerolo and the lands depending on it, and the marriage convention of the princess my daughter, with the appropriate renouncements.[1]

The French-Savoyard peace treaty had to be confirmed, not by a slight mention in one or two articles of the general Treaty, but by a specific part of the Treaty, in order to let everybody see that Piedmont's interests were essential to the concerned powers, and were a main part of the general peace. Moreover, it was necessary to modify the article in the Treaty of Münster, which tied Pinerolo to France.[2]

The conference was immediately troubled by the Imperial and Spanish ambassadors, who demanded this and that. William more or less found an agreement with France, and in spite of what the Emperor could say, ordered his ambassadors to sign.

On 20 September 1697:

---

1   Rep. in Carutti, *Diplomacy*, op. cit., p, 242.
2   Duke's instructions to President de la Tour and Count Frichignono for the conference in Rijsvijk, rep. in Carutti, *Diplomacy*, op. cit., ivi.

105. Victor Amadeus II Duke of Savoy at the age of at least 30

In the name of God and of the Most Holy Trinity to all the presents and to all next to come, let it be known that during the bloodiest war which Europe has long been afflicted by, it pleased Divine Providence to prepare for Christianity the end of its evils.[3]

Thus, thanks to the mediation of the glorious memory of Charles XI, by the grace of God King of Sweden, of the Goths and the Vandals, it was agreed that: Dutch and Spaniards would jointly guard a band of fortresses – the Barrier – on the border between the Spanish Low Countries and France, to deter and stop from the start any French offensive against the Netherlands. France lost a small part of the lands gained 20 years ago at Nijmegen and the Duchies of Lorraine and Bar, but kept Alsace and its border on the Rhine from Philippsburg to Basel. Louis XIV recognised William III as the legitimate King of England and abandoned James Stuart, who had been in France since 1688, and as far as Savoy was concerned:

Since it is important to the public tranquillity that the peace concluded in Turin on August 29th, 1696 between His Majesty and His Royal Highness is exactly observed, it was considered good to confirm it and include it in the present Treaty, and in all its points, such as they are contained in the copy signed and sealed by the Plenipotentiaries of Savoy, and which will be joint to the present Treaty, for the maintenance of which Treaty and the present Their Majesties give His Royal Highness their guarantee.[4]

Piedmont won, Victor Amadeus won. And as every good landlord would do, as soon as the problem ended, he immediately reduced his expenditure. His army decreased to fewer than 10,000 men. Corps paid by the Maritime Powers had already disappeared in 1696 as soon as he left the Grand Alliance, but now the decrease was far more consistent.

However the Duke kept – wisely – a hard core of well-trained infantry and cavalry units, whilst in 1697 he reorganised the artillery as a military corps and grouped field artillery into a regiment.

His army totalled again roughly 8,500 men, that is to say more or less the same as it had in 1690 before the war. It was at the same time a matter of saving

---

3   *Traité de paix entre Sa Majesté Catholique et Sa Majesté Très-Chrétienne*, done in Rijsvijk on 20 September 1697, premise, rep. in Solaro della Margarita, op. cit., vol. II, p. 174.

4   *Traité de paix entre Sa Majesté Catholique et Sa Majesté Très-Chrétienne*, cit., article XXXIII, rep. in Solaro della Margarita, op. cit., vol. II, p. 191. The same text, word by word, is in article XV of the other two treaties signed on the same day by France with the Netherlands and Britain.

money and manpower. The rate of people fit for duty inserted in the general list composing the Battalion of Piedmont, the militia, decreased. As we may remember, Victor Amadeus in 1690 ordered it to raise up to six percent of the men fit for duty, when two percent was considered as the safety standard to keep manpower available for agriculture. In 1690 that happened due to the needs of war and emergency; now the war was over and militiamen were sent back home to the countryside, for the harvest needed to be stored, and Victor could now happily look at the results he had achieved.

He started his rule as a mostly nominal chief of a client state, and now he was the real master of a truly independent state. Every foreign intrusive influence had been destroyed, and he could think of being considered as the most important Italian prince in Italy and abroad.

Of course, the country had been devastated and pillaged by friends and by enemies, damages were huge and losses and casualties too, but, with a lot of work and a bit of luck, one could trust the future to be not as bad as the recent past.

Everything ended well, or so it seemed, because there was already in the air a very serious question, which by itself alone had been the major incentive to achieve the end of hostilities. The European powers had to decide what to do about the succession to the throne of Spain. They would decide, but after another 12 years of bloody war fought on land and at sea in Europe, America, and on the coasts of Asia and Africa.

But this is another story.

Colour Plate Commentaries

A.
Garde du Corps, Campaign Dress, 1685–90
Since the 1670s, private guardsmen and NCOs, as well as all the Savoy–Piedmont's cavalry, wore the *bouffle* (buff coat) in training and on campaign. This dress became ever more common when the Duchy entered the war against France in 1690, to better identify its own troopers. The *Garde du Corps* maintained the musket's baldric in azure velvet and golden piping as specific distinctive items. (Reconstruction after Enrico Ricchiardi, *Il Costume Militare Sabaudo*, vol. 1, Turin, 1989)

B.
Garde du Corps, 1689
When engaged in official duty or as escort for the ruler family, the household troops wore a high uniform consisting in broad-brimmed hat with silver piping and white plume, scarlet coat with silver lace, buff waistcoat and scarlet breeches; a wide red cloak completed the clothing. The three companies of the *Garde du Corps* are the best documented units of the Savoy–Piedmont army regarding uniforms and equipment. Notwithstanding the lack of iconographic sources concerning the Duchy's army, the *Garde du Corps* appear in several contemporary paintings illustrating Victor Amadeus in his early phase of government. (Reconstruction after the painting 'Duke Victor Amadeus visits the galleys in Nice', 1689, by anonymous, preserved in Fondazione Umberto II e Maria Josè di Savoia, Geneve)

C.
Regiment of the *Guardie a Piedi, Senior Officer*, 1690–94
According to Italian historians of the 19th century, the foot guards of Savoy–Piedmont received a blue coat with red facing in 1659. These colours remained unchanged even when Louis XIV adopted a similar uniform for his *Gardes Françaises*. In the early 1690s senior officers carried partisans, while lieutenants carried a spoonton. An azure sash with gold fringe identified the Savoy–Piedmontese officer of all ranks. (Reconstruction after the painting 'Ostensione della Sindone', 1684, by Pieter Bolckmann, collection of the Castello Reale, Racconigi)

Infantry regiment *Monferrato*, Private Fusilier, 1690

Between 1688 and 1690, the national foot regiments foot received grey or white-grey coat with cuffs, breeches and stockings of different colours. In detail: blue for Regiments *Savoye* and *Monferrato* but the latter with red stockings; red for *Aosta, Piemonte, Nice, Fucilieri* and *Croce Bianca* but the latter with grey breeches; medium green for *La Marina* and yellow for *Saluzzo*. Regiment *Mondovì* had blue cuffs and breeches but grey stockings; *Chablaise* were uniformed completely in grey. Buttons were of white metal for all the regiments except *Savoye, Monferrato* and *Nice*, which had brass buttons. Flintlock muskets of new production, or modified matchlock muskets, were issued to the infantry from 1688. (*Livre de l'uniforme des Regiments d'Infanterie au service de S.M. le Roi de Sardaigne, selon l'etablissemnent qui en a etè fait en dernier lieu, et contenant la description des anciens uniformes des différents corps depuis leur fondation*, Turin, 1744)

D.

Regiment of the *Guardie a Piedi*, grenadier, 1690–95

Grenadiers were introduced into the Savoy–Piedmont infantry in 1684, as occurred in France. Private guards fusiliers wore a broad-brimmed hat, while the grenadiers are represented with a red *bonnet*. (Reconstruction after the painting 'Ostensione della Sindone', 1684, by Pieter Bolckmann, collection of the Castello Reale, Racconigi; Turin State Archive, *Biblioteca Antica*, Manuscript H-II-28)

Infantry regiment *La Marina*, 1695

Grey or light grey is often referred as *gris–blanc* in the archive sources, but some iconographic evidence sesems to represent the Savoy–Piedmont uniforms as darker than shown by many modern reconstructions. This infantryman has received the new equipment with the belt sword. The plug bayonet hung on the bandolier of the ammunition bag. (Turin State Archive, S. III, Camerale Piemonte Art. 315–320)

E.

Cavalry regiment *Savoia Cavalleria*, 1695–99, trooper and trumpeter

When the companies of mounted *Gendarmes* were formed into two regiments of heavy cavalry, they took the name of *Piemonte Reale* and *Savoye*. Troopers wore the same dark blue or buff coat of the original corps, but in late 1694 new uniforms were issued, worn alongside the buff coat when on campaign. The new coats were grey with tin buttons, cuffs and lining in red for *Piemonte* and blue for *Savoye*. The typical 'weave' livery in azure and silver of Savoy on the trumpeter's coat was common for both cavalry regiments. (Turin State Archive, S. I and II, *Materie Militari – Imprese Militari*)

F.

Infantry regiment *Croce Bianca*, drummer, 1695–97

Drum major, drummers and fifers of all foot regiments, Guards included, wore a red coat with Savoy's livery, blue cuffs and lining, blue breeches and stockings. In some regiments drummers wore breeches and stockings as the privates of their unit. (*Livre de l'uniforme des Regiments d'Infanterie au service de S.M. le Roi de Sardaigne, selon l'etablissemnebt qui en a etè fait en dernier lieu*, Turin, 1744)

Infantry regiment *Schulenburg* (German), NCO, 1695–99

Foreign regiments in ducal service received uniforms according to their traditional colours: red for Swiss and dark blue for Germans. Regiment *Schulenburg* sergeants were generally dressed as the soldiers with finer-quality cloth. Sometimes in national regiments the NCO's coat could be the colour of the cuffs while the privates wore grey. Corporals wore the private's coat and carried no polearm. They were usually distinguished by a lace hanging from the right shoulder. (Enrico Ricchiardi, *Il Costume Militare Sabaudo*, vol. 1, Turin, 1989)

G.

Dragoon regiment *Genevois*, dragoon in foot service, 1695
Dragoon regiment of *Sua Altezza Reale*, dragoon, 1695–99

Raised in the 1680s, the Savoy–Piedmont dragoons were dressed very similarly to their French counterparts, including leather gaiters instead of boots. Since the 1690s the dragoons were identified by their popular names of *Reds*, *Yellows*, or *Greens*, after the colour of their coat. The yellow regiment, or *Piemonte Reale*, had black cuffs and lining, but before 1690 this regiment was uniformed in blue with red facings. Buttons were of white metal for all the regiments. Usually, the Savoy–Piedmont dragoons' headgear was the broad-brimmed hat of black felt with white piping, but on campaign they frequently wore the red cloth bonnet. (Turin State Archive, S. I and II, *Materie Militari – Ufficio Generale del Soldo, Capitolazioni*; Enrico Ricchiardi, *Il Costume Militare Sabaudo*, vol. 1, Turin, 1989)

H.

Artillery, gunner and miner, 1697–99

The artillery, formed by independent companies, was joined later in 1696 in a battalion that included also a company of miners. They were uniformed with dark blue dress with facings, lining and breeches of the same colour, with brass buttons and red stockings for NCOs. Sergeants had a scarlet waistcoat and yellow–golden lace at the cuffs. The hat was bordered with gilt lace. Drummers, as in the infantry, wore the red coat with the ducal livery. (Reconstruction after Enrico Ricchiardi, *Il Costume Militare Sabaudo*, vol. 1, Turin, 1989)

Flags and Standards

I.

Ordinanza flags 1690

Each infantry regiment carried two flags, one *colonnella* and one *ordinanza* when fielded as a single battalion, and when it deployed a second battalion it carried two *ordinanze*. Flags with a white cross on a blue or red field were common in the late 1680s and early 1690, with the cross extended to the end of the field or interrupted.

J.
Infantry regiment *Piemonte, Ordinanza* flag 1697–99
Infantry regiment *Savoye, Ordinanza* flag 1699
The new style of the Savoy–Piedmont infantry flags is well represented by these items, which carried the province's coat of arms on the quarters. Usually the heraldry occupied the lower quarter furthest from the pole, but in some cases flags with a different scheme are documented

K.
Infantry regiment *Schulenburg*, Colonel's flag 1694
The *Ordinanza* flag was in red and blue with the same pattern

Unknown infantry regiment (possibly the *Religionari Miremont* or *Montauban* regiment), *Ordinanza* flag, 1694.

L.
Infantry regiment *De Losche* (*Religionari*), *Ordinanza* flag (above) and Colonel's flag (below), 1694.
Regiment *De Losche* was formed from French Huguenots and other Protestants. In 1694 the regiment fielded a single battalion, which after the Battle of La Marsaglia was joined with another *religionari* regiment. The cost of raising, recruiting and equipping these regiments was largely borne by the British Crown, which assumed four fifths of the expense, and the remaining one fifth was borne by the States General of the United Provinces of the Netherlands.

M.
Infantry regiment *Lislemarais* (*Religionari*), Colonel's flag (above), and *Ordinanza* flag (below), 1694–95

N.
Ordinanza attributed to the German regiment *Heydelac*, lost, like the flag L, at the Battle of La Marsaglia on 4 October 1693.
A single flag in blue with a white cross belonged to this regiment, and has been classified by some scholars as a Colonel's ensign.

Bibliography

AA.VV., *La guerra della Lega di Augusta fino alla battaglia di Orbassano* (Turin, 1993)

Ales, Stefano, *Insegne militari preunitarie italiane* (Rome, 2001)

Assum, Clemente, *Eugenio di Savoia* (Turin, 1935)

Barberis, Walter, *Le armi del principe – la tradizione militare sabauda* (Turin, 1988)

Barine, Arvède, *Madame mère du Régent* (Paris, 1909)

Barone, Enrico, *I grandi capitani dell'età moderna* (Rome, 1982)

Bertin, Pierre, *Le fantassin de France* (1986)

Bertrand, Louis, *Luigi XIV* (Milano, 1962)

Berwick, James Fitz-James, duke of, *Mémoires du Maréchal de Berwick*, in *Collection de Mémoires pour servir à l'histoire de France, depuis l'avénement de Henri IV jusqu'à la Paix de Paris conclue en 1763 ; avec des notices sur chaque auteur, et des obsérvations sur chaque ouvrage*, par messieurs A. Petitot et Monmerqué (Paris, 1828)

Birlic Nolano, Giovanni, *Historia della vita di Carlo V duca di Lorena e Bar, generalissimo delle truppe imperiali* (Venice, 1699)

Black, Jeremy, *Britain as a military power 1688-1815* (London, 1999)

Black, Jeremy, 'War and warfare in the Age of Louis XIV: the global context', in *The Projection and Limitations of imperial Powers, 1618–1850*, edited by Frederick C. Schneid, collection 'History of Warfare', no. 75 (Leiden–Boston, 2012)

Bluche, François, *Louis XIV* (New York, 1999)

Boeri, Giancarlo, 'El ejército del Ducado de Milàn en 1693', on 'Dragona', year I, n. 2, 1993.

Botta, Carlo, *Storia d'Italia continuata da quella del Guicciardini sino al 1789*, 10 vols.(Parigi, 1832)

Bovio, Oreste, *Le bandiere dell'esercito* (Rome, 1981)

Breve cenno delle principali operazioni militari svoltesi nelle Valli Pellice, Chisone, Germagnasca e Dora Riparia, manuscript ny author unknown in AUSSME L 3.

Brezzi, Paolo, *La diplomazia pontificia* (Milan, 1942)

Brignoli, Marziano, *Savoye bonne nouvelle* (Milan, 1989)

Broglie, Emmanuel duc de, *Catinat, l'homme et la vie 1737–1712* (Paris, 1902)

Brugnelli Biraghi, G. – Denoyé Pollone, M. B., *La seconda Madama Reale Giovanna Battista di Savoia Nemours* (Turin, 1996)

Canale, Michel-Giuseppe, *Nuova istoria della Repubblica di Genova, del suo commercio della sua letteratura dalle origini all'anno 1797* (Florence, 1860)

Canosa, Romeno, *Storia del Mediterraneo nel Seicento* (Rome, 1997)

Carutti Domenico, Baron di Cantogno, *Storia del regno di Vittorio Amedeo II* (Florence, 1863)

Castelnuovo, Enrico (published by), *La reggia di Venaria e i Savoia – arte, magnificenza e storia di una corte europea* (Turin, 2008)

Cavalieri, Giorgio, 'Le uniformi dell`esercito di Vittorio Amedeo II', in *Rivista Militare*, year CXXIV, n. 5 1990.

Cavalieri, Giorgio, 'Le uniformi sabaude', in 'Rivista Militare', year CXXXIII, n. 1, 1989.

Cénat, Jean-Philippe, 'Les débuts d'une la carrière militaire hors du commun : l'ascension du marquis de Chamlay, conseiller militaire de Louis XIV (1672–1678)', in *Revue internationale d'Histoire Militaire*, no. 82, 2002, Paris, Comité International des Science Historiques – Commission Internationale d'Histoire Militaire, 2002.

Cerman, Markus, 'Rural economy and society', in *A Companion to Eighteenth-Century Europe*, edited by Peter H. Wilson (London: Blackwell, 2008)

Cipolla, Carlo Maria, *Storia economica dell'Europa preindustriale* (Bologna: il Mulino, 2002)

Coniglio, Giuseppe, *I Vicerè spagnoli di Napoli* (Napoli, Fiorentino, 1967)

Contessa, Carlo, *Progetti economici della seconda Madama Reale di Savoia fondati sopra un contratto nuziale (1678–1682)* (Turin, 1914)

Costantini, Claudio, *La Repubblica di Genova nell'età moderna* (Turin, 1991)

D'Artanville, *Memoirs of Prince Eugene of Savoy* (London, 1716)

De Lange, Albert (edited by), *I Valdesi: un'epopea protestante* (Florence, 1989)

De Riencourt, Simon, *Histoire de Louis XIV* (Paris, 1695)

Del Carretto, Carlo Gerolamo, marchese di Bagnasco, *L'assedio di Mommeliano 1690–91* (Rome, 1936)

Diaz, Furio, *Il Granducato di Toscana – I Medici* (Turin, 1987)

Dichiarazione dell'Ambasciatore dell'Imperatore Leopoldo per la quale dei due Trattati di Vigevano egli dichiara veritiero quello che dà al Duca di Savoia il diritto d'offrire la sua mediazione al Re di Francia per la pace generale, fatta a Vigevano il 9 ottobre 1696, in Solaro della Margarita (published by), *Traités publics de la Royale Maison de Savoie avec les puissances étrangères depuis la paix de Chateau Cambresis jusqu'à nos jours*, Vol. II (Turin, 1836)

Duboin, Felice Amato, *Raccolta per ordine di materie delle leggi, editti, manifesti, ecc., pubblicati dal principio dell'anno 1681 sino agli 8 dicembre 1798 sotto il felicissimo dominio della Real Casa di Savoia per servire di continuazione a quella del senatore Borelli*, 38 vols. (Turin, 1816–1869)

Dumoulin, *Recueil des campagnes des divers maréchaux de France*, 30 vols., Amsterdam (1760–1773)

Ehrman, John, 'William III and the Emergency of a Mediterranean Naval Policy 1692–4', in *Cambridge Historical Journal*, Vol. 9, n. 3, (1949), pp. 269–292.

Elias, Norbert, *La società di corte* (Bologna, 1980)

Ferguson, Niall, *Empire – the rise and demise of the British world order and the lessons for global power* (New York, 2003)

Ferrari, G., *Vita e campeggiamenti del Serenissimo Principe Francesco Eugenio di Savoja, supremo comandante degli eserciti Cesarei, e dell'Impero* (Naples, 1754)

Frey, Linda – Frey, Marsha, *Frederick I: the Man and his Times* (Boulder, 1984)

Frischauer, Paul, *Il principe Eugenio* (Milan, 1935)

Gariglio, Dario, *Battaglie alpine del Piemonte sabaudo* (Collegno, 1999)

Gariglio, Dario, *Le sentinelle di pietra – fortezze e cittadelle del Piemonte sabaudo* (Cuneo, 1997)

Giannone, Pietro, *Storia civile del Regno di Napoli*, 5 Vols. (Milan, 1844)

Giarelli, Francesco, *Storia di Piacenza, dalle origini ai nostri giorni* (Piacenza, 1989, anast. of 1890 edition)

Giglio, Vittorio, *Milizie ed eserciti d'Italia* (Milan, 1927)

Gisondi, Francesco Antonio, *Innocenzo XII – Antonio Pignatelli* (Rome, 1994)

Greene, Molly, 'Islam and Europe', in *A Companion to Eighteenth-Century Europe* (London: Peter H. Wilson, 2008)

Grilletto, Renato, 'La viabilità nella Valle di Susa e la fortezza di Exilles', in 'L'universo', year LI, n. 4, July–August 1971

Grilletto, Renato, 'Notizie storico-geografiche sulla sub-valle di Bellino (Valle Varaita)', in *L'universo*, year LIX, n. 2, March–April 1979.

Grilletto, Renato, 'La Valle del Chisone e la fortezza di Fenestrelle', in *L'universo*, year LII, n. 5, September–October 1972.

Guerrini, Domenico, *I Granatieri di Sardegna 1659–1900* (Rome, 1962)

Hanlon, Gregory, 'The Italian States', in *A Companion to Eighteenth-Century Europe* (London: Peter H. Wilson, 2008)

Hanlon, Gregory, *The twilight of a military tradition: italian aristocrats and european conflicts, 1560–1800* (London, 1998)

Haussonville, count d', *La duchesse de Bourgogne et l'alliance savoyarde sous Louis XIV* (Paris, 1898)

Henderson, Nicholas, *Prince Eugene of Savoy* (London, 1964)

Howard, Michael, *La guerra e le armi nella storia d'Europa* (Bari, 1978)

Ilari, Virgilio, *Storia del servizio militare in Italia* (Rome, 1991)

Jörgensen, Christer – Pavkovic, Michael F. – Rice, Rob S. – Schneid, Frederick C. – Scott, Chris L., *Fighting techniques of the early modern world AD 1500–AD 1763 – equipment, combat, skills, and tactics* (New York, 2007)

Jori, Ilio, *Eugenio di Savoia* (Turin, 1941)

Kamen, Henry, *How Spain became a world power 1492–1763* (New York, 2003)

Kennedy, Paul, *The rise and fall of the great powers – economic change and military conflict from 1500 to 2000* (New York, 1988)

L.C.D.C. (Bousquet), *Histoire de François Eugène prince de Savoie et de Piémont, marquis de Saluces*, 2 vols. (London, 1739)

La Hode, *Histoire de la vie et du regne de Louis le Grand*, 3 vols. (Frankfurt–Basel, 1740)

La Motte, Yves Joseph - La Martinière, Antoine Augustin Bruzen de, *Histoire de la vie et du régne de Louis XIV roi de France*, 5 vols. (The Hague, 1740)

Labarre, Carole, 'La frontière franco-savoyarde: trois exemples de frontières fluviales XV–XVIII siècle', in *Frontiere e fortificazioni di frontiera* (Florence, 2001)

Lami, Lucio, *L'amante del Re – la Signora di Verrua* (Farigliano, 1994)

Lamigue, Isaac, *Histoire du Prince d'Orange et de Nassau*, 2 vols. (Leuwarde, 1715)

Lamoral Le Pipre de Neuville, Simon, *Journal historique des deux compagnies des mousquetaires du Roy*, Paris, s.i.

Lemire, Beverly, 'Manufacturing, markets, and consumption', in *A Companion to Eighteenth-Century Europe* (London: Peter H. Wilson, 2008)

Lynn, John A., 'Foods, Funds and Fortresses: resource, mobilization and positional warfare in the campaigns of Louis XIV', in Lynn, John A. (published by), *Feeding Mars – Logistics in Western Warfare from the Middle Age to the Present* (Boulder, 1993)

Lynn, John A., 'Recalculating French Army Growth during the Grand Siècle 1600–1715', in *French Historical Studies*, vol. 18, n. 4 (Autumn 1994), pp. 881–906.

Lynn, John A., 'The other side of victory: honorable surrender during the wars of Louis XIV', in *The Projection and Limitations of imperial Powers, 1618–1850*, published by Frederick C. Schneid, series History of Warfare, no. 75, Leiden-Boston, 2012.

Macaulay, Thomas Babington, *Storia d'Inghilterra dall'avvenimento al trono di Giacomo II*, 2 Vols. (Turin, 1852)

Mandrou, Robert, *Luigi XIV e il suo tempo* (Turin, 1990)

Manifesto di s.a. reale di Sauoia ouero copia di lettera scritta dalla medema altezza al duca d'Orleans suo suocero; sotto li 24. di giugno 1690. Per giustificare le sue azzioni con la corona, e corte di Francia nelle congionture presenti, con altre lettere del rè, e di monsù di Cattinat. Tradotto dal francese, s.i., 1690.

Manucy, Albert, *Artillery throught the Ages* (Washington, 1985)

Manuele, Pierangelo, *Il Piemonte sul mare* (Cuneo, 1997)

Massonat, Claudio, *Ricordi storici delle Alpi Marittime*, manuscript in AUSSME, L 3.

Mauvillon, Eléazar, *Histoire du prince François Eugène de Savoye, Généralissime des Armées de l'Empéreur et de l'Empire*, 5 vols., vols 1 and 4 in Vienna, 1741 and 1770; vols. 2, 3 and 5 in Amsterdam, 1740

Menegazzi, Claudio, *Luigi XIV* (Verona, 1980)

Montù, Cesare Maria, *Storia dell'Artiglieria Italiana*, 1st vol. (Rome: Tipografia 1934)

Morandi Carlo (published by) *Relazioni di ambasciatori sabaudi, genovesi e veneti (1693–1713)* (Bologna, 1935)

Moscati, Ruggero, *Direttive della politica estera sabauda da Vittorio Amedeo II a Carlo Emanuele III* (Milan, 1941)

Mugnai, Bruno & Cristini, Luca, *L'esercito imperiale al tempo del principe Eugenio di Savoia 1690–1720 – La fanteria*, 3 vols. (Bergamo, 2010)

Mugnai, Bruno, *L'esercito imperiale al tempo del principe Eugenio di Savoia (1690–1720), parte II: la cavalleria*, 2 vols. (Bergamo: Soldiershop publishing, 2013)

Muratori, Lodovico Antonio, *Annali d'Italia dal principio dell'era volgare sino all'anno 1750*, 13 vols. (Naples, 1870)

Natali, Aurelio, *Castelli e fortificazioni* (Milano, 1974)

Naulet, Frédéric, 'Pierre Surirey de Saint-Rémy et les mémoires d'artillerie', in *Revue internationale d'Histoire Militaire*, no. 82, 2002, Paris, Comité International des Science Historiques – Commission Internationale d'Histoire Militaire, 2002.

Noailles, Adrien, duke de, *Mémoires politiques et militaires, pour servir à l'histoire de Louis XIV et de Louis XV, composées sur les pièces originales recuillies par Adrien Maurice duc de Noailles, maréchal de France et ministre d'Etat*, par l'abbé Millot, in *Collection de Mémoires pour servir à l'histoire de France, depuis l'avénement de Henri IV jusqu'à la Paix de Paris conclue en 1763; avec des notices sur chaque auteur, et des obsérvations sur chaque ouvrage*, par messieurs A. Petitot et Monmerqué, Tomes LXX-LXXIII (Paris, 1828)

Orioli, Emilio, *L'esilio di Emanuele Filiberto di Savoia-Carignano a Bologna* (Bologna, 1907)

Ottieri, Francesco Maria, *Istoria delle guerre avvenute in Europa e particolarmente in Italia per la Successione alla Monarchia delle Spagne dall'anno 1696 all'anno 1725*, 4 vols. (Rome, 1753)

Paoletti, Ciro & Boeri, Giancarlo, 'La battaglia di Staffarda', in *Panoplia*, year VIII, n. 24, 1996.

Paoletti, Ciro & Boeri, Giancarlo, 'La guerra della Grande Alleanza 1688 – 1697 e le campagne in Italia', in *Rivista Italiana Difesa*, n. 7, July 1997

Paoletti, Ciro & Boeri, Giancarlo, 'La Lega di Augusta e le operazioni in Piemonte', in *Panoplia*, year VIII, n. 26, 1996.

Paoletti, Ciro, 'Italy, Piedmont and French anti-Habsburg strategy, 1690–1748', in *The Projection and Limitations of imperial Powers, 1618–1850*, published by Frederick C. Schneid, series History of Warfare, no. 75, Leiden–Boston, 2012.

Paoletti, Ciro, 'Le conseguenze del Trattato di Lione sull'assetto difensivo dello Stato Sabaudo', in Mola, Aldo Alessandro (published by), *Il marchesato di Saluzzo – da Stato di confine a confine di Stato a Europa*, proceedings of the conference held to commemorate the IV centennial of the Peace of Lyon, Saluzzo, November 30th–December 1st 2001, Foggia, 2003.

Paoletti, Ciro, 'Logistica e assedi delle guerre del settecento', in 'Panoplia', year VIII, n. 27–28, August–December 1996.

Paoletti, Ciro, 'Storia dei trasporti militari italiani dalle origini all'Unità', in *Studi storico-militari 2007*, Rome, 2009

Paoletti, Ciro, 'Un cas de financement prolongé des activités belliques: l'alliance entre l'Angleterre et la Maison de Savoye (1688-1861)', in *Acta of the International Commission of Military History* XXX Annual Conference, Rabat, Commission Marocaine d'Histoire Militaire, 2005.

Paoletti, Ciro, 'War 1688-1812', in *A Companion to Eighteenth-Century Europe* (London: Peter H. Wilson, 2008)

Paoletti, Ciro, *A military history of Italy* (Westport, 2007)

Paoletti, Ciro, *Capitani di Casa Savoia* (Rome, 2007)

Paoletti, Ciro, *Dal Ducato all'Unità – tre secoli e mezzo di storia militare piemontese* (Rome, 2011)

Paoletti, Ciro, *Gli Italiani in armi – cinque secoli di storia militare nazionale 1494-2000* (Rome, 2001)

Paoletti, Ciro, *Il principe Eugenio di Savoia* (Rome, 2001)

Pastor, Ludwig Baron von, *Storia dei papi nel periodo dell'assolutismo* (Rome, 1933), vol XIV.

Pieri, Piero, 'L'evoluzione dell'arte militare nei secoli XV, XVI, XVII e la guerra del secolo XVIII', in *Nuove questioni di storia moderna* (Milan, 1966)

Pilgrim, Donald, 'The Colbert-Seignelay Naval Reforms and the Beginning of the War of the League of Augsburg', in *French Historical Studies*, vol. 9, n. 2 (Autumn 1975)

Price, J. L., 'The Dutch Republic', in *A Companion to Eighteenth-Century Europe* (London: Peter H. Wilson, Blackwell, 2008)

Puletti, Rodolfo, *Caricat! – tre secoli di storia dell'Arma di Cavalleria* (Bologna, 1973)

Quazza, Romolo, *La formazione progressiva dello Stato sabaudo*, (Turin, 1942)

Quazza, Romolo, *Storia politica d'Italia – preponderanze straniere* (Milan, 1938)

Rappaport, Michael, 'France', in *A Companion to Eighteenth-Century Europe* (London: Peter H. Wilson, 2008)

Reineri, Maria Teresa, *Anna Maria d'Orléans, regina di Sardegna, duchessa di Savoia* (Turin, 2006)

Ricaldone, E. Aldo di, *Annali del Monferrato 951–1708* (Turin, 1972)

Riotte, Torsten, 'Britain and Hanover', in *A Companion to Eighteenth-Century Europe* (London: Peter H. Wilson, 2008)

Rivoire, Mario, *Luigi XIV il Re Sole* (Milano, 1970)

Roimanmotier, R. May de, *Histoire militaire de la Suisse et celle des Suisses dans les differens sérvices de l'Europe* (Lausanne, 1788)

Rombaldi, Odoardo, *Aspetti e problemi di un secolo di governo estense a Modena e Reggio Emilia (da Alfonso IV a Rinaldo I – 1658–1737)* (Modena, 1995)

Rowlands, Guy, 'Louis XIV, Vittorio Amedeo II and French military failure in Italy 1689–96', in *The English Historical Review*, June 2000, pp. 534–69

Sabatini, Gaetano, 'La spesa militare nel contesto della finanza pubblica napoletana del XVII secolo', in Rossella Cancila (edited by), *Mediterraneo in armi* (Palermo, 2007)

Saint-Simon, Louis de Rouvroy duke de, *Mémoires (Mémoires complets et authentiques du Duc de Saint Simon)*, 20 Vols. (Paris, 1840)

Saluzzo, Alessandro count di, *Histoire militaire du Piémont*, 5 vols. (Turin, 1818)

Salzano, Michele Tommaso Vincenzo, *Corso di storia ecclesiastica dalla venuta di Gesù Cristo ai giorni nostri, comparata colla storia politica dei tempi* (Rome, 1861)

Sandri-Giachino, Roberto, *Un suddito sabaudo ambasciatore straordinario a Vienna e Commissario imperiale in italia: Ercole Turinetti di Priero*, in Mola di Nomaglio, Gustavo – Sandri Giachino, Roberto – Melano, Giancarlo – Menietti, Piergiuseppe, *Turin 1706: memorie e attualità dell'assedio di Torino del 1706 tra spirito europeo e identità regionale – Atti del convegno, Turin 29 e 30 settembre 2006*, 2 vols., Turin, vol. II

Santi-Mazzini, Giovanni, *La macchina da guerra dal Medioevo al 1914 – La macchina da guerra nel Medioevo – metamorfosi della macchina da guerra*, in *Militaria: storia, battaglie, armate*, 12 vols. (Milan, 2006), vol. 3rd and 4th.

Scala, Edoardo, 'Intendenti, commissari ed amministratori egli eserciti sabaudi', in *La guerra del 1866 e altri scritti* (Rome, 1981)

Sconfienza, Roberto, 'Sulla prima uniforme e lo stemma del Reggimento Dragoni di Piemonte', in *Armi Antiche – Bollettino dell'Accademia di San Marciano* (Turin, 1995 (1998))

Segre, Arturo, 'Negoziati diplomatici della Corte Sabauda colla Corte di Baviera dalle origini al 1704', in *Le campagne di guerra in Piemonte (1703–1708) e l'assedio di Torino (1706) – studi, documenti, illustrazioni,* vol. VI (Turin, 1912)

Segre, Arturo, Negoziati diplomatici della Corte Sabauda colla Corte di Prussia e colla Dieta di Ratisbona, in *Le campagne di guerra in Piemonte (1703-1708) e l'assedio di Torino (1706) – studi, documenti, illustrazioni,* vol. VI (Turin, 1912)

Sella, Domenico – Capra, Carlo, *Il Ducato di Milano* (Turin, 1984)

Sella, Domenico, *Lo Stato di Milano in età spagnola* (Turin, 1987)

Signorelli, Bruno, 'Giovanni Battista Gropello ministro di Vittorio Amedeo II e suo plenipotenziario durante l'assedio di Torino (giugno-settembre 1706)', in Mola di Nomaglio, Gustavo – Sandri Giachino, Roberto – Melano, Giancarlo – Menietti, Piergiuseppe, *Turin 1706: memorie e attualità dell'assedio di Torino del 1706 tra spirito europeo e identità regionale – Atti del convegno, Turin 29 e 30 settembre 2006,* 2 vols. (Turin, 2006), vol. II.

Sirtema De Grovestijns, *Histoire des luttes et rivalités politiques entre les Puissances Maritimes et la France durant da seconde moitié du XVII Siècle*, Paris, 1853, Vol. 6th

Solaro della Margarita, count Clemente (published by), *Traités publics de la Royale Maison de Savoie avec les puissances étrangères depuis la paix de Chateau Cambresis jusqu'à nos jours,* 5 vols. (Turin, 1836)

Storrs, Christopher, *War, diplomacy and the rise of Savoy, 1690–1720* (London, 1999)

Susane, Louis Auguste, *Histoire de l'artillerie française* (Paris, 1874)

Susane, Louis Auguste, *Histoire de l'infanterie française,* 5 vols. (Paris, 1876)

Susane, Louis Auguste, *Histoire de la cavalerie française,* 3 vols. (Paris, 1874)

Symcox, Geoffrey, 'L'età di Vittorio Amedeo II', in Giuseppe Galasso, (published by), *Il Piemonte Sabaudo – stato e territori in età moderna* (Turin, 1994)

Symcox, Geoffrey, 'La guerra in Europa', in Albert De Lange (published by), *I Valdesi: un'epopea protestante* (Florence, 1989)

Symcox, Geoffrey, *Vittorio Amedeo II e l'assolutismo sabaudo 1675–1730* (Turin, 1989)

Tabacco, Giovanni, *Lo stato sabaudo nel Sacro Romeno Impero* (Turin, 1939)

Tassoni Estense, Alessandro, *Eugenio di Savoia* (Milan, 1939)

Tessé, Charles de Froulay count de, *Mémoires et lettres du Maréchal de Tessé, contenantes des anedoctes et des faits historiques inconnus, sur partie des regnes de Louis XIV et de Louis XV*, 2 tomes (Paris: Imprimérie Crapelet, 1806)

The History of Francis Eugene, Prince of Savoy (London, 1742)

Topin, Marius, *L'Europe et les Bourbons sous Louis XIV* (Paris, 1868)

Torcy, *Mémoires du Marquis de Torcy pour servir à l'histoire des négociations depuis le Traité de Riswick jusqu'à la Paix d'Utrecht*, in *Collection de Mémoires pour servir à l'histoire de France, depuis l'avénement de Henri IV jusqu'à la Paix de Paris conclue en 1763; avec des notices sur chaque auteur, et des obsérvations sur chaque ouvrage*, par messieurs A. Petitot et Monmerqué, 2 Tomes (Tomes LXVII and LXVIII of the collection) (Paris, 1828)

Trattato concluso fra il Duca di Savoia Vittorio Amedeo e Carlo II Re di Spagna contro la Corona di Francia, fatto a Milano il 3 giugno 1690, in Solaro della Margarita, count Clemente (published by), *Traités publics de la Royale Maison de Savoie avec les puissances étrangères depuis la paix de Chateau Cambresis jusqu'à nos jours,* Vol. II (Turin, 1836)

Trattato d'accessione del Duca Vittorio Amedeo II al Trattato della Lega contro la Francia, concluso fra l'Imperatore, l'Inghilterra e gli Stati Generali dei Paesi Bassi, fatto all'Aja il 20 ottobre 1690, in Solaro della Margarita, count Clemente (published by), *Traités publics de la Royale Maison de Savoie avec les puissances étrangères depuis la paix de Chateau Cambresis jusqu'à nos jours*, Vol. II (Turin, 1836)

Trattato d'alleanza difensiva fra Vittorio Amedeo Duca di Savoia ed il Re di Francia, fatto a Torino il 24 novembre 1682, in Solaro della Margarita, count Clemente (published by), *Traités publics de la Royale Maison de Savoie avec les puissances étrangères depuis la paix de Chateau Cambresis jusqu'à nos jours*, Vol. II (Turin, 1836)

Trattato d'alleanza offensiva e difensiva fra Vittorio Amedeo Duca di Savoia e l'Imperatore Leopoldo contro la Corona di Francia, fatto a Turin il 4 giugno 1690, in Solaro della Margarita, count Clemente (published by), *Traités publics de la Royale Maison de Savoie avec les puissances étrangères depuis la paix de Chateau Cambresis jusqu'à nos jours*, Vol. II (Turin, 1836)

Trattato della Lega contro la Francia, concluso fra l'imperatore, l'Inghilterra e gli Stati Generali dei Paesi Bassi, fatto a Vienna il 12 maggio 1689, contenuto nel *Trattato d'accessione del Duca Vittorio Amedeo II al Trattato della Lega contro la Francia, concluso fra l'Imperatore, l'Inghilterra e gli Stati Generali dei Paesi Bassi, fatto all'Aja il 20 ottobre 1690*, in Solaro della Margarita, count Clemente (published by), *Traités publics de la Royale Maison de Savoie avec les puissances étrangères depuis la paix de Chateau Cambresis jusqu'à nos jours*, Vol. II (Turin, 1836)

Trattato di pace fra S.M. Cattolica e S. M. Cristianissima, fatto a Ryswich, il 20 settembre 1697, in Solaro della Margarita, count Clemente (published by), *Traités publics de la Royale Maison de Savoie avec les puissances étrangères depuis la paix de Chateau Cambresis jusqu'à nos jours*, Vol. II (Turin, 1836)

Trattato di pace fra Vittorio Amedeo II Duca di Savoia e Luigi XIV Re di Francia, fatto a Turin il 29 agosto 1696, in Solaro della Margarita, count Clemente (published by), *Traités publics de la Royale Maison de Savoie avec les puissances étrangères depuis la paix de Chateau Cambresis jusqu'à nos jours*, Vol. II (Turin, 1836)

Trattato di scambio e riscatto dei prigionieri di guerra fatti dalle truppe di Sua Maestà Cristianissima e quelle che compongono l'Armata di S.A.R. Monsignore il Duca di Savoia e dei suoi Alleati, tanto di qua che di là dei monti, fatto a Vigone il 19 ottobre 1690, in Solaro della Margarita, count Clemente (published by), *Traités publics de la Royale Maison de Savoie avec les puissances étrangères depuis la paix de Chateau Cambresis jusqu'à nos jours*, Vol. II (Turin, 1836)

Trattato fra S.A.R. Vittorio Amedeo II Duca di Savoia da una parte, l'Imperatore Leopoldo e Carlo II Re di Spagna dall'altra per una sospensione d'armi in Italia fra le Loro Maestà e la Corona di Francia, fatto a Vigevano il 7 ottobre 1696, in Solaro della Margarita, count Clemente (published by), *Traités publics de la Royale Maison de Savoie avec les puissances étrangères depuis la paix de Chateau Cambresis jusqu'à nos jours*, Vol. II (Turin, 1836)

Treno di provianda: schema cronologico dei provvedimenti presi, Manuscrpt in AUSSME, L 3, 8 Lavori svolti.

Trevelyan, George Macaulay, *La rivoluzione inglese del 1688–89* (Turin, 1940)

Trevelyan, George Macaulay, *Storia d'Inghilterra*, 2 vols., (Milan, 1973)

Vallant, Edward, *The Glorious Revolution* (London, 2006)

Valori, Aldo, *Condottieri e generali italiani del Seicento* (Rome, 1946)

Vaughan, D.M., 'Campaigns in the Dauphiny Alps: 1588–1747', in *The English Historical Review*, Vol. 28, n. 110 (April 1913)

Viglino Davico, Micaela (edited by), *La piazzaforte di Verrua* (Turin, 2001)

Voltaire, *Le siécle de Louis XIV*, 2 vols. (Paris, 1792)

Williams, Henry Noel, *A Rose of Savoy* (London, 1910)

Wills, John E., *1688: biografia di un anno* (Milan, 2000)

Wilson, Peter H. (published by), *A Companion to Eighteenth-Century Europe* (London, 2008)

Wilson, Peter H., 'The Empire, Austria, and Prussia', in *A Companion to Eighteenth-Century Europe* (London: Peter H. Wilson, 2008)